The Other in Contemporary Migrant Cinema

As a rapidly aging continent, Europe increasingly depends on the successful integration of migrants. Unfortunately, contemporary political and media discourses observe and frequently support the development of nationalist, Eurosceptic, and xenophobic reactions to immigration and growing multi-ethnicity. Confronting this trend, European cinema has developed and disseminated new transcultural and postcolonial alternatives that might help to improve integration and community cohesion in Europe, and this book investigates these alternatives in order to identify examples of good practices that can enhance European stability. While the cinematic spectrum is as wide and open as most notions of Europeanness, the films examined share a fundamental interest in the Other. In this qualitative film analysis approach, particular consideration is given to British, French, German, and Spanish productions, with a comparison of multiethnic conviviality in Chicano cinema.

Guido Rings is Professor of Postcolonial Studies, director of the Research Unit for Intercultural and Transcultural Studies (RUITS), and co-editor of *German as a Foreign Language* (www.gfl-journal.com) and *iMex* (http://www.imex-revista.com). He is the author of 50 refereed articles, 7 volumes/special issues, and 5 authored books, including *La Conquista desbaratada* (Iberoamericana 2010).

Routledge Advances in Film Studies

For a full list of titles in this series, please visit www.routledge.com.

15 **Stardom and the Aesthetics of Neorealism**
Ingrid Bergman in Rossellini's Italy
Ora Gelley

16 **Postwar Renoir**
Film and the Memory of Violence
Colin Davis

17 **Cinema and Inter-American Relations**
Tracking Transnational Affect
Adrián Pérez Melgosa

18 **European Civil War Films**
Memory, Conflict, and Nostalgia
Eleftheria Rania Kosmidou

19 **The Aesthetics of Antifascist Film**
Radical Projection
Jennifer Lynde Barker

20 **The Politics of Age and Disability in Contemporary Spanish Film**
Plus Ultra Pluralism
Matthew J. Marr

21 **Cinema and Language Loss**
Displacement, Visuality and the Filmic Image
Tijana Mamula

22 **Cinema as Weather**
Stylistic Screens and Atmospheric Change
Kristi McKim

23 **Landscape and Memory in Post-Fascist Italian Film**
Cinema Year Zero
Giuliana Minghelli

24 **Masculinity in the Contemporary Romantic Comedy**
Gender as Genre
John Alberti

25 **Crossover Cinema**
Cross-Cultural Film from Production to Reception
Edited by Sukhmani Khorana

26 **Spanish Cinema in the Global Context**
Film on Film
Samuel Amago

27 **Japanese Horror Films and Their American Remakes**
Translating Fear, Adapting Culture
Valerie Wee

28 **Postfeminism and Paternity in Contemporary US Film**
Framing Fatherhood
Hannah Hamad

29 **Cine-Ethics**
Ethical Dimensions of Film Theory, Practice, and Spectatorship
Edited by Jinhee Choi and Mattias Frey

30 **Postcolonial Film: History, Empire, Resistance**
Edited by Rebecca Weaver-Hightower and Peter Hulme

31 **The Woman's Film of the 1940s**
Gender, Narrative, and History
Alison L. McKee

32 **Iranian Cinema in a Global Context**
Policy, Politics, and Form
Edited by Peter Decherney and Blake Atwood

33 **Eco-Trauma Cinema**
Edited by Anil Narine

34 **American and Chinese-Language Cinemas**
Examining Cultural Flows
Edited by Lisa Funnell and Man-Fung Yip

35 **American Documentary Filmmaking in the Digital Age**
Depictions of War in Burns, Moore, and Morris
Lucia Ricciardelli

36 **Asian Cinema and the Use of Space**
Interdisciplinary Perspectives
Edited by Lilian Chee and Edna Lim

37 **Moralizing Cinema**
Film, Catholicism and Power
Edited by Daniel Biltereyst and Daniela Treveri Gennari

38 **Popular Film Music and Masculinity in Action**
A Different Tune
Amanda Howell

39 **Film and the American Presidency**
Edited by Jeff Menne and Christian B. Long

40 **Hollywood Action Films and Spatial Theory**
Nick Jones

41 **The Western in the Global South**
Edited by MaryEllen Higgins, Rita Keresztesi, and Dayna Oscherwitz

42 **Spaces of the Cinematic Home**
Behind the Screen Door
Edited by Eleanor Andrews, Stella Hockenhull, and Fran Pheasant-Kelly

43 **Spectacle in "Classical" Cinemas**
Musicality and Historicity in the 1930s
Tom Brown

44 **Rashomon Effects**
Kurosawa, Rashomon and Their Legacies
Edited by Blair Davis, Robert Anderson and Jan Walls

45 **Mobility and Migration in Film and Moving Image Art**
Cinema Beyond Europe
Nilgün Bayraktar

46 **The Other in Contemporary Migrant Cinema**
Imagining a New Europe?
Guido Rings

The Other in Contemporary Migrant Cinema
Imagining a New Europe?

Guido Rings

NEW YORK AND LONDON

First published 2016
by Routledge
711 Third Avenue, New York, NY 10017

and by Routledge
2 Park Square, Milton Park, Abingdon, Oxon OX14 4RN

First issued in paperback 2018

Routledge is an imprint of the Taylor and Francis Group, an informa business

© 2016 Taylor & Francis

The right of the editors to be identified as the authors of the editorial material, and of the authors for their individual chapters, has been asserted in accordance with sections 77 and 78 of the Copyright, Designs and Patents Act 1988.

All rights reserved. No part of this book may be reprinted or reproduced or utilised in any form or by any electronic, mechanical, or other means, now known or hereafter invented, including photocopying and recording, or in any information storage or retrieval system, without permission in writing from the publishers.

Trademark notice: Product or corporate names may be trademarks or registered trademarks, and are used only for identification and explanation without intent to infringe.

Library of Congress Cataloging-in-Publication Data

CIP data has been applied for.

ISBN 13: 978-1-138-59955-0 (pbk)
ISBN 13: 978-1-138-95163-1 (hbk)

Typeset in Sabon
by codeMantra

Contents

List of Figures ix
Acknowledgements xi

Introduction 1

1 Otherness in Contemporary European Cinema 8
　1.1 Questions of Traditional Othering 8
　1.2 Transcultural Identities in a Postcolonial Framework 10
　1.3 The Other in European Migrant Cinema 17

2 Potential and Limits of a New European in Nicolas Echevarría's *Cabeza de Vaca* 29
　2.1 Preliminary Remarks 29
　2.2 From Monocultural to Transcultural Perspectives 32
　2.3 Back to Monoculturality? 38
　2.4 The Postcolonial Heritage 42

3 Migrants in Europe: Breaking the Boundaries? 48
　3.1 Principles of Exclusion in Montxo Armendáriz's *Letters from Alou* and Carlos Saura's *Taxi* 48
　3.2 Assimilation Tendencies in Gurinder Chadha's *Bend It Like Beckham* 62
　3.3 From Principles of Coexistence and Limited Interaction before German Unification to Transcultural Exchange in Fatih Akın's *The Edge of Heaven* 77
　3.4 New Solidarity in Aki Kaurismäki's *Le Havre* 97

4 Inspiration from Abroad? Cultural Boundaries in Chicano Cinema 127
　4.1 Preliminary Remarks 127
　4.2 *My Family, Bordertown*, and the 'American Dream' 128
　4.3 Transcultural Potential 131
　4.4 Transcultural Limits 139
　4.5 Concluding Remarks 147

Conclusion 157

Index 165

List of Figures

2.2.1	Hybrid resurrection ritual in *Cabeza de Vaca*.	37
2.3.1	Christian exorcism ritual.	41
3.1.3.1	Claustrophobic migrant spaces in *Letters from Alou*.	53
3.1.4.1	Framing of Others in *Taxi*.	58
3.1.4.2	Paz in front of Carbonell's bronze relief.	60
3.2.2.1	Guru Nanak's blessing in *Bend It Like Beckham*.	65
3.2.4.1	The traditional wall.	73
3.3.3.1	Ayten and Lotte in *The Edge of Heaven*.	87
3.3.3.2	Susanne and Ayten in Nejat's bookshop.	90
3.4.2.1	Marcel and Idrissa in *Le Havre*.	99
3.4.2.2	Inspector Monet's investigation.	102
4.3.2.1	Eva and Lauren in *Bordertown*.	135
4.4.1.1	The Aztec encounter in *My Family*.	142

Acknowledgements

Above all, I would like to thank my wife, Cristina Blanca-Sancho, for all her support throughout the last years. Without her, this book would never have been written.

I am also particularly grateful to Anglia Ruskin University for granting a sabbatical, which allowed me to complete the work, and I would like to express my gratitude to the numerous colleagues and students, who gave me opportunities to present and discuss my ideas.

Finally, in the course of these years, I have published preliminary findings on individual films, which the reader will now find more elaborated, further developed, and interconnected in this monograph, and I would like to thank the publishers for giving me permission to draw on my earlier texts, which include: 'The West - A Transcultural Home for the Rest?', in: *Anglistik* 22/1 2011, pp. 167–186; 'Questions of Identity: Cultural Encounters in Gurinder Chadha's "Bend It Like Beckham"', in: *Journal of Popular Film and Television* 39/3 2011, pp. 114–123; 'Madrid: Neo-colonial Spacing in Contemporary Spanish Cinema?', in: Godela Weiss-Sussex, Katia Pizzi (eds.): *Cultural Identities of European Cities*, London: Peter Lang 2010, pp. 205–229; 'Möglichkeiten und Grenzen der Transkulturalität in Gregory Nava's "My Family"', in: Frank Leinen (ed.): *México 2010: Kultur in Bewegung – Mythen auf dem Prüfstand*. Düsseldorf: DUP 2012, pp. 269–288; '"Cabeza de Vaca" de Nicolás Echevarría', in: Christian Wehr (ed.): *Antología del Cine Mexicano* 2016. Madrid: Iberoamericana-Vervuert.

Introduction

As a rapidly aging continent, Europe depends increasingly on the successful integration of migrants; thus it is essential to overcome traditional oppositions and racist hierarchies between 'us' and 'them'. Unfortunately, contemporary political and media discourses observe and frequently support the development of nationalist, Eurosceptic, and xenophobic mindsets, which have led to spectacular election results of right-wing parties all over Europe. For example, the European elections in 2014 showed substantial gains for parties such as UKIP, Front National, the Danish People's Party, Austrian Freedom, Lega Nord, and Golden Dawn. However, these results have to be considered as part of a new trend that highlights a 'continent-wide rise of Euroscepticism' (Torreblanca/Leonard 2013) and the new popularity of 'The European far Right' (Ramalingam 2014), both of which continue to shape European politics, including anti-immigration policies of popular conservative governments. Confronting this trend, European cinema has become well known for new transcultural, postcolonial, and migrant orientation in contemporary films. These films provide answers that might help to improve integration and community cohesion in Europe, and in this work I propose to investigate them further.

Although the cinematic spectrum is as wide and open as most notions of Europeanness, there is a fundamental interest in the Other. This new interest draws on the loss of confidence in the authority of monocultural identity constructs, neoliberal politics, and neocolonial structures in contemporary Europe, within which cultural differences are portrayed as inferior. The cultural Other tends to be marginalized and suppressed. I find the fluid and transgressive character of migrant protagonists in cinema is particularly fruitful for the elaboration of mindsets better suited to address the opportunities and challenges in highly dynamic European societies that are characterized by fast-paced globalization and increasing international migration.

Meanwhile, directors, scriptwriters, and actors are not fully resistant to well-established cultural hierarchies and neocolonial perspectives that continue to shape contemporary forms of neo-liberalism, and commercial pressures on their productions have enhanced tendencies to melodramatic excess, which supports the reconstruction of monocultural subtexts even within diversity-embracing films. These subtexts deserve further exploration, as they may be the largest obstacle to the development of socio-political, cultural, and economic means of reducing the popularity of current right-wing strategies aimed at the destabilization of Europe.

In this qualitative film analysis approach, particular consideration will be given to British, French, and German productions, as their cinema studios have managed to develop the most successful migrant mediascape in Europe, both in terms of quantity and quality of productions, particularly because they include the invaluable input of directors and scriptwriters with migrant backgrounds. These films must, however, be analyzed within their European context, which is impressively rich in variety and has produced numerous outstanding examples of migrant cinema. As a country with relatively recent mass immigration, Spain illustrates the variety and excellent quality of migrant cinema from countries with relatively recent mass immigration particularly well and shall therefore be included in the case study analysis. I have selected the most recent period of European migrant cinema, from 1990 (*Letters from Alou*) to 2011 (*Le Havre*), and beyond, in order to facilitate the comparison of cinematic portrayals of new mass migration to countries like Spain with explorations of the diaspora in countries with traditionally high immigration such as Britain, Germany, and France.

Using Montxo Armendáriz's *Letters from Alou* as starting point, it is worth stressing that in the context of the Schengen Agreement (1987), the Single European Act (1987), and the Maastricht Treaty (1992) 'marks of a more unified Europe were particularly visible in the 1990s' (Harrod, Liz, and Timoshkina 2015: 4). This correlates with the foundation of the Council of Europe's cinematic key fund Eurimages (1989) and its aim to support the production of 'works which uphold the values that are part and parcel of the European identity' (Eurimages News 1990, in Jäckel 2015: 61). One such value is the recognition of European diversity, as expressed by the Council of Europe's mandate 'to strengthen human rights, racial tolerance and multicultural acceptance' (CoE 1991: 9), and *Letters from Alou* is certainly an excellent example for the defense of that value.[1] In this context, it is no coincidence that academic interest in European cinema 'as an entity in its own right emerged around 1990' (Harrod, Liz, and Timoshkina 2015: 6). On the other hand, *Le Havre* (2011) appears to be exemplary of a 'new wave' of European films, including *Blindgänger* and *Krüger aus Almanya* (both from 2015), which have started to explore transcultural solidarity constructs in greater depth by concentrating on the effects of globalization on national boundaries. It is understood that in this sense both 1990 and 2011—as suggested by *Letters from Alou* and *Le Havre*—can be regarded only as open reference points and not exclusive boundaries for new tendencies in film.

This is the first monograph to offer an in-depth examination of the potential and limits of transcultural identity constructs in contemporary European migrant cinema with a focus on four key countries for migrant film development—Germany, France, the UK, and Spain. The book will be able to build on numerous individual film interpretations in a wide range of journals and relatively few more extensive explorations of migrant cinema, albeit usually within one particular national framework that limits the scope (see Bourne 2001, Santaolalla 2005, Brandt 2007) or within a wider migration and diaspora framework of edited volumes and a few authored books that do not offer a comparable conceptual focus (Berghahn/Sternberg 2010, Hake/Mennel 2012, Loshitzky 2010, Ballesteros 2015).[2] There is a shortage of comparative studies of alternative concepts of Europe in contemporary migrant cinema. We can see, however, that film production has developed at a glocal level, and it has become clear that national film analysis is not well equipped to embrace questions linked to the legacy of colonialism or new fascism and cultural racism at the European level. Also, the ongoing marginalization of popular films in scholarly literature implies the exclusion of the films with the widest audience and impact, which does not help to explore key features of contemporary discrimination and xenophobia.

Drawing on intercultural and transcultural concepts of culture (Welsch 1999, Huggan 2006, Antor 2006/2010, Benessaieh 2010/2012, Moses/Rothberg 2014), postcolonial identity theory (Lazarus 2012, Singh/Kim 2015) and contemporary debates of postcolonial responsibility (Wallerstein 2003, Lazarus 2012, Menozzi 2014), this book will address the following key questions:

1 How well do contemporary films about migration and diaspora manage to blur traditional boundaries marked by monocultural concepts, ethnic discrimination, and gender stereotyping?
2 Which monocultural constructs remain resistant enough to new deconstruction efforts that they destabilize the cinematic output?
3 How do different portrayals of migration compete, and to what extent do they underpin opposing perspectives?
4 How do the films address Europe's role in our transcultural modernity with ever-shifting migrations and diasporas?

These questions will be discussed in four chapters: 'Otherness in Contemporary European Cinema' (Chapter 1) explores key concepts like 'monoculturality', 'multiculturality', 'interculturality', and 'transculturality' in a postcolonial framework that facilitates the analysis of films with focus on transgressive identities. It also provides a working definition for 'European migrant cinema' in its historical context. 'Potential and Limits of a New European in Nicolás Echevarría's *Cabeza de Vaca*' (Chapter 2) examines cultural patterns of European colonialism that continue to inform current debates about European identity and that have been reconstructed and deconstructed quite convincingly in Echevarría's *Cabeza de Vaca* (1990), hence the critical interrogation of this movie as the first film analysis. It is also worth noting that key examples of European migrant cinema, from Rainer Werner Fassbinder's *Fear Eats the Soul* (1974) and Gianni Amelio's *Lamerica* (1994) to Fernando León de Aranoa's *Princesas* (2005), have

4 Introduction

repeatedly highlighted the need to consider the wider spectrum of Othering, which goes far beyond the reduction of Otherness to migrants in contemporary Europe. In particular, protagonists like Emmi, Gino, and Candela have stressed the similarity of mechanisms of discrimination and exclusion that reach the supposedly privileged European Self, for example due to age and low economic capital, the loss of a passport, a profession that breaks with social norms, or simply unequal power relations that tend to underpin most patterns of exclusion that are at the forefront of *Cabeza de Vaca*. Finally, Echevarría's film can be regarded as an excellent example of the exploration of the possibilities and limitations of transcultural identity constructs in contemporary cinema.

The third and largest chapter, 'Migrants in Europe: Breaking the Boundaries?', offers an in-depth exploration of selected films on contemporary European migrant cinema. These works follow the development from an early focus on co-existence embedded in traditional multicultural perspectives still dominant in 1990s cinema (e.g., in Montxo Armendáriz's *Letters from Alou* and Carlos Saura's *Taxi* 1996) to new transcultural tendencies that increasingly shape European films in the new millennium, including Gurinder Chadha's *Bend It Like Beckham* 2002, Fatih Akın's *The Edge of Heaven* 2007, and Aki Kaurismäki's *Le Havre* 2011. As references to the wider cinematic context will highlight, my selection of films for each period follows shifts in identity concepts that I regard as characteristic of developments in contemporary European cinema and correspond to a preference for in-depth analysis of films rather than superficial reviews. Any attempt at reading the sequence of films as a reconstruction of cultural hierarchies that confirm the leading role of one national cinema over another would be misleading and would not consider that the internationalization of film funding and film production is increasingly blurring the boundaries of nation states.

Letters from Alou and *Taxi* have been selected because they exemplify a wide spectrum of European migrant films from the 1980s and the 1990s that promise a deconstruction of separatist concepts of culture and identity but tend to stop at levels of co-existence shaped by principles of (self-) exclusion. Armendáriz's and Saura's films also mark key periods in the development of Spanish Cinema about migration (see Santaolalla 2007), and they were popular in their respective periods of time, with *Letters from Alou* forming part of anti-racist education in Spanish schools. *Bend It Like Beckham* has been included because it is an excellent example of narratives promoting popular assimilation concepts rather than integration in the last two decades, and it is still in commercial terms the most successful British-Asian film. In many ways comparable to Damian O'Donnell's *East is East*, Hark Bohm's *Yasmin*, and Philippe Faucon's *Samia*, Gurinder Chadha's celebrated work ultimately falls into the trap of following monocultural patterns of thought that break with the transcultural perspectives embedded in the film and indicated in interviews.

With the analysis of *The Edge of Heaven*, this study turns to the most impressive transcultural work of famous Turkish-German director Fatih Akın, which prepares the ground for elaborations of solidarity messages in other European films and will be mapped against tendencies in German cinema before and after Unification, including Akın's earlier films *Short Sharp Shock*, *In July*, and *Solino*. There is evidence of a comprehensive subversion of nationality, gender, education, and age-related stereotypes by explorations of affect in *The Edge of Heaven*, which successfully started in Akın's *Head-On* (2004) and continues in Yasmin Samdereli's *Almanya* (2011). Finally, Aki Kaurismäki's *Le Havre* has been chosen as a popular example of more recent work on transcultural memory. This chapter examines the potential and limitations of 'the new trend' and suggests that the 'mise-en-scène' of new solidarity leitmotifs appears as a powerful link between films as different as *Le Havre*, Zübert's *Three Quarter Moon* (2011), and Kahane's *The Blind Flyers* (2015).

In Chapter 4, the study concludes with a debate of selected films of one of the most popular Chicano directors, Gregory Nava, who in his attempt to bridge Spanish, Native American, and US American heritage interrogates the link between hybrid cultures and the so-called American Dream. I argue that this approach could lead the way to fruitful research of the European Dream in European cinema, and questions of postcolonial responsibility linking the themes.

Notes

1. *Letters from Alou* is well known as a text for anti-racist education and intercultural education in Spanish schools. In his *Companion to Spanish Cinema*, Bentley argues that it is the first film 'to tackle the issue [of immigration from Africa] square on' (2008: 289).
2. Power criticises the 'multiplicity of viewpoints [...] and motivations' (2011) in Loshitzky's *Screening Strangers* (2010), which offers convincing individual film analyses but lacks the conceptual basis for in-depth explorations of European identity questions.

Filmography

Akın, Fatih (1998): *Short Sharp Shock/kurz und schmerzlos*. BRD: Wüste Filmproduktion.
Akın, Fatih (1999): *In July/Im Juli*. Germany: Wüste Filmproduktion.
Akın, Fatih (2002): *Solino*. Germany: Wüste Filmproduktion.
Akın, Fatih (2003): *Head-On/Gegen die Wand*. Germany: Wüste Filmproduktion.
Akın, Fatih (2007): *The Edge of Heaven/Auf der anderen Seite*. Germany/Turkey: Anka Film.
Amelio, Gianni (1994): *Lamerica*. Italy, France, Switzerland: Alia Film, Cecchi Gori Group Tiger Cinematografica, Arena Films.
Armendáriz, Montxo (1990): *Letters from Alou/Las cartas de Alou*. Spain: Elías Querejeta Producciones Cinematográficas S.L., Televisión Española (TVE).

Bochert, Marc-Andreas (2015): *Krüger aus Almanya*. Germany: Provobis.
Bohm, Hark (1988): *Yasemin*. Germany: Hamburger Kino Kompanie/ZDF.
Chadha, Gurindher (2002): *Bend It Like Beckham*. UK, Germany, US: Kintop Pictures.
Echevarría, Nicolás (1990): *Cabeza de Vaca*. Mexico, Spain, US, UK: Producciones Iguana.
Fassbinder, Rainer Werner (1974): *Fear Eats the Soul/Angst essen Seele auf*. Germany: Filmverlag der Autoren.
Kahane, Peter (2015): *The Blind Flyers/Blindgänger*. Germany: Polyphon.
Kaurismäki, Aki (2011): *Le Havre*. Finland, France, Germany: Sputnik, Pyramide Productions, Pandora Filmproduktion.
León de Aranoa, Fernando (2005): *Princesas*. Spain: Reposado Producciones.
Nava, Gregory (1995): *My Family*. US: American Playhouse, American Zoetrope, Majestic Films International.
Nava, Gregory (2006): *Bordertown*. US: Möbius Entertainment, El Norte Productions, Nuyorican Productions.
O'Donnell, Damien (1999): *East Is East*. Great Britain: FilmFour.
Samdereli, Yasmin (2011): *Almanya – Willkommen in Deutschland*. Germany: Roxy Film, Infa Film.
Saura, Carlos (1996): *Taxi*. Spain: Canal+.
Zübert, Christian (2011): *Three Quarter Moon/Dreiviertelmond*. Germany: BR, ARTE.

Bibliography

Antor, Heinz (2006): 'Multikulturalismus, Interkulturalität und Transkulturalität. Perspektiven für interdisziplinäre Forschung und Lehre', in: Antor, Heinz (ed.): *Inter- und Transkulturelle Studien: Theoretische Grundlagen und interdisziplinäre Praxis*. Heidelberg: Winter, pp. 25–39.
Antor, Heinz (2010): 'From Postcolonialism and Interculturalism to the Ethics of Transculturalism in the Age of Globalization', in: Antor, Heinz; Merkl, Matthias; Stierstorfer, Klaus; Volkmann, Laurenz (eds.): *From Interculturalism to Transculturalism: Mediating Encounters in Cosmopolitan Contexts*. Heidelberg: Universitätsverlag Winter, pp. 1–14.
Ballesteros, Isolina (2015): *Immigration Cinema in the New Europe*. Chicago: University of Chicago Press.
Benessaieh, Afef (2012): 'Après Bouchard-Taylor: multiculturalisme, interculturalismeettransculturalisme au Québec', in: Imbert, Patrick; Fontille, Brigitte (eds.): *Trans, multi, interculturalité, trans, multi, interdisciplinarité*. Québec: Presses de l'université Laval, 2012, pp. 81–98.
Benessaieh, Afef (2010): 'Multiculturalism, Interculturality, Transculturality', in: Benessaieh, Afef (ed.): *Transcultural Americas/Amériques transculturelles*. Ottawa: Ottawa University Press, pp. 11–38.
Bentley, Bernard P.E. (2008): *A Companion to Spanish Cinema*. Woodbridge: Tamesis.
Berghahn, Daniela; Claudia Sternberg (eds./2010): *European Cinema in Motion: Migrant and Diasporic Film in Contemporary Europe*. Basingstoke: Palgrave Macmillan.
Bourne, Stephen (2001): *Black in the British Frame: The Black Experience in British Film and Television*. London: Continuum.
Brandt, Kim (2007): *Weiblichkeitsentwürfe und Kulturkonflikte im deutsch-türkischen Film*. Saarbrücken: VDM.

COE (1991): *The Council of Europe and the Cultural Heritage Information Documents*. Strasbourg: CoE.
Hake, Sabine; Barbara Mennel (2012): *Turkish German Cinema in the New Millenium: Sites, Sounds, and Screens*. Oxford, New York: Berghahn.
Harrod, Mary; Mariana Liz; Alissa Timoshkina (2015): *The Europeanness of European Cinema: Identity, Meaning, Globalization*. London: Tauris. .
Huggan, Graham (2006): 'Derailing the "Trans"? Postcolonial Studies and the Negative Effects of Speed', in: Antor, Heinz (ed.): *Inter- und Transkulturelle Studien: Theoretische Grundlagen und interdisziplinäre Praxis*. Heidelberg: Winter, pp. 55–61.
Jäckel, Anne (2015): 'Changing the Image of Europe? The Role of European Co-productions, Funds and Film Awards', in: Harrod, Mary; Mariana Liz; Alissa Timoshkina (eds.): *The Europeanness of European Cinema: Identity, Meaning, Globalization*. London: Tauris, pp. 59–71.
Lazarus, Neil (2012): *The Postcolonial Unconscious*. Cambridge: Cambridge University Press.
Loshitzky, Yosefa (2010): *Screening Strangers. Migration and Diaspora in Contemporary European Cinema*. Bloomington, Indianapolis: Indiana University Press.
Menozzi, Filippo (2014): *Postcolonial Custodianship: Cultural and Literary Inheritance*. New York: Routledge.
Moses, Dirk; Michael Rothberg (2014): 'A Dialogue on the Ethics and Politics of Transcultural Memory', in: Bond, Lucy et al. (eds.): *The Transcultural Turn: Interrogating Memory Between and Beyond Borders*. Berlin: De Gruyter, pp. 29–38.
Power, Aidan (2011): 'Loshitzky, Yosefa: Screening Strangers. Migration and Diaspora in Contemporary European Cinema. Bloomington, Indianapolis: Indiana University Press 2010', in: *alphaville* 1 (http://www.alphavillejournal.com/Issue%201/ReviewsPDF/Review Power.pdf) (last accessed October 8, 2014).
Ramalingam, Vidhya (2014): 'The European Far Right is on the Rise, Again', in: *The Guardian*, February 13, 2014 (http://www.theguardian.com/commentisfree/2014/feb/13/european-far-right-on-the-rise-how-to-tackle) (last accessed October 8, 2014).
Santaolalla, Isabel (2005): *Los "Otros". Etnicidad y "raza" en el cine español contemporáneo*. Zaragoza: Prensas universitarias de Zaragoza.
Santaolalla, Isabel (2007): 'Inmigración, "Raza", y género en el cine español actual', in: Herrera, Javier; Cristina Martínez-Carazo (eds.): *Hispanismo y Cine*. Madrid, Frankfurt/Main: Iberoamericana/Vervuert, pp. 436–476.
Singh, Jyotsna; David Kim (eds./2015): *The Postcolonial World*. New York: Routledge.
Torreblanca, José Ignacio; Mark Leonard (2013): 'The Continent-Wide Rise of Euroscepticism', in: *ecfr.eu*, May 16, 2013 (http://www.ecfr.eu/page/-/ECFR79_EUROSCEPTICISM_ BRIEF_ AW.pdf) (last accessed October 8, 2014).
Wallerstein, Immanuel (2003): 'Knowledge, Power, and Politics. The Role of an Intellectual in an Age of Transition', in: *UNESCO Forum on Higher Education, Research and Knowledge Global Research Seminar "Knowledge Society vs. Knowledge Economy: Knowledge, Power, and Politics"*. Opening Presentation. Paris, December 8–9, 2003 (http://unesdoc.unesco.org/images/0018/001833/183329e.pdf) (last accessed July 27, 2015).
Welsch, Wolfgang (1999): 'Transculturalism – The Puzzling Form of Cultures Today', in: Featherstone, Mike; Scott Lash (eds.): *Spaces of Culture: City, Nation, World*. London: Sage, pp. 194–213.

1 Otherness in Contemporary European Cinema

1.1 Questions of Traditional Othering

Before analyzing selected examples of European cinema, this study will explore the different concepts of Self and Otherness that are quite explicitly reconstructed in most of the films in our corpus. As German philosopher Wolfgang Welsch reminds us, notions of culture

> are not just descriptive concepts but operative concepts. Our understanding of culture is an active factor in our cultural life. [...] If one tells us (as the old concept of culture did) that culture is to be a homogeneity event, then we practice the required co-ercions and exclusions. [...] Whereas, if one tells us [...] that culture ought to incorporate the foreign and do justice to transcultural components, then we will set about this task, and then corresponding feats of integration will belong to the real structure of our culture. The 'reality' of culture is [...] always a consequence too of our conceptions of culture.
>
> (Welsch 1999: 201)

Welsch summarizes here the basic distinction between monoculturality and his understanding of transculturality, concepts that could be located at the opposite ends of a cultural spectrum, with multiculturality and interculturality between these two poles. However, considering the wide spectrum of positions, which includes 'multiculturalists' like Stefan Neubert, Hans-Joachim Roth and Erol Yildiz (2013) and 'interculturalists' like Werner Delanoy (2006) taking on perspectives this study tends to categorize as 'transcultural', I suggest differentiating further by classifying the concepts in Welsch's study as 'traditional multiculturality' and 'traditional interculturality', which will be examined below. All four concepts remain very popular, and they are significantly different, although Welsch and Graham Huggan (2006: 58) tend to stress the continuity among monoculturality, (traditional) multiculturality, and (traditional) interculturality, whereas Heinz Antor (2006: 30f.) and Delanoy (2006: 239) regard contemporary notions of interculturality and transculturality as complementary, an idea this study supports. In principle all four scholars reject the notion of monoculturality that shaped nationalism in 19th and early 20th century Europe and well beyond that period in most so-called developing countries, including India, Pakistan, Bangladesh, and Turkey, as well as most African and Latin American states. By the end of the 18th century, philosopher Johann Gottfried Herder had defined monocultural mentality as follows:

> Everything which is still the same as my nature, which can be assimilated therein, I envy, strive towards, make my own; beyond this, kind nature has armed me with insensibility, coldness and blindness; it can even become contempt and disgust.[1]

The short passage describes a notion of culture that could be regarded as 'closed' (Benessaieh 2010: 13) or, more precisely, essentialist, homogeneous, and separatist in its link to the notion of a people. It appears both double-sided and hierarchical when sharply dividing a culturally and/or racially 'pure'/superior Self from an 'impure' and inferior Other, and it can be enhanced by the cultivation of a 'container culture' memory (Moses/Rothberg 2014: 31). Although all this is not representative of Herder's work,[2] he summarised the problematic side of this nationalist culture concept very well. Welsch rightly claims that such a traditional model is 'not only wrong but dangerous' in its assimilation and exclusion; in an increasingly global environment 'it is important to imagine cultures outside of the opposition of own and other cultures' (1997: 69, my translation), particularly beyond the well-known pattern of 'the heterogeneous and the own' (Adorno 1984: 192). With such remarks, both Welsch and Adorno imply that monoculturality is not a phenomenon of the past, although decolonization, mass immigration of non-European workforce, and the alternative culture concepts proposed by 1968 movements have contributed to a growing public acceptance of greater diversification in Europe.

By stressing the need for peaceful coexistence of different cultures within a society, traditional multiculturality re-establishes a relative distance to monocultural principles of purity and homogeneity, which is particularly important after long periods of extreme nationalist self-glorifications in the wider context of World War I and II mirrored in most British and US war movies from the 1940s to the 1960s could be cited as examples. However, the insistence on clearly definable cultural borders and on the perception of individual cultures as autonomous, self-sufficient, and coherent, reflected in so-called communitarian as well as left-wing progressive notions of multiculturality, remains a highly problematic aspect.[3] The focus on cultural difference and coexistence rather than on interaction does not address the new challenges of intercultural communication in increasingly diverse European societies marked by the diaspora of an immigrant workforce from former colonies and beyond, such as South-Asians in Britain, North-Africans in France, and Turks in Germany. In this context, it might be worth stressing that tendencies to self-enclosure in an 'imagined community'—to refer to Benedict Anderson's famous discussion on nationalism (1991)—cannot be regarded as a one-dimensional pattern only applicable to people from so-called host countries. British and British-Asian directors have repeatedly highlighted this in their portrayal of Pakistani communities in Britain (see Udayan Prasad's *My Son the Fanatic* 1997, Damian O'Donnell's *East is East* 1999, and Ken Loach's *Ae Fond Kiss* 2004), and research on Indian and Pakistani nationalism confirms the socio-historical and political background of such tendencies.[4] Similarly, Turkish-German directors have explored strong nationalist tendencies in immigrant communities (see Tevfik Baser's *40 Square Meters of Germany* 1985 and Hark Bohm's *Yasmin* 1988), and there is no shortage of portrayals of self-enclosure in other migrant films (such as Philippe Faucon's *Samia* 2000 and Tasma's *Fracture* 2010). Consequently, one must assess the social impact of cross-cultural nationalism and racism on screen with regard to the link to nationalist mentalities in the host and the migrants' home countries. In this framework, we should take note of the shift from biological to cultural racism (Hardt/Negri 2000: 189ff.), but it is also important to accept that the latter can be as essentialist and the former separatist.

The controversy about different concepts of culture increases when contemporary notions of interculturality are linked to Herder's elaborations on the 'culture of a folk' (1967[1774]: 45). Welsch criticises the (traditional) interculturalists' focus on cultural differences (1999: 196–197), which in my opinion is frequently mirrored in their leitmotif of 'bridging differences'. The leitmotif continues to shape a wide range of work from William B. Gudykunst's classic *Bridging Differences* (2004) and Patrick Schmidt's less convincing *In Search of Intercultural Understanding* (2007) to Bernd Springer's underresearched *Das kommt mir Spanisch vor* (2012). For Huggan, such a focus on dissimilarity implies a 'back-door to cultural essentialism' (2006: 58), whereas Antor stresses that contemporary forms of interculturality have abolished the idea of cultural oppositions and focus instead on a dialogue that intends to cross boundaries (2006: 29). Delanoy goes one step further when stressing that intercultural learning theorists have always shown a strong interest in 'cultural interdependence' and 'transcultural phenomena' (2006: 239). This theoretical discussion is of major relevance for the analysis of cultural representations in contemporary European migrant cinema because one often finds Huggan's assessment of interculturality in films up to the 1990s (Stuart Allen's comedy series *Love Thy Neighbour* from the 1970s, Ahmed A. Jamal's *Majdhar* 1983, and Armendáriz's *Letters from Alou* 1990). On the other hand, recent productions increasingly tend toward categorizing the way Antor or Delanoy suggest (e.g., Akın's *The Edge of Heaven* 2007 and Kaurismäki's *Le Havre* 2011).

1.2 Transcultural Identities in a Postcolonial Framework

Depending on the definition of interculturality, 'transculturality' can be defined in different ways: as a radical break with rather separatist notions of cultures (see Welsch 1999: 198), as the consequence of intercultural exchange (Delanoy 2006: 239), or as a significantly different concept that finally blurs the boundaries of individual cultures (Antor 2006: 30). This study supports Antor's perspective and acknowledges that transcultural notions focus on the interconnectedness of our increasingly global environment and on interactions and exchanges that contribute to the development of a pool of global cultures potentially facilitating cultural choices.[5] Instead of further enhancing separatist concepts of national cultures and 'bridging' the differences (Gudykunst 2004), Antor suggests starting explorations from the 'interlocking interdependence of cultures in the age of globalization' (Antor 2010: 12). This move would critically interrogate and destabilize the traditional binary construct of Self and Other and imply that questions of human agency versus collective structures have to be revisited and possibly revised. In this context, transculturality builds on well-established notions of hybrid societies, which have been discussed by Bhabha (1994) and García Canclini (1995), for example. However, it concentrates on questions of agency and remains process-orientated vis-à-vis a more results-oriented notion of hybridity. Contemporary urban landscapes such as New York and Tijuana, which García Canclini explores in *Hybrid Cultures* (1995), but also hybrid music and so-called fusion food could consequently be regarded results of transcultural dialogue and exchange. This correlates with enhanced cross-cultural agency in a period of increasing globalisation, including accelerated use of the Internet and virtual communication.

In his well-received documentary *Crossing the Bridge: The Sound of Istanbul* (2005), Fatih Akın provides us with excellent examples of such agents within Turkish music culture, because the bands interviewed here draw very consciously on so called 'traditional Turkish' music,[6] 'Western pop', and numerous other styles in order to create something new.[7] This new style is the result of ongoing explorations and negotiations and as such is never complete. It cannot culminate in a harmonious entity because it is never free of tensions, but it blurs traditional boundaries when joining different cultural elements within a shared cultural framework. In this context, the musicians remind us that transcultural agency depends not only on the ability to redefine culture as a highly dynamic, interconnected, and transitory 'relational web' (Benessaieh 2010: 11), but also on the capacity to critically interrogate one's own concepts of culture and identity. Films like *Crossing the Bridge* are able to support the development of such agency, because they help 'to dissolve the solidity of one's [...] identity and to share the experience of "the other"', which is a key aspect of transculturality for Epstein (2009: 340) and which is also a very important objective for the migrant film directors discussed in Chapter 3.

European migrant cinema can also facilitate the development and dissemination of 'multidirectional' memories (Rothberg 2009, 2011), which are key for implementing the 'ethics of transcultural memory' by acknowledging 'our implication in each other's suffering and loss' and 'our mutual experience of histories of destruction' (Moses/Rothberg 2014: 29). Rothberg defines the three-dimensional focus of the transcultural turn in memory studies as follows:

> The need for attention to theoretical definitions of actually existing transcultural and transnational connections; the ethical and political problems that attend the circulation of memories; and the possibilities for counter-narratives and new forms of solidarity that sometimes emerge when practices of remembrance are recognized as implicated in each other. (ibid. p. 31)

For cinema, this implies the need to critically interrogate, revise, and amend popular short-term memory of mass immigration to Europe as reflected and enhanced in contemporary mass media. The revision would include aspects of European emigration from conquest and colonization (in Echevarría's *Cabeza de Vaca* 1991) to 20th century fascist imperialism (in Amelio's *Lamerica* 1994 and Kaurismäki's *Le Havre*), which prepared the ground for postcolonial migration (Armendáriz's *Letters from Alou* 1990 and Saura's *Taxi* 1996) and postcolonial diaspora (Chadha's *Bend It Like Beckham* 2002). Such a multidirectional perspective allows the viewer to explore parallels in the negotiation of identities as well as the monocultural, traditional multicultural, and traditional intercultural obstacles to it.

In this context, it would be fundamentally misleading to regard globalization, transcultural exchange, individual agency, and transcultural memory development as intrinsically linked. In opposition to Welsch, this study argues that transcultural exchange and memory building can be traced back to ancient high cultures, i.e., it should not be regarded as 'a consequence of the inner differentiation and complexity of modern cultures' (Welsch 1999: 197). Also, one cannot assume that 'the global networking of communications technology' will necessarily further enhance transcultural dialogue and hybridization, because 'there is no longer anything absolutely foreign' (Welsch 1999: 198). The substantial use of global communications by the highly diverse spectrum of contemporary monocultural agents, from extreme European right-wing parties to Islamic fundamentalist organizations including Islamic State, is a clear example of the fragility of the potential link between globalization and transculturality. Working hypotheses of an intrinsic link are consequently based on a highly optimistic, if not naïve/glorifying, assessment of globalization and global communication, which tends to marginalize questions of economic, political, and military power, as well as the impact of socio-economic, political, and cultural discourses on individual and collective lifestyles, aims, and internalized hierarchies. Fundamental differences in education, cognitive abilities, and the instrumentalization of education in neo-liberal frameworks are other aspects that further limit transcultural agency. Delanoy reminds us that transcultural processes can be experienced in very different ways: as conscious or unconscious, self-chosen or forced, free or regimented, individual or collective, at surface or at a deeper level; they can be used for political empowerment or oppression, for a critique of the nation, or for the development of new nationalism (2006: 236–239; see also Delanoy 2012: 160–164). Although all these aspects need to be considered when exploring cultural exchange and memory development in film, it is worth stressing that they depend on subjective definitions ('free', 'surface level'?) and that the above outlined basic differentiation of identity concepts remains valid. If, for example, in the above-referenced context of music culture developments key representatives of the music industry tend to accept only a very particular (e.g., supposedly more market-oriented) form of hybrid music for dissemination, this should be discussed as a new monocultural orientation, not a transcultural development.

On the other hand, most transcultural processes—from music and food culture developments to the individual desire for (and personal change in) trans-ethnic relationships—might simply pass unacknowledged, which leads us to 'affective dimensions of shared human vulnerability' (Breger 2014: 66). I argue that by considering the preconscious 'unformed and unstructured' affect (Massumi 2002: 260) as a key factor of interpersonal interaction and cultural interconnectedness, transcultural studies help to prepare the ground for a new post-postmodernist perspective. Such a viewpoint can also be found in Gilroy's elaborations of 'conviviality' (2004: xi), Appiah's discussion of 'partial cosmopolitanism' (2007: xvii), and Breger's vision of 'transnational cosmopolitanism' (2014: 68). Although there are differences in Gilroy's, Appiah's, and Breger's viewpoints on the necessary balance between postmodernist deconstruction and post-postmodernist affirmative notions of belonging, there is major common ground with regard to their basic aims, which reflect transcultural objectives and the ethics of transcultural memory discussed above and are summarized by Gilroy as follows:

> We need to consider whether the scale upon which sameness and difference are calculated might be altered productively so that the strangeness of strangers goes out of focus and other dimensions of a basic sameness can be acknowledged and made significant. We also need to consider how a deliberate engagement with the twentieth century's histories of suffering might furnish resources for the peaceful accommodation of otherness in relation to fundamental commonality. (2004: 3)

For this, Gilroy suggests taking note of the 'creative, intuitive capacity among ordinary people who manage tensions' (2006), and Breger asks for a reconceptualization of the relatively 'fluid processes of affective encounter, which [...] never operate outside signification, but [...] also cannot be reduced to stable emotional capture' (2014: 70).[8] I argue that such a transcultural reconceptualization is possible within European migrant cinema if reimagined as a 'realm of affective encounters [and] signification'. This is the case in Breger's definition of narrative as 'a process of configuration through a world-making "assemblage" of affects, associations, images, sounds', which 'contributes to ongoing affective orientations in the (larger) world' (ibid. p. 69f.).

For most films under consideration, including *Bend It Like Beckham*, *Taxi*, *Letters from Alou,* and *Le Havre*, the tensions between traditional cultural binaries and transcultural perspectives of glocal life experience are inextricably linked to questions of neocolonialism and its critical interrogation by postcolonial scholars, who increasingly include key concepts of transcultural memory as well as affect studies and might therefore be well equipped to help prepare the ground for post-postmodernism. In this context, it is worth stressing that a majority of people of migrant background living in contemporary Western Europe originate from former colonies of those Western powers. Most of them migrated during or after the decolonization period, including Indians, Pakistanis, and Bangladeshis who settled in the UK in large numbers beginning in the 1950s, Algerians who went mostly to France starting in the 1960s, and Moroccans and Latin Americans who have left for Spain in substantial numbers since the 1980s. The same applies to Brazilian migration to Portugal, some sub-Saharan African migration to Belgium, South-African and South-Asian migration to the Netherlands, and Albanian migration to Italy, to name just a few demographic shifts that have been the topic of cinematic exploration. In all of these cases, postcolonial research can directly help shed light on the cultural encounters portrayed, whereas in cases without a shared history of colonialism, which includes Turkish migration to Germany, there is a strong indirect link due to the impact of European colonialism and neo-colonialism on the framing of Self and Other.[9]

In the 1960s, Kwame Nkrumah criticized the 'enormous dimension of finance-capital concentrated in a few hands' (1965: vi) and—paraphrasing him—Ashcroft and Tiffin stated that the new challenge could be linked to the aim of ex-colonial powers and superpowers such as the US 'to play a decisive role through international monetary bodies, (...) the fixing of prices on world markets, multinational corporations and cartels and a variety of educational and cultural institutions' (Ashcroft 1999: 162ff.). In his well-known work *Translation and Empire*, Robinson confirms that there is a 'continuing force of authority' at work, which shapes 'self concept, values, political systems and personalities' (1997: 22). In this sense, it might not be wrong to talk about a colonization of the mind. Not by coincidence Shankar states that 'economic subordination, cultural imperialism, and psychological anxiety survive (...) independence' (2001: 137), and Bhabha criticizes an 'ongoing colonial present' (1994: 128). On a representational level, this implies the continuity of binary constructs within which former colonizers and succeeding national elites tend to portray themselves to formerly colonized or neo-colonized 'Others' as rational, civilized, and male representatives of a superior order, which leaves more instinctive, barbarian, and female roles for those Others.[10] Within the image of 'the west and the rest' Said stresses the continuity of such dichotomies (1995: 20). The superficial inversion of colonial structures in some African dictatorships[11] or in some self-excluding migrant communities in Europe neither breaks with these binary patterns of thought nor is likely to improve the situation for the 'ex-colonized'. On the other hand, any intent to reduce the complex contemporary condition to a homogenic 'neocolonial' phenomenon, within which political independence appears as a minor event, would not only be wrong but is likely to serve the binary agenda of colonialism. Instead, I propose that we imagine that world in its complexity: 'successfully decolonized in some respects and still subject to updated colonial mechanisms in others' (Shankar 2001: 139), whereas the local nature of colonialism, decolonization, and/or neocolonialism and its cinematic portrayal might be significantly different in each case and ought to be explored individually.

After all, it would be blatantly simplistic to reduce the extreme variety of globalization processes to a form of Western neo-imperialism, and it might even be more misguided to regard hybridity as omnipotent guiding principle out of conflictive hierarchical relations. Kien Nghi Ha stressed the need for a more differentiated discussion of mainstream commercial forms of hybridity in architecture, music, and TV, which contribute to the stabilization of late-capitalist power relations by the instrumentalization of the Other as a 'funky-fresh' or 'exotic-erotic' object of consumption within the marketing patterns of a new American Dream (*Hype um Hybridität* 2005: 75–81).[12] There are, however, parallels and resemblances to colonial patterns of domination if we start considering imperialism as not simply 'a conscious and active ideology, but a combination of conscious ideological programs and unconscious "rhizomic" structures of unprogrammed connections and engagements'.[13] In this sense, a relatively obvious common denominator can be found in ongoing processes of colonization and commodification of 'nature' (to include animals), which despite increasing concerns amongst environmentalists, animal rights activists, postcolonialists, and affect studies scholars are still far from being solved.

Since the colonial process began, the expansion of the languages of the colonizers as well as the continuing mechanisms of language choice and use after political independence have been regarded as defining characteristics of and threats to identity, so it is not surprising that linguistic analysis and language policy have become key issues in postcolonial studies. Ashcroft, Griffith, and Tiffin stress that 'to name the world is to "understand" it, to know it and to have control over it' (2006: 261). This is by no means a new finding if we take into account Antonio Nebrija's perspective of language as 'companion of empire' ('compañera del imperio'), voiced in his famous *Gramática castellana* in the year in which the Spanish colonization of the 'New World' began (1992 [1492]: 99). In this context, Ngũgĩ wa Thiong'o's rejection of English as yet another imperial language probably needs no further elaboration (see his *Decolonising the Mind* 1986). The attempts by many directors and scriptwriters to integrate the language of the Other, often to the extent that film comprehension is reduced, could be regarded as an example of new language awareness. However, in the last decades many scholars have put forward arguments for a subversion of 'ex-colonial' languages to suit the needs of formerly colonized people without losing the imperial language's qualities. Its potential to give 'access to [...] desirable domains of power and knowledge' (Kachru 1990: 7) by, for example, 'indianizing' English, 'africanising' French or 'turkifying' German, is one example, which can be found in contemporary migrant narrative.[14]

Finally, it is worth questioning scholarly assumptions of an unavoidable shift from monoculturality to transculturality in the context of enhanced globalization and international mass migration. Footprints of monocultural concepts are widely visible, and up to a certain degree mentalities remain governed by them—as media portrayals of encounters in international football continue to show. French tabloid media coverage of African footballers in French clubs and British tabloid media coverage of English–German games provide numerous xenophobic accounts of culture clashes,[15] which lead us to doubt the idea of football as the cultural mediator advocated in *Bend It Like Beckham*. It is therefore legitimate to ask which tendencies are here to stay and develop further, monocultural or transcultural approaches. Although there is clear evidence of an increasing process of cultural hybridization, there are also many examples of growing xenophobia. There is a tendency to integrate hybrid texts (in particular songs and films) into neo-capitalist models that strengthen industries of a particular (usually Western) cultural geography, and this study suggests that comedies like O'Donnell's *East Is East* and Chadha's *Bend It Like Beckham* fit very well into this category. Certainly, if and when hybridity degenerates into a fashionable object of consumption, it is extremely likely to lose its destabilizing potential and enhance traditional boundaries instead, as Ha has argued with reference to the German-Turkish TV comedy series *Erkan & Stefan* (2005: 80). This, and the apparently never-ending attraction of monocultural perspectives, confirmed by spectacular right-wing success in the European Parliament elections in 2014, is in itself a phenomenon that breaks with current notions of linear and progressive developments from monocultural to transcultural societies. Major historical examples include the paradigmatic return of monocultural features in socio-political and cultural life from a relatively tolerant Muslim Spain to an exclusive Catholic Spain (1492), from the Ottoman Empire to the Turkish Republic in the 1920s, from Weimar to German National Socialism in the 1930s, and from Arab Palestine to the State of Israel in the 1940s. Other examples are the discrimination of foreign workers in 1950s and 1960s England (with 'No Blacks, no Irish, no dogs' signs on numerous Bed and Breakfasts), the post-9/11 increase in xenophobia against Muslims in the US and Europe, and the new rise of radical Islamist societies, from Afghanistan's Taliban to the Islamic State movement in Syria and Iraq. Despite their dissimilarities, all of these examples indicate a cyclical return to monocultural essentialism, homogeneity, and separatism—ranging from patterns of cultural exclusion to aggressive suppression and elimination of Others in periods of major crisis—and this ethnocentric tendency destabilizes the development of transcultural alternatives.

1.3 The Other in European Migrant Cinema

Europe has become 'multinational, multi-religious and multi-ethnic' (Elsaesser 2015: 21), and recent statistics confirm that despite the impact of the global financial crisis of 2007–2008 and the so- called Eurozone crisis, in which unemployment rates in Greece and Spain reached 27% (CBS 2013), mass immigration to Europe continues. Estimates for the number of immigrants to the EU-27[16] from non-EU countries are 1.7 million for 2012, which is very much in line with preceding years (1.73 in 2009, 1.81 in 2010 and 1.75 in 2011). Germany reports the largest numbers (592,200) well ahead of the UK (498,000), Italy (350,800), France (327,400), and Spain (304 100), although in Spain emigration rates were higher than immigration rates due to its national crisis (Eurostat 2015). These figures confirm substantial differences with regard to demographic change in Europe, which have to be examined in the framework of comparably strong migration between EU countries (also 1.7 million; ibid.).They also highlight the continuity of mass migration to the four countries for filmic case study analysis in this monograph. Finally, despite political rhetoric of exclusion, there can be little doubt about future mass migration to Europe given long-term migration trends to OECD countries with high Human Development Indexes,[17] the challenges linked to an aging European population, and the difficulties policing European borders.

In this context, media debates on the impact of large-scale migration are now a weekly (if not daily) news feature; films about the migrant Other have become part of a mainstream trend in European cinema and TV alike, and scholarly discussions have followed. The latter include critical interrogations of key concepts, in which even the very existence of 'European cinema' has been questioned. Although European cinema cannot be regarded 'as a cultural monolith or static unitary identity' (Everett 2005: 8), and I argue that scholars looking for such a homogenous entity might have to conclude that it does not exist, I value it as a very significant cultural and analytical concept. It is also a space for the articulation of extremely diverse and multifaceted European cultures, in which film 'becomes both the object of and the vehicle for Europe's fundamental quest for identity' (Everett 2005: 8, 13, 12). This implies a focus on European themes and, more precisely, a fundamental interest in 'reworking [...] the values and political ideals of the Enlightenment' (Elsaesser 2015: 31).These correlate with a shared history of nationalism and colonialism, including two world wars largely fought on European soil and the impact of decolonization and 'post-nationalism' shaping contemporary migration to Europe and its exploration in European migrant cinema. Another legacy is Christianity, which continues to be magnified in Islamophobic right-wing discourses as a key characteristic of European heritage,[18] and which remains a hot topic in European film. Wheatley outlines three main tendencies: 'the Christian narrative, the anti-Christian film and the Christian aesthetic' (2015: 91). These indicate the ongoing tensions surrounding ideas of modern Europe: At the one end of the spectrum, there is the fundamentalist Christian idea of modern Europe staying or falling with the defense of Christianity whereas, at the other end, a militant form of secularism is portrayed as the pillar of modern European identity. Serious discussions between those poles include the recognition of Christianity as 'the privileged faith in Western society and culture' (Wheatley 2015: 89). From this fruitful starting point one can critically interrogate the conscious and often one-sided portrayals of Christian myths, narratives, and imagery in European cinema as well as the often less consciously employed Christian aesthetics informing European movies that remain ambiguous: 'These films incorporate Christianity; they do not appropriate it' (Wheatley 2015: 98). According to Elsaesser, such cinematic explorations of shared European history have led to a 'common heritage of story types and myths, of deep structures of feeling, genres of symbolic action and narrative trajectories that create recognizably European protagonists and destinies' (2005: 25).

European funding programs and European film awards, which aim to support explorations of Europe's shared history and diversity in film, provide more common ground. The spectrum of funding programs ranges from the foundation of MEDIA in 1987, which led to successful pre- and post-production initiatives such as the European Script Fund (SCRIPT) and the European Film Distribution Office (EFDO) and to the setup of Eurimages (1988) that helps to develop co-productions between partners from different member states.[19] Similarly, the impact of awards such as FELIX (from 1988) and the LUX prize (from 2007) on cinematic themes should not be underestimated. Directors who want to compete for them have to 'illustrate or question the founding values of our European identity, illustrate the diversity of European traditions, and/or provide insights into the debate on the EU integration process'.[20] On the other hand, the heterogeneous membership of most funding panels and award committees as well as the openness of such guidelines, mirrored in the norms for funding initiatives and linking with the Council of Europe's wider mandate to human rights and multicultural acceptance (CoE 1991: 9), leave a wide space for the development of individual film projects. With regard to the impact of Eurimages, Jäckel stresses the irony 'that a pan-European fund with a mandate to "promote European identity" with references to "a single culture" often gives its support to films that foreground rather than obliterate cultural differences' (2015: 65).

Finally, there is a tendency toward low budget and small-scale films in Europe, which correlates with a long tradition of 'auteur' cinema (Everett 2005: 11) that is again gaining strength. Not by coincidence, Bergfelder starts his exploration of 'popular European cinema in the 2000s' with comments on the 'reinvigorated championing of auteurism' and the 'renewed orientation towards art cinema practices' that help us understand European cinema as 'a productive category for academic enquiry, as a viable form of cinema and as an object of cinephilic attention' (2015: 33). Also, his long list of most popular European films from 2004 to 2011 (2015: 46–57) confirms the strength of this highly diverse, small-scale cinema in the 21st century. Although it would be wrong to portray this tendency as the absolute opposite of Hollywood, which has developed its own tradition of auteurism with Scorcese, De Palma, and Cimino exemplifying New American Cinema, it makes sense to talk about differences in preferred production styles with auteur cinema on the one hand and corporate productions on the other hand. Everett summarizes the discrepancy as follows:

> Whatever the financial and other pressures, many European directors continue to make essentially personal films in an entirely individual even idiosyncratic way. And this simply does not sit easily with a large studio system or with current pressures to produce big budget, commercially successful films. (2005: 11)

It is worth adding that European small-scale productions can be financially successful, as one film from our case study analysis demonstrates very clearly: *Bend It Like Beckham*, a $5 million production, generated around $350 million in its first year (silicone team 2003: 15) and is as such an excellent example of low-budget success. In contrast, bigger corporate productions with Hollywood stars like Jennifer Lopez and Antonio Banderas do not necessarily have to offer a recipe for success, as the major loss from *Bordertown* (2006) illustrates ($21 million budget vis-à-vis $8.3 million box office gross; IMDB 2015).

Although Hollywood manages to keep more than a 60% market share of the global box office,[21] categorizing European cinema as 'the big loser' and discussing it predominantly as part of 'world cinema' (Elsaesser 2005: 485ff., 495) is not convincing. Instead, it could be regarded as a thriving cinema that fosters a 'transnational European film culture' through co-productions and exports (Bergfelder 2015: 45). There can be no doubt that in a period of increasing migration in Europe and a growing virtual culture, its cultural observations are of key importance, as potential reflections of popular attitudes, ideas, and preoccupations or as regards their likely impact on popular views and opinions on the topic.[22]

When this study refers to 'European migrant cinema', it is very much in line with our exploration of European cinema that I argue for an open definition, for which I draw on recent debates about Chicano cinema. In her study, 'Allison Anders and the Racial "Authenticity" Membership-Test', Pitman (2012) argues that the same critics, who produce outstanding non-essentialist theorizations of Chicano identity in film, still occasionally struggle to disentangle themselves from using essentialist arguments in their own work. A prime example is the debate over definitions of Chicano cinema, which seems frequently reduced to films produced for, by, and about Chicanos. Pitman argues that such a racial limitation (by and for Chicanos) can no longer be upheld and proposes a less restrictive definition linked to Chicano diaspora themes. Similarly, and in opposition to traditional concepts, I suggest a definition of European migrant cinema that embraces films about 'migration' to/from 'Europe', regardless of the cultural background of directors, scriptwriters, producers, cast, or potential viewers.

In this sense, migrant cinema should be regarded neither as a genre nor as a homogenous entity. It cannot be categorized as part of Third Cinema or Accented Cinema as defined by Nacify, because it does not necessarily attempt to 'create a nostalgic, even fetishized, authentic prior culture—before contamination by the West in the case of the Third Cinema, and before displacement and emigration in the case of the accented cinema' (2001: 31). Also, it does not have to follow Marxist or socialist perspectives, which tend to characterize Third Cinema (ibid.). It is not driven by Accented Cinema's 'aesthetics of juxtaposition', which include binary structures that 'nostalgically repress, fetishize, and favorably compare [...] home with exile' and correlate with particular 'accents' in plot, narrative structure, visual style, and character development (Nacify 2001: 6, 21). Finally, the director's 'displacement' is not a prerequisite, nevermind first generation forced displacement, which frequently leads to traumas that inform Nacify's notions of exilic and diasporic identities.

None of this excludes the possibility of exploring selected migrant films from an Accented Cinema perspective. However, this study concentrates on films by directors with second-generation migrant background, such as Gurinder Chadha and Fatih Akın, whose work cannot be understood solely on the basis of personal traumas of displacement, and on movies by directors without migrant background and personal experience of international displacement, including Montxo Armendáriz and Aki Kaurismäki. It is worth adding that in countries with relatively recent mass immigration, like Spain, Portugal, Italy, Sweden, Denmark, and Finland, cinematic explorations of migration and diaspora are largely left to directors and scriptwriters without migrant background, which implies that in a reductionist view of migrant cinema a wide spectrum of European perspectives would have to be excluded. The above-proposed wider definition of migrant cinema allows the inclusion of non-European directors, such as Nicolas Echevarría, whose work on European colonialism and potential alternatives stands at the beginning of our explorations of the migrant Other in film.

Notes

1. 'Alles was mit meiner Natur noch gleichartig ist, was in sie assimiliert werden kann, beneide ich, strebs an, mache mirs zu eigen; darüber hinaus hat mich

die gütige Natur mit Fühllosigkeit, Kälte und Blindheit bewaffnet; sie kann gar Verachtung und Ekel werden' (Herder 1967[1774]: 45, own translation).
2. Such statements by the German philosopher should be assessed within the broader context of his ideas on humanity elaborated in his later work; precisely because of this need for contextualization it would be misleading to categorize him as some kind of master-mind of 19th and 20th century European nationalism, as Welsch does (1999). However, conservative Herder-researchers, national school reformers, and social Darwinists have done precisely that over the last centuries. For a discussion of Herder reception see Gaier (2007) and Proß (2007).
3. See Welsch (1997: 70); Epstein describes the result as 'cocoonization of each culture within itself' (2009: 329). Neubert/Roth/Yildiz highlight essentialist, separatist, and fundamentalist orientations of communitarian and left-wing progressive multiculturalists and opt instead for a 'critical self-reflexive multiculturalism discourse' with transcultural tendencies (2013: 16–17).
4. For a discussion of Indian and Pakistani nationalism see Srivastava (2008: 37f.).
5. Whereas Huggan (2006: 58f.) claims a direct link between transculturalism and individual choice, Ritzer's *McDonaldization of Society* highlights the limits of individuality set by glocal business (2011). I argue that there is a tendency toward cultural choice, but the gap between rhetoric and factual limits of choice must be considered, and each individual case has to be assessed in its own right.
6. In its discussion of so-called traditional Turkish music as a hybrid, which integrates Egyptian sounds; the film 'brilliantly illustrates that past cultural production also relied on borrowing, influencing and exchanging of "other" cultural traditions' (Mennel 2010: 52).
7. Isenberg highlights the innovative potential when she argues that 'Akın adeptly eludes the trap of ethnic essentialism by revealing the fertile cross-pollination of traditions: the Romani influence on Turkish folk music, the import of Seattle grunge by the rock band Duman and the speed rapping of Ceza' (2011: 61).
8. The importance of affects for our study lies particularly in the fact that they are 'ways of connecting to others and to other situations' (Massumi, in: Zournazi 2003), which are not individually or discursively controlled. Furthermore, their intensity and fluidity directs our attention to a potential that is likely to open new ground in cultural studies.
9. In the case of Turkish-German relations, I suggest to consider potential continuities from Kemalist nationalism, which has been shaped by French colonialism and Italian fascism (see Zeydanlıoğlu 2007), as well as German nationalism and colonialism within the context of European colonial discourse. The former is well reflected in Baser's *40 Square Meters of Germany*, when Dursun summarizes the threat of moral corruption facing his wife if she were to leave the flat and catch the German 'disease'.
10. See Chateaubriand (1966: 159) for a romantic perception of such binaries. For a detailed analysis of hierarchical, polar images in (neo-) colonial encounters see Todorov (2013).
11. Zimbabwe has become an example of institutionalized black racism and an inversion of colonial relations when after numerous murders of white farmers and illegal occupation of their land Mugabe confirmed that 'whites … will not be allowed to own land' (Chidzha 2014).
12. For a summary of main ideas in English language see Ha (2007).

13. Drawing on the botanical rhizome, Ashcroft (2001: 50) refers here to a concept developed by Deleuze and Guattari that allows for multiple, non-hierarchical perspectives in interpretation.
14. See for example Feridun Zaimoğlu's *Kanak Sprak* (1999[1995]) and Lars Becker's film *Kanak Attack* (2000, based on Zaimoğlu's script).
15. See Boli's remarks on the lack of public acceptance of African footballers in French clubs due to 'préjugés proches des discours racialistes' (2010: 29) and Taylor's discussion of Englishness and football (2013: 394) with British media coverage of the 1996 European championship as a xenophobic peak. He comes to the conclusion: 'Just like British society, it [football] seems to be in a perpetual state of crisis and imminent collapse' (2013: 430).
16. Croatia joined as the 28th member state in January 2013.
17. See Martin's overview of migration trends from 1956 to 2004, which shows an overall increase in net migration rates to OECD countries that gains particular strength in the 1990s (2008: 24). UNEP (2012) highlights the continuity of net migration to Europe with a particular impact on Spain and Italy from 2005 to 2010, and the UNDP's (2014) *Human Development Report* suggests a correlation with HDI data insofar as mass migration tends to flow from lower to higher scoring HDI countries. Also, all four countries for case study analysis are still rated in the top 15% of 187 countries assessed, with Germany in sixth place before the UK (14), France (20), and Spain (27), which mirrors current net migration rates to these countries, although this has to be explored further in the context of other push and pull factors as well as political attempts to reduce immigration.
18. See for example the Islam versus Europe (2013) blog with the subtitle 'Where Islam spreads, freedom dies' and numerous Islamophobic comments as a reaction to the assault of a Catholic priest in Avignon.
19. See Jäckel (2015: 61) and Vincendau (1995: 133–134).
20. European Parliament website (2010), in: Jäckel (2015: 67).
21. In the last few years, there is again a relatively strong continuity in the Hollywood market share, which stays between 63% and 67%. *The Guardian* (2013) offers the following data: 2009: 63.9%; 2010: 67.4%; 2011: 66.9%; 2012: 62.7%.
22. The potential impact of cinema seems today as strong as once outlined in the Moyne Committee Report, according to which film is 'undoubtedly a most important factor in the education of all classes of the community, in the spread of national culture and in presenting national ideas and customs to the world' (Cinematograph Act 1927, quoted in Aldgate 2002: 1). In this 'educational' sense, Junkelmann categorizes films like *Gladiator* as a primary medium for shaping general ideas about the Ancient World: Film is 'perhaps the medium with the biggest impact on reception of Ancient World that has ever existed' (2004: 63).

Filmography

Akın, Fatih (1998): *Short Sharp Shock/kurz und schmerzlos*. BRD: Wüste Filmproduktion.
Akın, Fatih (1999): *In July/Im Juli*. Germany: Wüste Filmproduktion.
Akın, Fatih (2002): *Solino*. Germany: Wüste Filmproduktion.
Akın, Fatih (2003): *Head-On/Gegen die Wand*. Germany: Wüste Filmproduktion.

Akın, Fatih (2005): *Crossing the Bridge – The Sound of Istanbul*. Germany: corazón international/intervista digital media/NDR.
Akın, Fatih (2007): *The Edge of Heaven/Auf der anderen Seite*. Germany/Turkey: Anka Film.
Allen, Stuart; Ronnie Baxter; Anthony Parker et al. (1972–76): *Love Thy Neighbour*. UK: Thames Television for ITV.
Amelio, Gianni (1994): *Lamerica*. Italy, France, Switzerland: Alia Film, Cecchi Gori Group Tiger Cinematografica, Arena Films.
Armendáriz, Montxo (1990): *Letters from Alou/Las cartas de Alou*. Spain: Elías Querejeta Producciones Cinematográficas S.L., Televisión Española (TVE).
Baser, Tefvik (1985): *40 Square Meters of Germany/40 Quadratmeter Deutschland*. Germany: Letterbox Filmproduktion.
Becker, Lars (2000): *Kanak Attack*. Germany: Becker & Häberle Filmproduktion GmbH.
Bochert, Marc-Andreas (2015): *Krüger aus Almanya*. Germany: Provobis.
Bohm, Hark (1988): *Yasemin*. Germany: Hamburger Kino Kompanie/ZDF.
Chadha, Gurindher (2002): *Bend It Like Beckham*. UK, Germany, US: Kintop Pictures.
Echevarría, Nicolás (1990): *Cabeza de Vaca*. Mexico, Spain, US, UK: Producciones Iguana.
Fassbinder, Rainer Werner (1974): *Fear Eats the Soul/Angst essen Seele auf*. Germany: Filmverlag der Autoren.
Faucon, Philippe (2000): *Samia*. France: Canal+.
Jamal, Ahmed A. (1983): *Majdhar*. UK: Retake Film.
Kahane, Peter (2015): *The Blind Flyers/Blindgänger*. Germany: Polyphon.
Kaurismäki, Aki (2011): *Le Havre*. Finland, France, Germany: Sputnik, Pyramide Productions, Pandora Filmproduktion.
León de Aranoa, Fernando (2005): *Princesas*. Spain: Reposado Producciones.
Loach, Ken (2004): *Ae Fond Kiss*. Great Britain, Belgium, Germany, Italy, Spain: Bianca Film.
Nava, Gregory (1995): *My Family*. US: American Playhouse, American Zoetrope, Majestic Films International.
Nava, Gregory (2006): *Bordertown*. US: Möbius Entertainment, El Norte Productions, Nuyorican Productions.
O'Donnell, Damien (1999): *East Is East*. Great Britain: FilmFour.
Prasad, Udayan (1997): *My Son the Fanatic*. UK, France: Arts Council of England.
Samdereli, Yasemin (2011): *Almanya – Willkommen in Deutschland*. Germany: Roxy Film, Infa Film.
Saura, Carlos (1996): *Taxi*. Spain: Canal+.
Tasma, Alain (2010): *Fracture*. France: ACSE, CNC.
Zübert, Christian (2011): *Three Quarter Moon/Dreiviertelmond*. Germany: BR, ARTE.

Bibliography

Adorno, Theodor W. (1984): *Negative Dialektik.Gesammelte Schriften*. Vol. 6. Frankfurt a. M.: Suhrkamp.
Aldgate, Anthony, and Jeffrey Richards (2002): *Best of British. Cinema and Society from 1930 to the Present*. London, New York: Tauris.

Anderson, Benedict (1991[1983]): *Imagined Communities*. London: Verso Books.
Antor, Heinz (2006): 'Multikulturalismus, Interkulturalität und Transkulturalität. Perspektiven für interdisziplinäre Forschung und Lehre', in: Antor, Heinz (ed.): *Inter- und Transkulturelle Studien: Theoretische Grundlagen und interdisziplinäre Praxis*. Heidelberg: Winter, pp. 25–39.
Antor, Heinz (2010): 'From Postcolonialism and Interculturalism to the Ethics of Transculturalism in the Age of Globalization', in: Antor, Heinz; Matthias Merkl; Klaus Stierstorfer; Laurenz Volkmann (eds.): *From Interculturalism to Transculturalism: Mediating Encounters in Cosmopolitan Contexts*. Heidelberg: Universitätsverlag Winter, pp. 1–14.
Appiah, Kwame Anthony (2007): *Cosmopolitanism: Ethics in a World of Strangers*. New York: Norton.
Ashcroft, Bill; Gareth Griffiths; Helen Tiffin (1999): *Key Concepts in Post-Colonial Studies*. Oxford, New York: Routledge.
Ashcroft, Bill; Gareth Griffiths; Helen Tiffin (eds./2006): *The Post-Colonial Studies Reader*. 2nd edition. Oxford, New York: Routledge.
Ballesteros, Isolina (2015): *Immigration Cinema in the New Europe*. Chicago: University of Chicago Press.
Benessaieh, Afef (2010): 'Multiculturalism, Interculturality, Transculturality', in: Benessaieh, Afef (ed.): *Transcultural Americas/Amériques transculturelles*. Ottawa: Ottawa University Press, pp. 11–38.
Bentley, Bernard P.E. (2008): *A Companion to Spanish Cinema*. Woodbridge: Tamesis.
Bergfelder, Tim (2015): 'Popular European Cinema in the 2000s: Cinephilia, Genre and Heritage', in: Harrod, Mary; Mariana Liz; Alissa Timoshkina (eds.): *The Europeanness of European Cinema: Identity, Meaning, Globalization*. London: Tauris, pp. 33–57.
Berghahn, Daniela; Claudia Sternberg (eds./2010): *European Cinema in Motion: Migrant and Diasporic Film in Contemporary Europe*. Basingstoke: Palgrave Macmillan.
Bhabha, Homi (1994): *The Location of Culture*. New York: Routledge.
Boli, Claude (2010): 'Les footballeurs noirs africains en France. Des années cinquante à nos jours', in: *hommes & migrations* 1285, pp. 14–30 (http://hommesmigrations. revues.org/ 1173#tocto1n5) (last accessed September 26, 2014).
Bourne, Stephen (2001): *Black in the British Frame: The Black Experience in British Film and Television*. London: Continuum.
Brandt, Kim (2007): *Weiblichkeitsentwürfe und Kulturkonflikte im deutsch-türkischen Film*. Saarbrücken: VDM.
Breger, Claudia (2014): 'Configuring Affect: Complex World Making in Fatih Akın's "Auf der anderen Seite (The Edge of Heaven)"', in: *Cinema Journal* 54/1, pp. 65–87.
CBS (2013): 'Eurozone Unemployment at Record High in May', in: *CBS News* (http:// www.cbsnews.com/news/eurozone-unemployment-at-record-high-in-may/) (last accessed October 8, 2015).
Chateaubriand, François-René de (1966): *Génie du christianisme*. Paris: Gallimard.
Chidza, Richard (2014): 'No Land for Whites – Mugabe', in: *The Zimbabwe Mail*, July 3, 2014 (http://www.thezimmail.co.zw/2014/07/03/no-land-for-whites-mugabe) (last accessed November 14, 2014).
COE (1991): *The Council of Europe and the Cultural Heritage Information Documents*. Strasbourg: CoE.

Dagnino, Arianna (2013): 'Global Mobility, Transcultural Literature, and Multiple Modes of Modernity', in: *Transcultural Studies* 2, pp. 130–160.
Delanoy, Werner (2012): 'From "Inter" to "Trans"? Or: Quo Vadis Cultural Learning?', in: Eisenmann, Maria; Theresa Summer (eds.): Basic Issues in EFL Teaching and Learning. Heidelberg: Winter, pp. 157–167.
Elsaesser, Thomas (2005): *European Cinema: Face to Face with Hollywood*. Amsterdam: Amsterdam University Press.
Elsaesser, Thomas (2015): 'European Cinema into the Twenty-First Century: Enlarging the Context?', in: Harrod, Mary; Liz Mariana; Alissa Timoshkina (2015): *The Europeanness of European Cinema: Identity, Meaning, Globalization*. London: Tauris, pp. 17–32.
Epstein, Mikhail (2009): 'Transculture. A Broad Way between Globalisation and Multiculturalism', in: *American Journal of Economics and Sociology* 68/1, pp. 327–351.
Eurostat (2015): 'Migration and Migrant Population Statistics', in: *Eurostat Statistics explained* (http://ec.europa.eu/eurostat/statistics-explained/index.php/Migration_and_migrant_population_statistics) (last accessed October 8, 2015).
Everett, Wendy (ed./2005): *European Identity in Cinema*. Bristol: intellect.
Gaier, Ulrich (2007): 'Herder als Begründer des modernen Kulturbegriffs', in: Stauf, Renate; Berghahn, Cord-Friedrich (eds./2007): *Johann Gottfried Herder: Europäische Kulturtheorie zwischen historischer Eigenart und globaler Perspektive*. Heidelberg: Winter, pp. 5–18.
García Canclini, Néstor (1995): *Culturas Híbridas. Estrategias para entrar y salir de la modernidad*. Buenos Aires: Sudamericana.
Gilroy, Paul (2004): *After Empire: Melancholia or Convivial Culture?* London: Routledge.
Gilroy, Paul (2006): 'Colonial Crimes and Convivial Cultures', in: *Rethinking Nordic Colonialism Exhibition. Keynote Speech* (http://www.rethinking-nordic-colonialism.org/files/pdf/ ACT2/ESSAYS/Gilroy.pdf) (last accessed July 28, 2015).
Gudykunst, William (2004): *Bridging Differences: Effective Intergroup Communication*. 4th edition. London: Sage.
Ha, Kien Nghi (2005): *Hype um Hybridität. Kultureller Differenzkonsum und postmoderne Verwertungstechniken im Spätkapitalismus*. Bielefeld: Transcript Verlag.
Ha, Kien Nghi (2007): 'Crossing the Border? Hybridity as Late-Capitalistic Logic of Cultural Translation and National Modernisation', in: *Inter Activist Info Exchange* (http://eipcp.net/transversal/1206/ha/en) (last accessed October 8, 2014).
Hake, Sabine; Barbara Mennel (2012): *Turkish German Cinema in the New Millenium: Sites, Sounds, and Screens*. Oxford, New York: Berghahn.
Hardt, Guy; Antonio Negri (2000): *Empire*. Cambridge, Massachusetts: Harvard University Press.
Herder, Johann Gottfried (1967[1774]): *Auch eine Philosophie der Geschichte zur Bildung der Menschheit*. Frankfurt a.M.: Suhrkamp.
Huggan, Graham (2006): 'Derailing the "Trans"? Postcolonial Studies and the Negative Effects of Speed', in: Antor, Heinz (ed.): *Inter- und Transkulturelle Studien: Theoretische Grundlagen und interdisziplinäre Praxis*. Heidelberg: Winter, pp. 55–61.
IMDB (1990–2015): *International Movie Database* (http://www.imdb.com) (last accessed October 9, 2015).
Isenberg, Noah (2011): 'Fatih Akın's Cinema of Intersections', in: *Film Quarterly* 64/4, pp. 53–61.

Islam versus Europe (2013): 'France: Priest Attacked by Muslim' (http://islamver suseurope.blogspot. co.uk/2013/05/france-priest-attacked-by-muslim.html) (last accessed July 27, 2015).

Jäckel, Anne (2015): 'Changing the Image of Europe? The Role of European Co-productions, Funds and Film Awards', in: Harrod, Mary; Mariana Liz; Alissa Timoshkina (2015): *The Europeanness of European Cinema: Identity, Meaning, Globalization*. London: Tauris, pp. 59–71.

Junkelmann, Marcus (2004): 'Träume von Rom. Ridley Scotts "Gladiator" und die Tradition des römischen Monumentalfilms', in: Baumgaertner, Ulrich; Monika Fenn (eds.): *Geschichte und Film*. München: Herbert Utz, pp. 63–89.

Kachru, Braj B. (1990): *Alchemy of English. The Spread Functions and Models of Non-Native Englishes*. Urbana: University of Illinois Press.

Lazarus, Neil (2012): *The Postcolonial Unconscious*. Cambridge: Cambridge University Press.

Loshitzky, Yosefa (2010): *Screening Strangers. Migration and Diaspora in Contemporary European Cinema*. Bloomington, Indianapolis: Indiana University Press.

Martin, John P. (2008): 'Migration and the Global Economy', in: *Canadian Diversity* 6/3, pp. 22–25.

Massumi, Brian (2002): *Parables for the Virtual*. Durham: Duke UP.

Mennel, Barbara (2010): 'The Politics of Space in the Cinema of Migration', in: *GFL* 3, pp. 39–55.

Menozzi, Filippo (2014): *Postcolonial Custodianship: Cultural and Literary Inheritance*. New York: Routledge.

Moses, Dirk; Michael Rothberg (2014): 'A Dialogue on the Ethics and Politics of Transcultural Memory', in: Bond, Lucy et al. (eds.): *The Transcultural Turn: Interrogating Memory Between and Beyond Borders*. Berlin: De Gruyter, pp. 29–38.

Nacify, Hamid (2001): *An Accented Cinema. Exilic and Diasporic Filmmaking*. Princeton: Princeton University Press.

Nebrija, Elio Antonio de (1992[1492]): *Gramática castellana. Introducción y notas por Miguel Angel Esparza y Ramón Sarmiento*. Madrid: Fundación Antonio de Lebrija.

Neubert, Stefan; Hans-Joachim Roth; Erol Yildiz (2013): 'Multikulturalismus – ein umstrittenes Konzept', in: ibid. (eds.): *Multikulturalität in der Diskussion: neuere Beiträge zu einem umstrittenen Konzept*. Wiesbaden: Springer, pp. 9–29.

Nkrumah, Kwame (1965): *Neo-Colonialism: The Last Stage of Imperialism*. London: Thomas Nelson & Sons.

Pitman, Thea (2012): 'Allison Anders and the 'Racial "Authenticity" Membership-Test': Keeping *Mi vida loca/My Crazy Life* (1994) on the Borders of Chicano Cinema', in: *iMex* 1/2, pp. 12–30.

Power, Aidan (2011): 'Loshitzky, Yosefa: Screening Strangers. Migration and Diaspora in Contemporary European Cinema. Bloomington, Indianapolis: Indiana University Press 2010', in: *alphaville* 1 (http://www.alphavillejournal.com/ Issue%201/ReviewsPDF/Review Power.pdf) (last accessed November 8, 2014).

Proß, Wolfgang (2007): 'Herder und die moderne Geschichtswissenschaft', in: Stauf, Renate; Cord-Friedrich Berghahn (eds./2007): *Johann Gottfried Herder: Europäische Kulturtheorie zwischen historischer Eigenart und globaler Perspektive*. Heidelberg: Winter, pp. 19–44.

Ramalingam, Vidhya (2014): 'The European Far Right Is on the Rise, Again', in: *The Guardian*, February 13, 2014 (http://www.theguardian.com/commentisfree/2014/

feb/13/european-far-right -on-the-rise-how-to-tackle) (last accessed October 8, 2014).
Ritzer, George (2011): *The McDonaldization of Society*. 6th edition. London: Sage.
Robinson, Douglas (1997): *Translation and Empire. Postcolonial Theories Explained*. Manchester: St Jerome Publishing.
Rothberg, Michael (2009): 'Introduction: Theorizing Multidirectional Memory in a Transnational Age', in: Rothberg, Michael (ed.): *Multidirectional Memory: Remembering the Holocaust in the Age of Decolonization*. Stanford: Stanford University Press, pp. 1–29.
Rothberg, Michael (2011): From Gaza to Warsaw: Mapping Multidirectional Memory', in: *Criticism* 53/4, pp. 523–548.
Said, Edward (1995[1978]): *Orientalism. Western Conceptions of the Orient*. London: Penguin.
Santaolalla, Isabel (2005): *Los "Otros". Etnicidad y "raza" en el cine español contemporáneo*. Zaragoza: Prensas universitarias de Zaragoza.
Santaolalla, Isabel (2007): 'Inmigración, "Raza", y género en el cine español actual', in: Herrera, Javier; Cristina Martínez-Carazo (eds.): *Hispanismo y Cine*. Madrid, Frankfurt/Main: Iberoamericana/Vervuert, pp. 436–476.
Schachtner, Christina (2015): 'Transculturality in the Internet: Culture Flows and Virtual Publics', in: *Current Sociology Monograph* 63/2, pp. 228–243.
Schmidt, Patrick (2007): *In Search of Intercultural Understanding. A Practical Guidebook for Living and Working across Cultures*. Montreal: Meridian.
Shankar, Shalinki (2001): 'Decolonization', in: Hawley, John C. (ed.): *Encyclopaedia of Postcolonial Studies*. London: Greenwood, pp. 131–139.
silicone team (2003): 'Bend It Like Beckham', in: *siliconindia* 5, p. 15.
Singh, Jyotsna; David Kim (eds./2015): *The Postcolonial World*. New York: Routledge.
Springer, Bernd F. W. (2012): *Das kommt mir Spanisch vor. Einführung in die deutsch-spanische Kommunikation*. München: Iudicium.
Srivastava, Neelam Francesca Rashmi (2008): *Secularism in the Postcolonial Indian Novel. National and Cosmopolitan Narratives in English*. London: Routledge.
Taylor, Matthew (2013): *The Association Game: A History of British Football*. London: Routledge.
The Guardian (2013): 'Hollywood's Hold over Global Box Office – 63% and Falling', in: *The Guardian*, April 2, 2013 (http://www.theguardian.com/film/filmblog/2013/apr/02/ hollywood-hold-global-box-office) (last accessed July 27, 2015).
Thiong'o, Ngugi wa (1986): *Decolonizing the Mind. The Politics of Language in African Literature*. London: James Currey.
Todorov, Tzvetan (2013[1982]): *La conquête de l'Amerique. La question de l'autre*. Paris: Seuil.
Torreblanca, José Ignacio; Mark Leonard (2013): 'The Continent-Wide Rise of Euroscepticism', in: *ecfr.eu*, May 16, 2013 (http://www.ecfr.eu/page/-/ECFR79_EUROSCEPTICISM_ BRIEF_ AW.pdf) (last accessed October 8, 2014).
UNDP/United Nations Development Index (2014): *Human Development Reports* (http://hdr.undp.org/en/content/table-1-human-development-index-and-its-components) (last accessed April 29, 2015).
UNEP (2012): *The UNEP Environmental Data Explorer. United Nations Environment Programme* (http://people.hofstra.edu/geotrans/eng/ch2en/conc2en/global_net_migration. html) (last accessed July 27, 2015).

Vincendau, Ginette (ed./1995): *Encyclopedia of European cinema*. London: BFI.

Wallerstein, Immanuel (2003): 'Knowledge, Power, and Politics. The Role of an Intellectual in an Age of Transition', in: *UNESCO Forum on Higher Education, Research and Knowledge Global Research Seminar "Knowledge Society vs. Knowledge Economy: Knowledge, Power, and Politics"*. Opening Presentation. Paris, December 8–9, 2003 (http://unesdoc.unesco.org/images/0018/001833/183329e.pdf) (last accessed July 27, 2015).

Welsch, Wolfgang (1997): 'Transkulturalität. Zur veränderten Verfassung heutiger Kulturen', in: Schneider, Irmel; Christian W. Thomson (eds.): *Hybride Kulturen. Medien – Netze –Künste*. Köln: Wienand, pp. 67–90.

Welsch, Wolfgang (1999): 'Transculturalism – The Puzzling Form of Cultures Today', in: Featherstone, Mike; Scott Lash (eds.): *Spaces of Culture: City, Nation, World*. London: Sage, pp. 194–213.

Wheatley, Catherine (2015): 'Christianity and European Film', in: Harrod, Mary; Liz, Mariana; Timoshkina, Alissa (eds.): *The Europeanness of European Cinema*. London: Tauris, pp. 87–99.

Zaimoğlu, Feridun (1999[1995]): *Kanak Sprak. 24 Mißtöne vom Rande der Gesellschaft*. Rotbuch: Hamburg.

Zeydanlıoğlu, Welat (2007): *Kemalism's Others: The Reproduction of Orientalism in Turkey*. Cambridge: Anglia Ruskin University (unpublished PhD thesis).

Zournazi, Mary (2003): 'An Interview with Brian Massumi', in: *International Festival* (http://www.international-festival.org/node/111) (last accessed July 28, 2015).

2 Potential and Limits of a New European in Nicolas Echevarría's *Cabeza de Vaca*

2.1 Preliminary Remarks

As contemporary migration from Latin America, Africa, and Asia to Europe and its cinematic portrayal are frequently shaped by former colonial relations, films on early colonialism might help to shed light on key questions associated with media portrayals of (neo-/post-)colonial discourse and identity construction. This became particularly clear in the context of international celebrations of 500 years of 'discovery' of the 'New World' in 1992, which concentrated on European conquest and colonization as new Spanish banknotes with images of Cortés and Pizarro confirmed, but did not always culminate in glorifications of the conquest in the tradition of 1892 events. Instead, organizers of festivities in Seville, Washington, and New York, as well as film directors who continued to portray Columbus as representative of European enlightenment, modernity, and human progress (like Ridley Scott in *1492* and John Glen in *Christopher Columbus*, both from 1992), encountered often fierce resistance from politicians, authors, and directors celebrating decolonization.

Nicolás Echevarría's *Cabeza de Vaca* (1991), Luis Alberto Lamata's *Jericho* (1991), and Salvador Carrasco's *The Other Conquest* (1998) are films aimed at deconstructing Europeans as 'makers of history' and Non-Europeans as 'more or less childlike [who] could be brought to adulthood, to rationality, to modernity, through a set of learning experiences' (Blaut 1993: 1, 96). However, *Cabeza de Vaca* did this particularly well in its portrayal of the European conqueror and colonizer as migrant Other, and it could be argued that Echevarría's film is exemplary in its construction of a transcultural protagonist who overcomes traditional boundaries and manages to bridge cultural differences while drawing on common cultural ground. This transformation includes a profound respect for the native cultures he encounters, and it is precisely this 'opening up' to other societies and mentalities that could serve as inspiration for the imagination of a new Europe on screen and will be further explored in this chapter. On the other hand, it is clear that Echevarría does not manage to deconstruct all of the stereotypes he reconstructs in his film. This is also a common feature of contemporary migrant cinema, which deserves further exploration.

Just like Álvar Núñez Cabeza de Vaca's historical report *Shipwrecks* (1999[1542]), Echevarría's *Cabeza de Vaca*[1] tells the story of a failed conquest. The narrative perspectives are fundamentally different: The autobiographical report concentrates on the protagonist's shipwreck and survival in the New World, which leads to long descriptions of geography and climate, whereas the film deals primarily with Cabeza de Vaca's interaction with the natives and his personal transformation from conqueror to slave and shaman. The transformational journey allows him to understand key aspects of native societies that remained unknown to his fellow Spaniards. Particularly, this transformation leads Bruce-Novoa to conclude that the protagonist has Chicano attributes (1993: 5), which allows the report to be categorized as a founding text of Chicano literature (ibid. 5, Herrera 2011: 184) and invites us to reconsider *Cabeza de Vaca* as part of Chicano cinema. In his portrayals of the Other, Mexican director Echevarría stresses cultural differences between Europe and the so-called New World that was being assimilated into the Spanish empire (as New World/New Spain), but he also indicates cultural varieties in that world, which contradict popular reductionist views. Not by coincidence, scriptwriter Sheridan (August 27, 1950, Mexico City) highlights that there was 'a rich, complex and sophisticated world' in America,[2] and the director's attempt to elaborate on that cultural variety is mirrored in the iconography, which links the natives' tribes to their environment. One example is the desert tribe that connects to Mother Earth by covering bodies in mud; another is natives in the jungle who wear feathers of local birds. These portrayals confirm that 'the' (good or bad) Indian does not exist and that all attempts to create such an Indian in colonial and neo-colonial discourse have to be explored as methods to establish and/or sustain unequal power relations. In this respect, *Cabeza de Vaca* forms part of Echevarría's socio-critical work, which aims to bring Mexican native cultures from the margins of governmental politics into the center of popular attention.[3]

The differences between *Shipwrecks*, which remains embedded in Spanish colonial discourse, and postcolonial *Cabeza de Vaca* have to be assessed within their historical backgrounds. Núñez writes his report to 'his Majesty' King Carlos I (1516–1556; Núñez 1999: 4) to achieve political and economic benefits from his large odyssey through territories that now form part of Florida, Texas, New Mexico, Arizona, and California,[4] with some success. The King makes him governor of one of the new territories ('Segundo Adelantado del Río de la Plata') and then leader of another expedition to the Americas (1540–1545). However, Nicolás Echevarría directs *Cabeza de Vaca* shortly before the Fifth Centenary celebrations, which are overshadowed by debates about neo-colonialism and its manifestation in Spanish governmental subsidies for films like Scott's *1492* and Glen's *Christopher Columbus*. One could argue that the subsidies given for *Cabeza de Vaca* by the same institution that funds neo-colonial films (the Sociedad Estatal del Quinto Centenario) are an attempt at political correctness (see Grenier

1991 and Carr 1992). However, it also appears to be a good choice insofar as *Cabeza de Vaca* received better reviews and more prestigious awards (e.g. DICINE and ACE) than the more expensive Hollywood-style movies by Scott and Glen.

Differences between *Shipwrecks* and *Cabeza de Vaca* are particularly visible at the level of narration: The historical report describes the long voyage from one tribe to the next in clearly separated episodes and strict chronological order in true baroque style, whereas the film's structure follows patterns that have been widely disseminated by New Historical Narratives (see Rings 2010). The hyperrealist dimension is particularly explicit in the numerous ruptures of narrative illusion and the metaphorical use of the circle in a film that overall maintains a chronological order to facilitate its reception by a larger audience. Reviewers have identified key aspects of this hyper-realism, but it is clear that many are not able to connect these aspects to postmodern philosophies and related narrative theories. Examples include Fernández's criticism of the 'few attempts at narrative' (1992: 72), Tallmer's complaints about 'rudimentary continuity' (1992: 32), and Billings's rejection of 'huge gaps in the story' (1997), which highlight how critics tend to apply values of 19th century narrative traditions for the assessment of contemporary films. Although Echevarría uses fewer alienation techniques for the portrayal of his Cabeza de Vaca than, for example, Sanchis Sinisterra in his theatrical work on the same conqueror (*Naufragios de Álvar Núñez* 1991), his aims remain very clear, and there are ruptures with narrative illusions from the very beginning of the film. One example is the presentation of a black background to Spanish military march music, which mirrors the protagonist's perception of Spanish militarism at the end of his long journey through native indigenous territories. After having been kept as a slave by Native Americans for many years, Cabeza de Vaca has to observe the even more violent and inhuman treatment of Indian slaves kept by the Spaniards. Instead of being able to embrace 'Spanish civilization' again, he is alienated by a new form of barbarity that shatters his earlier concepts of humanity and linear progress. The continuity of inhuman violence under Spanish rule is such a disturbing aspect for a character who has entered deeply into the world of Indian tribes that he reacts in a very emotional manner—with a scream of pain that culminates in desperate laughter. All of this helps viewers recognize a cyclical concept of time shaped by inhuman violence and suppression, despite the film's concentration on more constructive forms of conviviality that shape the protagonist's odyssey. It is probably due to these scenes that most critics mistakenly categorize Echevarría's film as indigenist text (Kempley 1992, Grenier 1991) and/or regard the protagonist as 'conquistador gone native' (Nogueira 2006, Floeck 2003, Valverde 1999).

Immediately after his emotional outburst, the flashback starts, and most of the film is devoted to the protagonist's seven-year-long travel experience, which is being told from his point of view. However, the radical change from one scene to the next, indicated by a strong contrast in brightness and narrative style especially in the theatrical presentation of the disaster of Pánfilo de Narváez's fleet, make it extremely difficult for viewers to identify fully with the protagonist. Afterwards the credits continue, but viewers listen now to indigenous drums, which indicate a shift from the pseudorationality of Spanish militarism to the magic of indigenous rituals and lead the viewer to mixtures of the two cultures, in particular in the protagonist's experience. In this context, it is no coincidence that the film's title draws our attention to the protagonist and his viewpoint rather than to the shipwreck and its consequences.

For Schäffauer (2007: 104), the paradigmatic change of Echevarría's protagonist happens in a cave after 60 minutes narration time, i.e., roughly halfway through the original film length. Cabeza de Vaca experiences hallucinations (provoked by exhaustion, hunger, and thirst) that appear to be crucial for him to reach a critical distance from the colonial patterns of thought that have so far shaped his behavior. Key is the voice of his dead grandfather Pedro de Vera who is now in hell because he ordered the genocide of the native population on the Canary Islands but—despite ongoing persecution—remains unable to show any remorse as his retrospective view shows: 'that is the only way to conquer'.[5] The scene is a warning to the protagonist not to follow his grandfather's monocultural mentality, which is likely to lead to similar atrocities and similar eternal suffering in hell. Only after physical liberation by the Indian trickster and mental liberation through 'insanity' in the cave, Cabeza de Vaca seems to be able to find his own way as a wizard serving a humanity shared by all cultures, which corresponds to the notion of transculturality disseminated by Welsch (1999). Not unlike Jesus in the New Testament, viewers see Cabeza de Vaca healing ill people and even bringing the dead back to life, although the protagonist draws on Christian and Indian traditions simultaneously to perform his miracles. All this implies that Echevarría's conquered conqueror has to be distinguished from the majority of failed anti-heroes from the New Historical Narrative, including Carpentier's Columbus in *The Harp and the Shadow*, Armas Marcelo's Rejonistas in *Burnt Ships,* and Sanchis Sinisterra's Cabeza de Vaca in *Shipwrecks of Álvar Núñez*, who aim for assimilation, exploitation, and/or marginalization of the Other.

2.2 From Monocultural to Transcultural Perspectives

When he arrives in territories that will much later form part of Florida, Echevarría's protagonist shares the separatist perspective of his companions. The theatrical scene immediately before the shipwreck indicates the prevailing insular mentality quite explicitly when Spanish sailors confirm their cultural boundaries with reference to their severely damaged ships: 'This is all of Spain that is left for us. These ships are Spain', exclaims an anonymous seaman, whereas Captain Pánfilo de Narváez affirms from his ship 'Spain ends here'.[6] Viewers have to wait until the end of the film to hear from the protagonist a much more open definition of boundaries that include the Other of the so-called New World. Facing the commanding officer of the military unit he encounters at the end of his journey, he exclaims 'you are Spain', but he then turns around and declares with reference to surrounding lands 'this is Spain', before he includes the rest of the New World by indicating the far away mountains: 'that is also Spain'.[7] Taking into account that in this scene a furrow separates the commanding officer and his subordinate from Cabeza de Vaca, the protagonist's crossing of that boundary confirms his new transcultural perspective. This is further enhanced when he rejects the Spanish justice system with the comment: 'I have seen examples of your justice all the way'.[8]

Here and elsewhere, the film critically interrogates the cultural hierarchy, discrimination, expulsion, forced assimilation, destruction, and other forms of socio-political, cultural, and economic injustice associated with the new Spain shaped by conquest, colonization, and the fundamentalist Catholic rule of Isabel and Ferdinand,[9] which Posse's Columbus rejected in *Dogs of Paradise* (1983). Consequently, the viewer is encouraged to transfer a young soldier's categorization of New World Indians as 'savages' to the new Spain, portrayed as a country in which the human nature of those Indians remains under discussion. The 'discussion' takes place not only in the immediate context of Cabeza de Vaca's expedition in the 1520s and 1530s, but during and after the famous public debates between Las Casas and Sepúlveda in 1550 and 1551.

Clear proof of the protagonist's internalization of colonial patterns of thought are provided later on in the film when he discovers that he cannot escape the magic powers of his Indian master and is therefore likely to remain a slave at his mercy. In this situation, Cabeza de Vaca re-confirms the cultural hierarchy that shapes Spanish colonial discourse when arguing 'I am more human than you [...] I have a world [...] and a God'.[10] His statement summarizes a viewpoint that helped to justify the conquest and colonization of the New World, including exploitation, enslavement, and elimination of the Other and that can be found again in (neo-)fascist 'folk' concepts of the 20th century mirrored in Saura's *Taxi* (see Chapter 3.1). Also, it might not be a coincidence that Echevarría selects the deformed dwarf Malacosa as one of the aggressors against whom the Spanish protagonist's judgment is directed. 'In my country they would have already impaled you',[11] says Cabeza de Vaca to a person who in the Spanish society of his time and in most Western industrialized societies until the end of the 20th century would be marginalized, if not discriminated, for his 'imperfection'. In pre-Colombian indigenous societies, however, such differences were usually interpreted as a particular expression of divine will, which demanded acceptance and respect. The circular concept of time enhances this interpretation with its reference to ongoing repetitions of cultural hierarchies and discriminations of the 'imperfect' Other, while 'perfection' continues to be measured in the image of the monoculturally imagined Self. In

Echevarría's film, this monocultural construct is based on the assumption of the superiority and unique legitimation of Christianity. This assumption implies the right and duty to Christianize 'pagan' Others and/or drive them off their land and enhances a xenophobic perspective that continues to shape Islamophobic and fundamentalist Christian concepts of Europe briefly discussed in Chapter 1.3 and mirrored in Gutiérrez's *Poniente* (2002) and Glenaan's *Yasmin* (2004). '"Reborn" as critical subject' (Alvaray 2004: 62), Cabeza de Vaca has a monumental task in front of him if he wants to fight the key concepts behind the cultural imperialism that shapes Spanish and European conquest of his time. However, despite substantial progress in the field of human rights and anti-discrimination laws, for example, the critical intervention by contemporary authors and directors in favor of more transcultural societies has not necessarily become a much smaller task, because monocultural tendencies have not been broken. Instead, as outlined in Chapter 1, they have frequently found a new (more acceptable) base in outdated multicultural and intercultural concepts, and it is largely left for Echevarría's successors in contemporary migrant cinema to address the challenge in disguise.

With these remarks in mind, it is necessary to explore the mental voyage of Cabeza de Vaca in greater detail. The first encounter of the shipwrecked Spaniards with American Indians seems to confirm the stereotypical views that Christian soldiers of the 16th century—as well as contemporary ethnocentric Western viewers of the film—might have internalized about the brutal, barbarous savage. In the middle of the jungle, black servant Estebanico discovers human skin hanging from a tree, which fills all members of the small expedition with such horror that the priest starts exorcism rituals. Shortly afterwards, the group encounters a mutilated human cadaver in a trunk, which they last saw on the captain's ship, and the priest gives the order to burn everything, including the symbols of Indian magic found nearby. This leads to an assault by enemies that appear at first invisible: The viewer mainly sees arrows entering into human targets until most of the Spaniards are dead, with the exception of Cabeza de Vaca and three of his companions who are captured for sale on a slave market. The portrayal of Indians as barbarians continues as the Spaniards are shown in cages and treated like animals waiting for merciful customers to buy them. However, the giant sorcerer who buys Cabeza de Vaca shows no empathy, and his deformed servant Malacosa is perceived by the Spaniards as a demon. It is only much later, after many months of humiliation and the protagonist's failed attempt to escape his master, that a close shot indicates empathy and compassion. Although the two Indians cannot grasp the meaning of the words shouted by their Spanish slave, they seem to understand his desperation, and this marks a substantial shift in their relationship, which is now characterized by mutual respect.

This humanization of the Other, which follows a humanization of the Self (in the protagonist's desperate emotional outburst) and culminates in the release of Cabeza de Vaca, is an essential first step for further change and reminds us of the importance of affects explored in greater detail in Akın's *The Edge of Heaven* more than 15 years later. The next step is the protagonist's self-discovery in the cage scene, which separates the film into two parts and ends with his desire to overcome the demons of conquest and colonization. The viewers are witness to a spiritual conflict reminiscent of the life of the famous hermit San Antonio Abad, and the tree on fire in the last cage scene makes reference to God's appearance in front of Moses. However, in contrast to the historical report, in which such biblical references are used to underline the Christian mentality of author and protagonist, the film transfers them to Indian culture. Instead of the Christian God, an Indian sorcerer is being presented, and he shows the Spaniard a tree on fire (rather than bushes) so that he can warm himself up (rather than receive instructions of how to liberate the Jewish people). Common interpretations speak of the protagonist's wish to redeem himself.[12] However, this study argues that the deep spiritual link between the sorcerer and the protagonist, i.e., two people from very different cultures, confirms the blurring of traditional racial and religious boundaries and that Cabeza de Vaca's 'insanity' opens up the necessary space to critically interrogate the monoculturality of 16th century Catholic discourse and European colonialism.

The film follows a tendency in Latin American narrative that can be traced back to exemplary work by Asturias, Yáñez, and Rulfo in the first part of the 20th century (see Rings 1996: 215, 291). This tendency rejects the notion of European and North American superiority and draws on different expressions of so-called insanity ('locura') to reveal the irrationality within Western rationality. In this sense, Cabeza de Vaca's emotional outbursts can be regarded as affect-based expressions of his unconsciousness, which rebels against the inhumanity of monocultural colonial discourse personified by Pedro de Vera, the commanding officer responsible for the mass killings during the conquest of the Canary Islands. All of this leads to an inversion of colonial hierarchies, because it is Pedro de Vera who is in this scene genuinely insane (in the sense of ill and irrational) as he continues to justify the genocide of the natives, not the protagonist in his search for alternatives to the vicious circles of pre-Columbian, colonial, and neocolonial violence.

In his search for a 'Third Space' (Bhabha 1994), Cabeza de Vaca enters into indigenous worlds, but I argue that he never assimilates into Indian society and even less 'runs away' from his Spanish identity or 'abandons' it.[13] Instead, he goes through a transculturation process during which he negotiates different identities and out of which emerges a new protagonist who cannot simply be classified as Spaniard or Indian. Consequently, it is not convincing to describe him as somebody 'gone native' (Floeck 2003: 272).[14] The idea that the protagonist of the 16th century report is more of a 'cultural mediator' than Echevarría's Cabeza de Vaca (Jablonska Zaborowska 2004: 22) is similarly unconvincing. The former stresses that he heals the wounded with the help of his Christian God and that indigenous rituals have no magic power whatsoever, whereas the latter draws on the religious heritage of both Spanish and Indian cultures in a new synthesis that blurs traditional boundaries. In this sense, the report mirrors the monocultural mentality of the Spanish Court and 16th century European colonialism,[15] whereas the film approaches the negotiation of different identities in situations that reduce the pressure of cultural hierarchies. This exchange follows tendencies to hybrid constructs in postmodern narrative, but it is not representative of colonial cinema, which tends to reconfirm monocultural concepts.

One example of the protagonist's hybridity, which this study would like to explore further, is the mixture of symbols, amulets, and languages in religious acts. In his role as wizard, Cabeza de Vaca wears the Christian cross around his neck but also carries smaller Indian amulets. While clothes (or the lack of them), amulets, and his hairstyle reflect his adaptation to indigenous customs, the cross and Christian gestures remain key for his 'miracles'. When he heals the Indian wounded by the nameless 'blue tribe', the protagonist puts his hands together and looks up to the sky as if praying to the Christian God and, at the end, he gives his 'patient' a symbolic bath that reminds one of christening. Similar gestures can be observed when he enters a cave in order to bring a dead woman back to life, an act reminiscent of Jesus's resurrection of Lazarus. Similarities include parallels in place (the cave) and symbolic acts (both untie their 'patients' as part of the resurrection ritual), as well as accompanying prayers, including in this scene fragments of the *Ave María* ('benedictus fructus ventris'), before he exclaims repeatedly in Spanish that she is alive ('está viva'). However, all this appears mixed with supposedly Indian words and gestures, which makes it impossible to decide which religion has more impact and leads to the conclusion that the healer's incredible success story depends precisely on the combination and fusion of two powerful traditions, rather than on separatist, homogenous, and essentialist concepts of one of them.

It would be an error to assume that the film's miracles depend solely on the Christian beliefs that guide the protagonist of the historical report. It would also be misleading to link them to indigenous magic exclusively.[16] All this confirms that Echevarría's protagonist has not 'abandoned' his Christian heritage in order to assimilate into Indian heritage, but he offers a synthesis based on 'multidirectional memory' (Rothberg 2011) that 'blurs' the boundaries of the two cultures (Antor 2006: 30). In contrast to the hero from *Shipwrecks*, who gains power from an ideal of purity, including his refusal to 'contaminate' his Christian belief system, the filmic protagonist draws power from transculturation. The cross, a magic formula from his former master, Christian prayers, and a magic stone placed on the 'patient's' throat all work together to achieve the desired outcome. The successful resurrection ritual indicates the importance of overcoming monocultural history constructs by an ethics of transcultural memory (Moses/Rothberg 2014: 29), which will be further examined in films like *Le Havre*.

Potential and Limits 37

Figure 2.2.1 Hybrid resurrection ritual in *Cabeza de Vaca*.

It remains unclear why Grenier summarizes Echevarría's America as 'choreographed paradise' of 'coffee-table Indians' (1991: G4), because the environment in which Cabeza de Vaca and his companions try to survive is extremely challenging and dangerous for Spaniards and Indians. Be it in the jungle, the mountains, or the desert, life is characterized as hard and short, not only due to assaults by brutal warriors, but because of a surrounding nature that does not provide sufficient water, food, and shelter for everybody. Also, Echevarría refuses to follow Hollywood's lead in its depiction of adventurous and romantic plots, dazzling swordplay, a simplistic binary separating (good) Christian heroes from (bad) pagan villains, and ultimately heroic death, which shape swashbuckler films from *Captain from Castile* (King 1947) to *Cristopher Columbus* (Glen 1992). The story of the conquest in Cabeza de Vaca bears in this sense no resemblance to traditional adventure films led by the numerous re-editions of the *King Arthur* legends and *The Three Musketeers*, which provide the chivalric tales of Medieval Europe with narrative continuity. This includes the portrayal of Cabeza de Vaca as anti-hero in opposition to, for example, Glen's Columbus, who—in his interpretation by Georges Corraface as outstanding fighter and womanizer—shows clear parallels to *Captain from Castile*'s Pedro de Vargas played by Tyrone Power. Also, neither the cannibal Esquivel, the Spanish troop dedicated to the hunt and enslavement of Indians, nor the show-off Dorantes who invents fantastic stories about sexual encounters with native 'women with three tits' ('mujeres de tres tetas'), is able to serve as a heroic model for the viewer. The same applies to the Indians, who either demonstrate too much brutality (from the warriors of the first assault and the sorcerer to all members of the blue tribe) or have such marginal roles (including the protagonist's nameless 'patients') that they cannot convincingly work as role models.

The academic discussion on the cannibalism of the 'tribe of the blue people' ('la tribu de los hombres azules') sheds additional light on the narrative strategies employed. For Gordon (2002) the tribe's cannibalism is so obvious and meaningful that he dedicates an entire chapter of his book to the comparison of *Cabeza de Vaca* and Pereira dos Santos's *How Tasty Was My Little Frenchman* (1971). However, the superficiality of this comparison leads directly to the ambiguity Echevarría aims to achieve: In his portrayal of the 'blue tribe', Indian cannibalism is indicated, never elaborated or explicitly proven. The viewer does not see any Indians actually eating human flesh (as in Pereira's *Hans Staden* 1999), he does not hear stories about it (as in the 16th century report *Hans Staden's True History: An Account of Cannibal Captivity in Brazil* 2008), and there is no 'confession' (as in Esquivel's elaborations on Spanish cannibalism). Taking into account that Esquivel's story about starving Spanish soldiers eating the flesh of their own companions is well documented in Cabeza de Vaca's report, this might actually be the only example of anthropophagy worth discussing.[17] However, the film plays very consciously with the popular stereotype of Indian cannibalism when warriors of the blue tribe kill Esquivel with a blow to the head by a stick in 'Jwera Pemme' form, which reminds critical viewers of an anthropophagus ritual explored in Staden's report (2007: book 2, chapter 28) and in Pereira's *Hans Staden*. Shortly afterwards, we see two Indians carrying a big pot, but it remains unclear whether the pot contains water to cook Esquivel or the drink that everybody takes during the ritual dance. I suggest linking these scenes of Indian life with the very first example of the topic, which shows— to the great disgust of the Spaniards—human skin hanging from a tree. In all of these scenes, viewers are invited to re-activate their stereotypes about Indian inhumanity, including its worst form: cannibalism. However, I argue that Echevarría reconstructs such stereotypes only for the purpose of deconstruction, because ultimately it becomes clear that Spanish soldiers can be as brutal and inhuman as the worst Indians they encounter, which dissolves the dichotomy between European civilization and Indian barbarity.

2.3 Back to Monoculturality?

It remains difficult to evaluate the 'effectiveness' of narrative deconstruction, because it cannot be done based on text analysis alone, as Gordon (2002: 93) highlights. In particular, it would be necessary to also conduct major empirical research with 'representative' groups of viewers in different locations and over longer periods of time, possibly including the impact of comparable films, which is well beyond the scope of this book. However, even without such additional studies, it is fair to say that Echevarría does not work on deconstruction persistently enough and that he seems to 'forget' some stereotyped groups completely. Probably one of the best examples is his objectification of Indian women as exotic creatures. Admittedly, his protagonist keeps a critical distance from Dorantes' fantastic stories at the campfire and keeps a 'professional' attitude as healer in his encounters, which could be regarded as a productive alternative to the interethnic love stories shaping commercial cinema from King's *Captain from Castile* (1947) to Juárez's *Hijos del Viento* (2000). Nevertheless, at the end, traditional stereotypes of the Other remain in place, which have led Walter to criticize the portrayal of women in the first part of the film as 'passive, nurturing, and freely sexual', whereas female sexual Otherness in the second part appears 'exotic, tantalizing, and extremely threatening' (2002: 144).

The last part of this quote makes particular reference to the women of the 'blue tribe', who move constantly around male prisoners, touch them, and—during the attack of the Spaniard-friendly tribe—try to kill one of them. This implies a radical change from female passivity in the first part to active aggression in the second part, but it does not necessarily mean that Indian women have lost their status as objects. In this context, it is worth stressing that 'blue tribe' women come out of their hut at the request of their (male) cacique like dangerous animals temporarily freed to kill the prisoners, and this allegory is enhanced by their instinct-led aggressive behavior. Just like the woman resurrected in the first part, they are mostly young and athletic, and they present their naked bodies from different perspectives. In all these scenes, the subject of history remains male, while women are presented as objects of a male gaze.

Very much like these women, the black servant Estebanico is framed as someone who suffers from history or occasionally benefits from certain events but appears unable to change the course of history. Considering the film's reputation as postcolonial text, in which 'the voice of the other can be rescued' (Miguel Magro 2004: 62), it is surprising to see that Estebanico has only received very marginal attention in the scholarly debate. Although Miguel Magro refers to indigenous perspectives, there can be little doubt that the black servant belongs to the group of subalterns, whose viewpoints tended to be excluded from European historiography. Echevarría's film does not mention Estebanico's origin, but the author of *Shipwrecks* describes him as Arab negro from Azamor,[18] which implies an intensification of Othering: Not only is he a black slave and, as such, very different in race and class, but being Arab he could also be perceived as arch-enemy of the Christian soldier. I argue that the film portrays the black subaltern as loyal colonial subordinate, who—guided by his instincts—remains always next to his white master without any sign of independent judgment. To some degree he complies with the role, which the Atheneist Martín Luis Guzmán summarized for Mexican Indians in his essay *La querella de México* as 'that of the loyal dog following blindly his master in whatever he does'.[19]

Just like the Indian women discussed above, Estebanico does not question anything, he does not act but react, and he always remains loyal to his master, regardless of whether it is Cabeza de Vaca (in the film) or Dorantes (in *Shipwrecks*). Estebanico's marginal passive role is highlighted when he goes to play with Indian children after the successful liberation from the 'blue tribe', while the protagonist talks to the winning tribe's priests, and Dorantes and Castillo enjoy the companionship of the Indian women sent to them. All this follows traditional social hierarchies, which can be traced back to medieval chivalry tales featuring a celibate knight, subordinates shaped by sexual instincts, and marginalized servants, but in associating innocent-loyal Estebanico's place closer to children than to rational adults Echevarría draws in particular on colonial perspectives. Estabanico's subaltern position is further stressed in the resurrection scene, in which he remains at first close to his master while Dorantes leaves in protest, but then fearfully runs out of the cave when the woman is brought back to life. In both scenes his behavior is instinct-driven and of limited help, whereas Cabeza de Vaca demonstrates superior rational control. Defined by emotions and in desperate need of protection, Estebanico confirms key ideas of (neo-)colonial discourse, because these attributes do not appear as results of enslavement, but as part of a natural condition (born to serve), which ultimately justifies that enslavement. We can summarize that in the portrayals of both Indian women and Estebanico, Miguel Magro is wrong in assuming that *Cabeza de Vaca* allows for the voice of the Other to be heard (2004: 62, see above).

Other challenging aspects of the film include the 'mise-en-scène' of Indian magic, which can be understood as a system of Otherness that shapes body painting, clothes, and ritual dances, but its origin, symbolic meaning, and impact are never explained. This omission protects it against simplistic attempts of occidental rationalization and categorization, including appropriation by the binary patterns of European colonial discourse. Also, Otherness is reduced when the importance of magic is highlighted on both sides: Not only Indians, but Spaniards too believe in miraculous healings as well as resurrections of the dead, and both practice rituals that are supposed to help 'the good' and fight 'the bad'.

However, camera shots on indigenous rituals are far more frequent and considerably longer than shots dedicated to comparable practices on the Spanish side. For example, the viewer is confronted with the Spanish priest's exorcism rituals and Dorantes' similarly irrational performance of cross signs when Malacosa approaches his cage. The duration of both scenes is less than one minute, whereas the sorcerer's rituals featuring the lizard, the drawing of a giant in the sand, and the burning tree take around eight minutes in total. There is also room for improvement in the presentation of Núñez's hybrid healings, because far too often indigenous elements come more to the fore than Christian aspects.

Finally, neither the inspiration of Indian clothing by Théodore de Bry's drawings (1528–1598), which have been discussed in their colonial framing

Figure 2.3.1 Christian exorcism ritual.

of the exotic Other, nor the invention of indigenous languages by the director (Restrepo 2000: 198, 197), support the protagonist's transcultural orientation in the second part of the film. Although the portrayal of indigenous languages as incomprehensible sounds might have formed part of the narrative reconstruction of colonial stereotypes for the purpose of deconstruction, key aspects of colonial iconography remain so strong that traditional Othering shapes the portrayal of Echevarría's Native Americans until the very end of the film. Restrepo summarizes that 'Amerindian bodies are turned into rich, exotic, and erotic textures that can be gazed at [...] by the metropolitan spectator' (2000: 189).

However, such assessment remains limited because it does not consider the narrative framework. On the one hand, the portrayal of Indians is clearly marked by humanization, which is very explicit in the change of the protagonist's Indian companions from an incomprehensible brutal-exotic sorcerer, who only reveals human empathy later on, to one of Cabeza de Vaca's patients. The latter is a significantly more comprehensible and human emotions foregrounding character and, as such, an example for most other Indians in the second half. On the other hand, the Spanish Self is characterized by dehumanization, which culminates in the portrayal of conquerors who unscrupulously take advantage of their military superiority in order to enslave or kill the Indians they encounter, including women and children. Interestingly enough, these are soldiers from the troop seen at the very beginning of the film. In the first scenes the camera focuses on joint and peaceful working together of Indians and Spaniards, whereas in the last scenes there are wide and mid shots of Indians jailed in cages, and the confrontation between Cabeza de Vaca and the commanding officer about social (in-) justice appears as melodramatic climax. This way, Echevarría guides the viewer from internalized stereotypes of the barbarous Other to the barbarity of the Self, not to simply invert moral authority, but to examine the continuity of human barbarity, while he proposes transcultural Cabeza de Vaca as 'postcolonial custodian' (Menozzi 2014: 3–4), who intervenes to overcome the vicious circles of mutual violence and destruction. In this context, the director wants to avoid the presentation of his Indians as romantic heroes in the tradition of Chateaubriand's *Atala*, without falling into the trap of traditional indigenist binaries in which they are reduced to the role of innocent and inherently good civilized victims of European greed and cruelty. Some critics regard the film as neocolonial text confirming European superiority,[20] whereas others label it as indigenist work.[21] This confirms that Echevarría was at least partially successful in his attempt to create a critical study that cannot be easily assimilated into colonial or indigenist master narratives, although viewers might try hard to make it fit into their binary patterns of thought. On the downside, there is little doubt that numerous stereotypes have survived Echevarría's attempts at deconstruction.

2.4 The Postcolonial Heritage

Echevarría's portrayal of a European conqueror who rejects monoculturality and embarks on a transcultural quest, could help to guide European cinema in its attempt to develop similar and possibly even better alternatives to internalized patterns of neocolonial discourses that continue to shape interactions between migrants and so-called host cultures in a postcolonial modernity. In this context, it is worth stressing that one must not categorize Cabeza de Vaca as a 'cultural renegade' (Floeck 2003) or conqueror 'gone native' (Valverde 1999), i.e. somebody who gives up his cultural heritage to assimilate into the host culture. We should recognize him as a new character who consciously draws on European and Indian cultures in his negotiation of a third way, including religious syncretism within which the cross and Christian prayers meet Indian symbols and rituals on equal footing. On a structural level, the film convinces in its attempt to combine traditional chronological narrative, which tends to accommodate mainstream viewing habits, with alienation techniques that destabilize linear perceptions of colonial history and question the mythification of European modernity as human progress. Particularly helpful are the flashback from the protagonist's perspective, which highlights the subjectivity of the story, and the use of silence and images that break with the wordiness of colonial discourse.[22] Other alienation techniques include the use of black backgrounds to Spanish or Indian drums at the beginning of the film and surrealist scenes ranging from Spanish horsemen without faces to the enormous silver cross carried by Indians at the end of the movie. Unfortunately, the deconstruction of stereotypes remains incomplete and allows for neo-colonial continuities, both with regard to the portrayal of Indian women as passive and erotic (or aggressive irrational) and the 'black man' as passive, emotional and obedient. However, one could argue that *Cabeza de Vaca* mirrors here traditional exotic objectifications of non-Europeans in European films that appear in contemporary migrant cinema as well. Consequently, European directors might be able to learn as much from Echevarría's failed attempts at deconstruction as from the more successful aspects of transcultural identity construction. The latter includes not only the narrative development of the protagonist's inner journey based on common cultural grounds, rather than differences, but also the Mexican-Spanish co-production, which transgresses national, continental and—above all—former colonial boundaries.

Notes

1. This study refers to the original 138 minute version of Cabeza de Vaca disseminated by Producciones Iguana and cited as 'Echevarría 1991'. There are numerous shorter editions of the film, in which for example the important encounter between the protagonist and his grandfather Pedro de Vera are not shown. This reduces the film to 112 or even 104 minutes, which might increase its appeal to a wider audience but clearly distorts its meaning and potential impact.
2. 'En América, existía un mundo rico, complejo, sofisticado' (Sheridan 1994: 10). All translations from Spanish, German, and French are mine, unless explicitly referenced as other scholars' work.
3. Examples include *Judea* (1973), *María Sabina* (1979), and *El niño Fidencio* (1980).
4. Vargas (2007) indicates the potential military benefits of such detailed descriptions of geography and climate, although his assessment of the report as a military handbook is not convincing.
5. '¡Condenadme en paz!', and 'Sólo se conquista así'.
6. 'Esto es toda la España que nos queda. Estos barcos son España', and 'aquí termina España'.
7. 'Tú eres España', 'esto es España', 'aquello también es España'.
8. 'La muestra de vuestra justicia la he visto yo en todo el camino'.
9. This interpretation has to be read in contrast to Nogueira, who misunderstands the protagonist's statements as questions (2006: 153) and asks 'Where exactly is Spain? Can Spain be transplanted? Can it be left behind?' (p. 154). However, I would agree with her concluding statement, 'Cabeza de Vaca cannot escape Spain and [...] neither can America' (p. 154), because this is confirmed by the symbolic scene at the very end of the film, in which Indians carry an enormous silver cross into an unknown future.
10. 'Soy más humano que vosotros [...] tengo un mundo [...] y un Dios'.
11. 'En mi país ya te hubieran empalado'.
12. For such an interpretation see Nogueira (2006: 149 s.). This study rejects Nogueira's 'redemption theory' for two reasons: 1) The film does not mention any sin committed by the protagonist or his companions that indicated a need for redemption. Instead, the massacre of the shipwrecked Spaniards and the

enslavement of the few survivors by Indians appears inhuman and unjustifiable. 2) The idea that the protagonists suffers like Jesus to redeem the sin of other conquerors or the viewers (due to their 'contributions [...] to colonialism', p. 155) starts from a Christian-centric viewpoint, which the film suggests overcoming.
13. See his categorization as 'cultural renegade' ('tránsfuga cultural') in Floeck's study (2003: 272). In contrast, a clear example of assimilation is provided by the young protagonist in Chadha's *Bend It Like Beckham*; see our analysis in 3.2.
14. See also Valverde (1999: 61), Jablonska Zaborowska (2004: 22), and Nogueira (2006: 157).
15. There are clear parallels between Cabeza de Vaca's *Naufragios* written for the Spanish King and Hans Staden's *História de duas viagens ao Brasil* directed at Count Philipp I from Hessen (Staden 2007 [1557]). In particular, the authors present themselves as noble Christians surviving in an extremely hostile environment. The question is in how far they have selected and even invented new episodes in order to enhance this image, for example in the description of extreme hunger in Núñez's text or fierce cannibalism in Staden's work.
16. Gordon argues: 'The film shows the power of Cabeza de Vaca's healing to come only from the magic taught to him by the shaman' (2002: 114).
17. See Núñez (1999: 89): 'The others cut those into pieces who died, and the last one who died was Sotomayor, and Esquivel cut him into pieces, and by eating from him he survived until first of March' ('Los que morían, los otros los hacían tasajos; y el último que murió fue Sotomayor, y Esquivel lo hizo tasajos, y comiendo de él se mantuvo hasta primero de marzo').
18. 'Negro alárabe, natural de Azamor' (Núñez 1999: 222).
19. 'La del perro fiel que sigue ciegamente los designios de su amo' (Guzmán 1984: 15).
20. See Restrepo's discussion of colonial iconography (2000: 198) and Jablonska Zaborowska's exploration of the film as a text, which 'denies the violence of the Conquest' and the fact that European culture imposed itself on Indian culture (2004: 23).
21. See Kempley, who argues that the film supports the portrayal of Indians as victims of 'greedy, cross-kissing Euro-savages' (1992: 32), which is enhanced by Grenier's categorization of Echeverría's America as 'choreographed paradise' of 'coffee-table Indians' (1991: G4).
22. Monsalvo criticizes 'the empire of the Spanish word [which] condemns all non-Western languages to live in the shadows, in misery and disregard' ('el imperio de la palabra española [que] condenó a todos los lenguajes del mundo no occidental a vivir entre las sombras, entre la miseria y el desprecio') (2010: 104).

Filmography

Akın, Fatih (2007): *The Edge of Heaven/Auf der anderen Seite*. Germany/Turkey: Anka Film.
Carrasco, Salvador (1998): *The Other Conquest/La otra conquista*. Mexico: ADO.
Chadha, Gurindher (2002): *Bend It Like Beckham*. UK, Germany, US: Kintop Pictures.
Echevarría, Nicolás (1973): *Judea*. Mexico: Centro de Producción de Cortometraje.
Echevarría, Nicolás (1979): *María Sabina*. Mexico: Centro de Producción de Cortometraje.

Echevarría, Nicolás (1980): *Child Fidencio, the Healer of Espinazo/El niño Fidencio*. Mexico: Centro de Producción de Cortometraje.
Echevarría, Nicolás (1990): *Cabeza de Vaca*. Mexico, Spain, US, UK: Producciones Iguana.
Glen, John (1992): *Christopher Columbus: The Discovery*. UK/US/Spain: Quinto Centenario.
Glenaan, Kenneth (2004): *Yasmin*. UK, Germany: Parallax Independent, EuroArts Medien.
Gutiérrez, Chus (2002): *Poniente*. Spain: Amboto Audiovisual.
Juárez, José Miguel (2000): *Hijos del viento*. Italy/Portugal/Spain/Mexico: Campoy/ Pozueco.
Kaurismäki, Aki (2011): *Le Havre*. Finland, France, Germany: Sputnik, Pyramide Productions, Pandora Filmproduktion.
King, Henry (1947): *Captain from Castile*. US: Twentieth Century Fox.
Lamata, Luis Alberto (1990): *Jericho/Jericó*. Venezuela: Foncine.
Pereira, Luís Alberto (1999): *Hans Staden*. Brasil, Portugal: Instituto Português da Arte Cinematográfica e Audiovisual (IPACA).
Pereira Dos Santos, Nelson (1971): *How Tasty Was My Little Frenchman/Como era gostoso o meu francês*. Brazil: Condor Filmes.
Saura, Carlos (1996): *Taxi*. Spain: Canal+.
Scott, Ridley (1992): *1492: The Conquest of Paradise*. UK/France/Spain: Gaumont.

Bibliography

Alvaray, Luisela (2004): 'Imagining Indigenous Spaces: Self and Other Converge in Latin America', in: *Film &History* 34/2, pp. 58–64.
Antor, Heinz (2006): 'Multikulturalismus, Interkulturalität und Transkulturalität. Perspektiven für interdisziplinäre Forschung und Lehre', in: Antor, Heinz (ed.): *Inter- und Transkulturelle Studien: Theoretische Grundlagen und interdisziplinäre Praxis*. Heidelberg: Winter, pp. 25–39.
Armas Marcelo, Juan José (1982): *Burnt Ships/Las naves quemadas*. Barcelona: Argos Vergara.
Bhabha, Homi (1994): *The Location of Culture*. New York: Routledge.
Billings, Thomas (1997): 'Cabeza de Vaca', in: *Internet Movie Database* (http://www.imdb.com/reviews/09/0997.html) (last accessed January 8, 2015).
Blaut, James M. (1993): *The Coloniser's Model of the World: Geographical Diffusionism and Eurocentric History*. New York: The Guilford Press.
Bruce-Novoa, Juan (1993): 'Shipwrecked in the Seas of Signification: Cabeza de Vaca's "La Relación" and Chicano Literature', in: Herrera-Sobek, María (ed.): *Reconstructing a Chicano/a Literary Heritage*. Tucson: University of Arizona Press, pp. 3–23.
Carpentier, Alejo (1985[1979]): *The Harp and the Shadow/El arpa y la sombra*. La Habana: Letras Cubanas.
Carr, Jay (1992): 'Cabeza de Vaca', in: *The Boston Globe*, September 21, 1992, p. 32.
Fernández, Enrique (1992): 'Cabeza de Vaca', in: *Village Voice*, May 26, 1992, p. 72.
Floeck, Wilfried (2003): *Estudios críticos sobre el teatro español del siglo XX*. Tübingen: Francke.
Gordon, Richard Allen (2002): *Reviewing the Colony/Revising the Nation: Mexican and Brazilian Cinematic Dialogues with Colonial Texts*. Ann Arbor: ProQuest.

Grenier, Richard (1991): 'Politically Correct Conquistador', in: *The Washington Times*, May 16, 1991, p. G4.
Guzmán, Martín Luis (1984[1915]): 'La querella de México', in: Fondo de Cultura Económica (ed.): *Martín Luis Guzmán. Obras Completas*. Vol. I. México D.F.: FCE, pp. 31–107.
Herrera, Spencer R. (2011): 'Chicano Writers', in: Ihrie, Maureen; Oropesa, Salvador A. (eds.): *World Literature in Spanish: An Encyclopedia*. Vol. 1. Santa Barbara: ABC-CLIO, pp.183–184.
Jablonska Zaborowska, Alexandra (2004): 'La representación de los procesos de construcción de la identidad en los contextos interculturales de dos películas mexicanas sobre la Conquista', in: *Cultura, lenguaje y representación: revista de estudios culturales de la Universitat Jaume I* 1, pp. 19–28.
Kempley, Rita (1992): 'Cabeza de Vaca: An Explorer's Self-Discovery', in: *The Washington Post*, November 20, 1992, p. C7.
Menozzi, Filippo (2014): *Postcolonial Custodianship: Cultural and Literary Inheritance*. New York: Routledge.
Miguel Magro, Tania de (2004): 'Religion as a Survival Strategy in "Los Naufragios" and in Echevarría's Film "Cabeza de Vaca"', in: *Torre de papel* 14/1–2, pp. 52–63.
Monsalvo, Jenifer; Wendy Salas; Alberto González (2010): 'La presencia de la subalternidad en los cambios mostrados por los mitos cosmogónicos de las etnias Ye'kuana, Yukpa y Yanomami al ser transcritos como literatura infantil', in: *Revista Ciencias de la Educación* 20/35, pp. 83–109.
Moses, Dirk; Michael Rothberg (2014): 'A Dialogue on the Ethics and Politics of Transcultural Memory', in: Bond, Lucy et al. (eds.): *The Transcultural Turn: Interrogating Memory Between and Beyond Borders*. Berlin: De Gruyter, pp. 29–38.
Nogueira, Claudia Barbosa (2006): *Journeys of Redemption: Discoveries, Re-Discoveries, and Cinematic Representations of the Americas*. Ann Arbor: ProQuest.
Núñez, Álvar Cabeza de Vaca (1999[1542]): 'La relación que dio Álvar Núñez Cabeza de Vaca', in: Adorno, Rolena; Patrick Pautz (eds.): *Álvar Núñez Cabeza de Vaca: His Account, His Life and the Expedition of Pánfilo de Narváez*. Vol. I, Lincoln: University of Nebraska Press, pp. 13–291.
Posse, Abel (1987[1983]): *Dogs of Paradise/Los perros del Paraíso*. Barcelona: Plaza & Janés.
Restrepo, Luis Fernando (2000): 'Primitive Bodies in Latin American Cinema: Nicolás Echevarría's "Cabeza de Vaca"', in: Camayd-Freixas, Eric; José Eduardo González (eds.): *Primitivism and Identity in Latin America: Essays on Art, Literature and Culture*. Tucson: The University of Arizona Press, pp. 189–208.
Rings, Guido (1996): *Erzählen gegen den Strich. Ein Beitrag zur Geschichtsreflexion im mexikanischen Revolutionsroman*. Frankfurt am Main/New York: Peter Lang.
Rings, Guido (2010): *La conquista desbaratada. Identidad y alteridad en la novela, el cine y el teatro hispánicos contemporáneos*. Madrid: Iberoamericana.
Rothberg, Michael (2011): From Gaza to Warsaw: Mapping Multidirectional Memory', in: *Criticism* 53/4, pp. 523–548.
Sanchis Sinisterra, José (1991): 'Naufragios de Álvar Núñez', in: Serrano, Virtudes (ed./1996): *José Sanchis Sinisterra. Trilogía Americana*. Madrid: Cátedra, pp. 91–176.
Schäffauer, Markus K. (2007): 'Bilder des Unsagbaren: "Cabeza de Vaca"', in: Fendler, Ute; Monika Wehrheim (eds.): *Entdeckung, Eroberung, Inszenierung. Filmische Versionen der Kolonialgeschichte Lateinamerikas und Afrikas*. München: Meidenbauer, pp. 101–115.

Sheridan, Guillermo (1994): *Cabeza de Vaca* (script). México D.F.: El Milagro/ IMCINE.
Staden, Hans (2008): *Hans Staden's True History: An Account of Cannibal Captivity in Brazil*. Translated by Neil L.Whitehead and Michael Harbsmeier. Durham: Duke University Press.
Tallmer, Jerry (1992): 'Cabeza de Vaca', in: *New York Post*, May 15, 1992, p. 32.
Valverde, César (1999): 'Del relato a la pantalla: la alteridad en Cabeza de Vaca', in: *Káñina* 23/3, pp. 59–63.
Vargas, Claret M. (2007): '"De muchas y muy bárbaras naciones con quien conversé y viví": Álvar Núñez Cabeza de Vaca´s "Naufragios" as a War Tactics Manual', in: *Hispanic Review* 75/1, pp. 1–22.
Walter, Krista (2002): 'Filming the Conquest: "Cabeza de Vaca" and the Spectacle of History', in: *Literature/Film Quarterly* 30/2, pp. 140–145.
Welsch, Wolfgang (1999): 'Transculturalism – The Puzzling Form of Cultures Today', in: Featherstone, Mike; Scott Lash (eds.): *Spaces of Culture: City, Nation, World*. London: Sage, pp. 194–213.

3 Migrants in Europe
Breaking the Boundaries?

3.1 Principles of Exclusion in Montxo Armendáriz's *Letters from Alou* and Carlos Saura's *Taxi*

3.1.1 Preliminary Remarks

This chapter argues that, despite claims for substantial transcultural developments enhanced by contemporary mass migration, European Cinema of the 1990s is still shaped by traditional multicultural concepts,[1] which are reflected in the cinematic landscape and can be examined particularly well in work by Armendáriz and Saura. As in British, French, and German migrant films, the multicultural tendency in Spanish cinema is toward neocolonial paradigms of cultural separatism that continue to inform governmental and city council discourse. They can be found as re-inscriptions in the films, even if they fight patterns of neocolonial exploitation and racial discrimination within the boundaries of what is supposed to be the prime example for cosmopolitan life in Spain: Madrid (see Empresa Municipal 2008 and Madrid Destino 2014 below). The examples chosen for this exploration are *Letters from Alou* (1990) and *Taxi* (1996), because they mark key periods in the development of Spanish cinema about migration (see Santaolalla 2007, Burkhart 2010), promise a deconstruction of separatist concepts, and include the Spanish capital in their focus.

The speed of Spain's demographic transformation in the last three decades has turned immigration into a topic of major and often polemic controversy in Spanish media discourse. This despite the fact that the ongoing economic crisis in Spain has temporarily led to modest negative migration and some media attention is currently devoted to the relatively small numbers of predominantly younger Spanish adults emigrating to other European countries. Particularly since the 1990s, Spanish films have substantially contributed to the migration debate, not only with critiques of social, economic, and political discrimination, but through portrayals of alternatives characterized by tolerance and mutual respect. Many of these films focus on Madrid, partially because of its higher than average percentage of foreign residents, but surely also because the capital remains the center of Spanish film production, and the necessary resources for the production of standard feature films are more easily and cost-efficiently available there. *Letters from Alou* and *Taxi* have developed images about contemporary Madrid that seem to point out the distance Spanish migrant cinema keeps from city council's narratives. This might be linked to the fact that the films tend to focus on groups whose cultural, economic, and especially symbolic capital is relatively low (e.g., simple manual workers, taxi drivers)[2] and who, therefore, remain marginalized in 'esMadrid.com' and other official texts aimed at promoting the city—despite their numerical dominance in Madrid's workforce. On the other hand, there is far less need to hide cultural or economic conflicts in contemporary cinema as neither box office success nor financial support from cultural institutions depends necessarily on such a manipulation of space, whereas the city authorities' interest in attracting investors certainly correlates with it. Instead, there are other factors to be taken into account for cinematic success, such as tendencies toward melodramatic structures and excess, which are objects of this film analysis.

3.1.2 No Boundaries in Madrid? A Review of City Narratives

In their marketing of Madrid, city authorities have created a concrete image of the city, which is disseminated via brochures, leaflets, posters, TV adverts, and the official website 'www.esMadrid.com'. As 'portal of the city of Madrid' (Empresa Municipal Promoción de Madrid 2008) and 'official tourism website' (Madrid Destino 2014), 'esMadrid.com', better known under its new title ¡Madrid!, seems a good starting point to approach the city council imagery of the capital as a cosmopolitan center with major opportunities for everybody. The capital's cosmopolitanism is already stressed in the introductory sections with numerous statements that remain without contextualization or proof. For example, under 'Plan your trip', visitors are prepared for an 'experience in multiculturalism', and under 'Discover Madrid' the capital is presented as an 'unprejudiced city'.[3] Further reading in the latter section leads to the Lavapiés neighborhood in the city center being singled out as a positive example of 'a melting pot of cultures and traditions'. There Madrid's popular heritage is said to live 'in perfect harmony with the customs and traditions that accompanied immigrants coming from different countries who settled in the area' (see Madrid Destino 2014, 'Discover Madrid'—'Madrid Neighborhoods'—'Lavapiés'). This is very much in line with older editions of the website that highlighted Madrid as 'a place for everyone because nobody asks where you come from'[4] and, ultimately, 'a cosmopolitan city embracing new cultures, where […] more than six million people from 172 different nationalities live side by side harmoniously' (Empresa Municipal 2008, 'Business'—'Invest in Madrid'—'Why choose Madrid?'). Regrettably, the website has so far not given any explicit examples of such harmonious multicultural city life supposedly enhanced by the anonymity of life in the big city.

Data from the National Institute of Statistics 'INE' (2014) confirms that 62% of foreigners with official residence in Madrid province originate from

Latin America (600,000), followed by 36% from other European countries (347,000), and 13% from Africa (126,000).[5] The city report adds that this is mainly a result of immigration in the last decades,[6] and that the percentage of new residents per district varies enormously.[7] Although 'esMadrid.com' insists on the harmonious coexistence of all different cultures, there is a rigid selection of places of interest. Usera, Carabanchel, and Tetuán, three of the four districts with the highest number of immigrants in Madrid, do not appear at all on the list of neighborhoods on the website. Whereas the fourth, 'Centro', which due to its economic and symbolic capital is difficult to ignore, appears in fragmentary form with focus on the historical importance of the Plaza del Dos de Mayo in Malasaña, the New Year celebration on the Puerta del Sol square, the commercial and high-culture history of La Latina, and architectural remarks on Austrias.[8] As a consequence, cultural diversity seems to be limited to Lavapiés in the city center, although this impression neither correlates with the general enthusiasm about Madrid's multiculturalism stressed in the introductory statements, nor sits easily with the less enthusiastic comment about Madrid's history being 'closely associated with cultural cross-breeding'.[9]

The harmonization of cultural encounters combined with a marginalization of ethnically mixed communities and a classification of interracial relations as 'cross-breeding' is reminiscent of the 'hispanismo' discourse that governed the centenaries of the so-called discovery of America, including the heavily criticized celebration of the fifth centenary in 1992 in Seville. However, the official website suggests taking the traditional Hispanic focus on harmonious Spanish-Latin American relations under Spanish colonialism and postcolonial present to the next level: global cosmopolitanism under Spanish patriarchal guidance and protection, with Madrid as a prime example. Although the website has improved substantially over the last years, especially with the suppression of photos that confirmed explicit ethnic and gender discrimination and the very strong business focus of the city council, there are still neocolonial continuities.

Less convincing is the confusion between notions of multiculturalism, interculturalism, and transculturalism in a website that begins with the idea of living 'side by side' and then stresses Lavapiés as an admirable 'melting pot of cultures'.[10] At first glance, the traditional multicultural concept of coexistence seems to be outdated in a website that invites people from all over the world to participate actively in city life, but there is suggestive evidence (starting with the portrayal of interracial relations as 'cross-breeding') that city authorities might favor a combination of private co-existence and public interaction. After all, the marketing focus of the current *esmadrid.com* website is geared toward tourists spending a considerable amount of money on high-culture attractions and luxury products,[11] whereas its original business investments focus has been enhanced by the development of a new 'Invest in Madrid' website (see Invest in Madrid 2014). Also, the claim that the city has no integration problems questions attempts to enhance integration by 'get to know your neighbor' campaigns and subsidized Spanish as a Foreign Language and/or intercultural support classes. In other words, the 'cosmopolitan' character of the city council, which should be re-defined as openness to foreign investment, meets provincial monoculturalism when it comes to 'living with each other'.

The historical high-culture focus of city authorities is not directly new, because Madrid's 'cultural capital'—to draw on a term proposed by influential sociologist Bourdieu (1987: 212f.)—has been promoted as a key aspect of the city by numerous intermediators, and Spanish as a Foreign Language course books provide many good examples. However, in line with Bianchini's assessment of royal events as constructions that stabilize a mindscape of traditional nationhood by transforming urban surroundings into a fictitious space of pre-modern state power (2006: 18), I see a similarly fictitious image of a high-culture past in city council narratives that favor groups with high economic and cultural capital. Citizens with low economic and cultural capital might have perceived Madrid already in the 16th century as a place in which a decent life is difficult to achieve, rather than the city of Velázquez in 'Golden Age' Spain. However, Echevarría's *Cabeza de Vaca* (1991) reminds us that the same Europeans who emigrated to the New World in order to improve their often precarious and miserable life at home seemed very open to disseminate colonial superiority constructs. In these, civilized, rational, and patriarchal Spain assumed the divine right and duty to invade, occupy, and govern less civilized, rather irrational, and female imagined territories. Understandably, authorities prefer to marginalize the importance of colonialism in neoliberal developments of cities like Madrid and Seville, which links to an obligation for migrant cinema to revisit history and facilitate the development of 'transcultural memory' (Moses and Rothberg 2014).

3.1.3 Neocolonial Structures *in* Letters from Alou

The first film that draws wider attention to challenges for black migrants in Spain is Armendáriz's *Letter's from Alou*, which Ballesteros categorizes convincingly as a 'road movie' that questions the rationale behind the 'Fortress approach [...] within the EU' (2015: 24). A significant part of it was shot in Madrid, and no other feature film was to treat the reception of non-white migrants in the capital in a comparable way until Saura's *Taxi*. Armendáriz handed over the copyright to SOS Racismo in exchange for SOS members giving advice during all production periods. Maybe in this context it is not surprising that the film has become a tool of anti-racist education and intercultural training in the school environment and beyond (see Santaolalla 2007: 468f.). However, despite claims of being close to 'reality',[12] it should be treated as what it is: a fictional product that primarily mirrors non-governmental perspectives on migration to Spain. In opposition to portrayals of globalization as de-limitation and dissolution of borders, the film emphasizes the strength of traditional boundaries and the mechanisms used to (re-)erect new ones in an effort to protect privileges. This is clear and rather dramatic in the case of illegal black immigrant Alou, whose travels from Africa via Almeria to Madrid and Barcelona province appear as a major quest for a place to live with human dignity. Until he meets his Spanish girlfriend Carmen toward the end of the film, Spaniards tend to make money from him or tell him where he does not belong. This may happen with the lorry driver who finds him on 'his' vegetable plantation somewhere in Almeria, the worker in Madrid who detects him on 'his' building site, or the owner of a village pub near Barcelona who does not want to serve black immigrants. Alou's challenges are well reflected in the difficulties of his journey: the dangerous nightly boat-trip to reach Spain, the travel to Madrid where his travel bag and money are stolen, or the long nightly walk along Catalan railways. The montage accentuates the lack of Spanish hospitality and the immigrant's role as a victim of inhuman conditions and hostilities. This is the case not only in his own country (which forced him to leave) but also in Spain, where people seem to have forgotten their own history of emigration during and after the Spanish Civil War. A remark to this effect appears in Gutiérrez's *Poniente* (2002). All this reminds us of comparable patterns of exclusion even for 'legal' immigrants from the former colonies in 1960s England, which Chadha's *Bend It Like Beckham* (2002) indicates via Mr. Bhamra's memory of being kicked out of a white cricket club 'like a dog'. On the other hand, most 21st century migrant cinema, including Chadha's work, Akın's *The Edge of Heaven* (2007), and Kaurismäki's *Le Havre* (2011), claim a fundamental change in popular perceptions of immigration in the 21st century. In the context of increasing right-wing success, this claim may correspond more to the directors' wishful thinking than to empirically measurable shifts in mentality.

In Madrid, Alou is exposed to the anonymity of a metropolis with masses of people who ignore each other. The camera's focus on hectic street life and claustrophobic accommodations creates a filmic geography of the capital, i.e., a 'cinematic city' (Dear 2000: 183f.), which does not concentrate on the tourist attractions highlighted in city council narratives. Alou's ejection from the building site is symbolic, because that site mirrors the fast growing capital the city authorities wish to project. Consequently, it is always a non-white migrant who helps him find a space to live and work, be it the vegetable plantation in Almeria, the fruit plantation or sewing business in Barcelona, or the pubs and streets of Madrid, where he sells cheap goods—just like the nameless African in *Taxi*. In all cases, Alou is relocated into colonial space, in particular as a manual worker exploited by white plantation owners, but also as a tradesman on streets controlled by white police.

Surely, 'investinmadrid.com' does not refer directly to these jobs when it tries to sell the city by stressing its low labor costs,[13] but there is no doubt that the availability of cheap labor can be a strong argument for investing in Madrid. Opportunities include running a business (for which Nena's role as shop assistant in Gutiérrez Aragón's *Things I Left in Havana* 1997 might be a good example), purchasing goods (see Alou as tradesman on the street), or caring for children and elderly (Olga in Pérez Rosado's *Salt Water* 2005). Recalling colonial times, all of this comes with a strict separation of white and non-white living space. On the plantation in Almeria, a tiny house far away from the accommodations of white bosses and village people holds more than a dozen workers from Africa; in Barcelona province the substructure of a former aqueduct serves as a shelter for several dozen immigrants, and in Madrid a room in a cheap hotel accommodates at least half a dozen. The latter's landlady stresses the binary further by asking Alou and his friend to speak in 'cristiano', a term that should not only be considered as an 'ideological leftover from the days of Franco', as Deveny (2012: 28) suggests. It is a synonym for Spanish that dates back to colonial times and suggests drawing a dividing line between Christian Spaniards and less Christian or simply pagan Others.[14] However, even if they speak Spanish, finding a place is not easy for these Others, as emphasized in *Things I Left in Havana*, in which Igor seduces single women in order to get shared accommodations, whereas individual living space is nearly impossible to get.[15] As Alou's experience highlights, non-whites are usually kept in larger groups, like herds, within relatively small and rather dark claustrophobic spaces, which stresses the narrow boundaries set for them and underlines their difficulties in recovering subjectivity.[16]

Figure 3.1.3.1 Claustrophobic migrant spaces in *Letters from Alou*.

Cultural separatism is also highlighted through the quality of accommodations, which Alou's Moroccan companion from the crossing pointedly summarizes toward the end as 'bad smell and dirty? – our place!'('¿mal olor y sucio?– ¡nuestro lugar!'). Exceptions are associated with cross-cultural relations and the immigrants' assumption of neocolonial roles from the whites. However, unlike his pen pal Mulai, who has succeeded by marrying a Spanish woman and opening a small sewing business, Alou remains illegal and thus an extremely vulnerable outcast, stressed by his deportation to Africa. At the very end, the film shows him again on a boat returning to his girlfriend Carmen who represents both his love and his chance to start a life with human dignity by achieving legal status through marriage.[17]

Alou's body—the last place the migrant can retreat to—is very integrated into this system of neocolonial exploitation, in particular as an incredibly economic and very flexible picking and collecting 'machine' on the plantations, that can be easily disposed of after the harvest, or earlier in case of malfunction. However, the same corporal strength that distinguishes him as a good worker can resist humiliation, especially in the scene in which Alou fights the Spanish worker who does not want him to eat a pear from the plantation. As symbol of Alou's rebellious ego, his body becomes a place of postcolonial resistance against arbitrary use of white authority when he forces the white man to eat that pear, an action that recalls Raúl's rebellion against a global consumerist re-inscription of his body in *Jamon Jamon* (1992).[18] On the other hand, just like in colonial times, the fight leads to an immediate loss of working and living space and the inability to find a 'good patron' (one of the first words Alou learns in Spanish) to work for, and this might mean the same as deportation back to Africa: living in subhuman conditions or simply starving to death.

Despite the rhetoric of friendship, the job as a tradesman employed by his new African 'friend' in Madrid does not break with these patterns of authoritarian exploitation, which reminds the audience of the replacement of white colonizers and neocolonial plantation managers by black successors. At the same time, Alou is a sexual object for a couple of Spanish women who look for him and his 'friend' only when they want to have sex. Admittedly, the clever tradesman who gives Alou a place to sleep and then teaches him to sell his watches on the streets is not comparable to a Mugabe in Zimbabwe, but behind the superficial notion of black brothers united in their fight to survive in a white-dominated economy there is the bitter taste of 'internalized Orientalism'.[19] Not by coincidence, Alou's rebellion against economic and sexual exploitation is categorized as the action of an ill mind in front of the Spanish women: 'I don't know what's wrong with him' ('No sé lo que le pasa.'). Similarly, the Cuban aunt in *Things I Left in Havana* rejects Nena because she does not accept the place of neocolonial exploitation reserved for her, but her Othering of fellow countrymen culminates in an excessive rejection of Cuban food and customs that remains in conflict with her desire for it.

Unfortunately, the framing of Alou as a sexual object is not limited to the perspective of some characters in the film—like Zulema's description in

Princesses—but remains part of the filmic message. Whilst evoking empathy with Alou's destiny, e.g., by the 'mise-en-scène' of his emotional and psychological subjectivity mirrored in the letters to his family and friends (the 'letters' from the title), Armendáriz constantly highlights his protagonists' black body as an object of desire. Overall, he places Alou in an imagined pre-civilized corporal world that belongs to the central and highly ambiguous aspects of colonial fantasy.[20] Shortly after Alou's arrival in Spain, the camera leads the viewer to Alou's naked torso and frames it in detail when he cleans himself in the sea stressing his muscles and dark skin. As Santaolalla remarks, there is no direct shot at the genital zone (2007: 469), but colonial stereotyping is confirmed when Spanish women in Madrid argue that he would be ideal to 'comfort widows' ('consolar viudas'). In fact, Alou succeeds in winning Carmen's affection in a pub in which most clients are white, and there are strong allusions to the importance of sex in this love story.

Finally, Alou's difficulties with the Spanish language and customs are problematic. They contribute to this traditional framing of black people as stronger in a corporal than in an intellectual sense, in particular because there is no major exception to this rule until the 'mise-en-scène' of the black diplomat in *Taxi* and the Cuban sisters in *Things I Left in Havana*. Spanish cinema has certainly developed alternatives to the erotic portrayal of Alou; Uribe's non-sexual projection of black Ombasi as an extremely peaceful nature-bound being in *Bwana* (1996) is a good example. However, *Bwana* draws on colonial stereotyping as well when Ombasi is reconstructed as a 'noble savage' by Uribe to explore the weaknesses of the contemporary Spanish family and society, rather than only those of 'the white Spanish man in crisis' as Santaolalla argues (2005: 159). Like Chateaubriand's Atalá, Ombasi is governed by a superior link to nature that gives him the strength to resist the moral corruption of European citizens represented by a cowardly, racist, and hypocritical Antonio, who leaves him in the dramatic end at the mercy of skinheads and who is anything but a role model for his family. Alou is too ambitious and self-centered to fit into this image, but his fight against neocolonial exploitation provides him too with an aura of moral superiority. In this sense, both of the protagonists from *Letters from Alou* and *Bwana* can be regarded as examples of an inversion of colonial hierarchies, which neither breaks with the binary structure of colonial discourse, nor offers a clear and feasible alternative to white mainstream society. Instead, noble savage Ombasi and fighter Alou invite occidental society to reform itself and, in particular, to work against moral corruption in order to return to its traditional role of an exemplary civilization.

3.1.4 *Neofascist Racism in* Taxi

The popular thriller *Taxi* by famous director Carlos Saura, for which Ingrid Rubio as Paz won two major awards, places discrimination patterns into a wider context than *Letters from Alou*. Instead of targeting migrants only, the fascist taxi drivers want to 'clean' the streets of Madrid from all kinds of 'human garbage', their definition of drug addicts, homosexuals, transvestites, and particularly non-white immigrants. What matters with respect to foreigners is clearly not so much their status (legal, illegal, diplomatic), ethnic origin (African, American), or foreign passport but the color of their skin or, to be more precise, their race. As confirmed by data from the Observatorio de la Inmigración Marroquí en España (2007), at the time *Taxi* was produced Moroccans formed numerically the strongest group of non-white immigrants in Madrid, which helps to explain why their illegal settlement in the capital's suburbs becomes the main target for Calero's fascists. The dramatic scene is representative for excessive racist violence in many other films about migration like *Bwana* and *Poniente*, which both end on such a note, and it reconstructs very similarly—for the purpose of deconstruction—the monocultural discourse upon which this violence is based.

The stereotypical arguments for the Others' expulsion or elimination are quickly summarized by Calero: 'they are the ones who steal your job and rape your women'.[21] Neither the former nor the latter corresponds to the taxi drivers' personal experiences, but precisely this lack of confirmation leads viewers to understand the extreme nationalism portrayed as expression of traditional Othering within which racist aggression is justified as part of Spain's 'bellum iustum'. This can be traced back to colonial dichotomies stressing the supposedly illegal aggressive and barbarian nature of the Other against the legal, peaceful, and civilized character of the Self, although the image of the barbarian seems to have changed from cannibal to rapist.[22] The cinematic de-construction follows Calero's binary by inverting each aspect of it: 'illegal' are in particular the fascists' assaults, they are the only aggressive group in the film, and their murders of the supposed 'human garbage' as well as their own people (such as Velázquez) could easily be categorized as barbarian.

The fact that most victims are caught as taxi passengers is symbolic. This modern public transportation is used for a racist purpose by a pre-modern person-centered group. Modern societies tend to concentrate on people's functions rather than on their social roles, a topic nicely examined in Pepe Danquart's *Fare Dodger* (1993), in which a racist woman is expelled from a tram by a supervisor checking tickets without concern for passengers' race. *Taxi* outlines that precisely the opposite might apply: The trust in modern functionality combined with the relative isolation and anonymity of clients and drivers in taxis in a modern metropolis appears to be the ideal environment for fascists to implement their own laws. The value of Madrid's anonymity—which city council narratives stress as the facilitator of contemporary integration (see 3.1.2)—is here reversed as it protects traditional enemies of transcultural societies from persecution.[23] The fascists follow a strictly hierarchical monocultural and person-centered structure inspired by traditional forms of caudillismo: at the bottom new 'soldiers' like Dani and quickly recruited skinheads; in the middle senior members like Niño, Reme, and Velázquez. All of this is headed by the former policeman (probably under Franco) and now 'mini-caudillo' Calero. Considering the rigid centralization of the Spanish nation under fascism, which is still visible in contemporary Madrid, the 'family's' ambition to 'clean' the capital can be read as an attempt to complete the work fascist propaganda promised to deliver after the Civil War: 'liberate' the nation from 'enemies' and 'parasites'.

However, the setting of boundaries is arbitrary, and in the news shown on TV at the end of the film, a Spanish fascist demands Europe as a whole to be white: 'Europa blanca'. All of this facilitates a discussion of *Taxi* as an examination of European right-wing tendencies, which have enjoyed astonishing popularity again nearly two decades after Saura's film (see Ramalingam 2014). I find attempts to discuss it under headers like 'The European Family in the Face of Otherness' (Ballesteros 2015: 24) less convincing, because the extreme racism of Calero's group goes well beyond opportunistic treatments of immigrants. Above all, the exclusion of non-white immigrants and other black people in the taxi drivers' world could be regarded as an expression of neofascist perspectives. However, as social Darwinist race theories were already extremely popular when European colonialism reached its culminating point, i.e., in a largely democratic period in 1920s Europe—long before German and Spanish fascism came to power—the biological racism portrayed should also be examined in its correlation with colonial discourse. Parallels can be drawn as far back as the famous debate between the Head of the Spanish Inquisition Sepúlveda and bishop Las Casas in the mid-16th century, in which Sepúlveda explicitly questioned the Native Americans' human character, thereby feeding common doubts of conquerors and colonizers in the centuries to come (see Rings 2005: 58). As Campra summarizes, being classified an 'Other' in colonial discourse implied being not only different but less: 'less strong, less intelligent … less human' (1991: 82). By drawing on such principles, Calero's fascists link up to popular reconstructions of white European superiority, which are mirrored in recent right-wing tendencies again, but their extremely aggressive and undifferentiated monoculturality should not be misunderstood as a reflection of national or EU policies in Europe.

Unfortunately, in its focus on monocultural perspectives and group dynamics, Saura's film reduces immigrants and other target groups so excessively to the role of victims that they are left as objects of historical processes, just like the helpless stagnant Other in colonial discourse, in which Europe appears as a progressive 'maker of history' (Blaut 1993: 1). Caught in the traditional Las Casas-style dichotomy of bad white perpetrators and good colored victims, the Africans from *Taxi* remain in desperate need of white patriarchal protection, ironically offered by female protagonist Paz who defends the passive black African in the pub from her aggressive boyfriend. In this way the dramatically objectified African becomes a prime example of colonial and neocolonial claims about the whites' right to and duty of leadership.

58 Migrants in Europe

Figure 3.1.4.1 Framing of Others in *Taxi*.

Certainly, the Moroccans in their illegal settlement fight back, and so does the African diplomat. Both are, however, examples of a rather instinctive resistance, a spontaneous reaction more than an action. This does not develop them as subjects with own aims, agendas, and culture, and brings them closer to Ombasi and Alou, than to Adbembi in *Poniente*, who stresses his Berber history and culture. The framing of all victims in public spaces, rather than inside their own homes, confirms their lack of subjectivity. Even the African diplomat remains at the mercy of Spanish negotiations, in which the confrontation between Paz and Calero can be read as a new, albeit distorted, contemporary cinematic edition of the clash between Las Casas and Sepúlveda. At the end, their access to space depends on Spanish civil courage and good will: mainly by Paz, but also by the Spanish government, which welcomes the diplomat and reduces Calero's activities to nightly clandestine crimes. Comparable binaries of white subject and colored object are reconstructed well before and after *Taxi*, for example in Bohm's *Yasemin* (1988), in which German 'knight' Jan rescues his Turkish girlfriend, and in Kaurismäki's *Le Havre*, in which Marcel helps the child-refugee Idrissa. However, the monocultural opponents tend to be different, the colonial link might be less explicit, and above all in contrast to transcultural approaches in the first part of *Yasemin* and the adoption process based on transcultural memory in Kaurismäki's film, *Taxi* proposes to leave neocolonial cultural separatism unchallenged.

It is worth remembering that key scenes of *Taxi* are shot in the Retiro, originally designed for the Spanish Court's recreational use but opened to the public during the revolution of 1868. Rebellious Paz and her boyfriend Dani kiss for the first time in front of the Crystal Palace in the center of the park, and Paz retreats to the same place when hunted by Calero, all at night shaped by the expressionist lighting and color of cinematographer Vittorio Storaro. The building, originally erected to display fragile flower species from the Philippine Islands for the International Exhibition in 1887, presented a chance to prove to the rest of the world the greatness of Spain. Paz's new relationship builds on such symbolism: The love between the female rebel (who fights all forms of patriarchal authority—her father's at home or Calero's outside) and Dani (the new unwilling fascist recruit) is extremely fragile, but it also has enormous potential. If the two can find a way to be together, the vicious circle of hate and violence can be broken, and Calero's organization could be finished—provided the two report him to the police.

Only five minutes from the end, when Paz breaks up with Dani and Calero starts hunting her, it looks as if such prospects are unattainable, which is confirmed by her not finding shelter in front of the well-lit palace and giving up on her attempt to run way. However, the fact that she awaits Calero at the monument to Alfonso XII, the so called 'Peacemaker' ('Pacificador') who—only aged 17—ended the fighting in a country shaken by the 'Revolutionary Sexenial' (1868–1874), reflects more than the director's choice of a 'dramatic location' (Deveny 2012: 42). Paz reminds viewers of Alfonso, not only by her name and young age but by fighting those who reject the concept of peaceful coexistence of different (sub-) cultures as betrayal of patriotic values.[24] Her location during this scene, exactly underneath Pedro Carbonell's bronze relief in which La Patria praises the restoration of Alfonso's monarchy as re-establishment of peaceful patriotism, highlights the absurdity of the fascists' belief.

In this respect, the film follows the city authorities' portrayal of Madrid as deeply rooted in a history of peaceful coexistence, bound to continue after Paz' victory. However, there are at least two weaknesses in Saura's dramatic contribution to sell Madrid as a good place for investors and tourists alike: one is linked to Madrid's colonial past and another to its neocapitalist present. Although the location for Calero's death—at the statue of Alfonso XII—suggests that the film wishes to frame fascist nationalism as an aberration of a history of peaceful patriotism represented by the constitutional monarch, it is difficult to ignore the park's numerous reminders of Spanish colonialism,[25] which played an important role in the historical justification of Franco's regime. On the other hand, Fraser—who does not explore the park's colonial or 19th century symbolism at all—refers

60 *Migrants in Europe*

Figure 3.1.4.2 Paz in front of Carbonell's bronze relief.

to an unacknowledged 20th century history of 'class conflicts'. They shine through as soon as the 'bourgeois' taxi drivers and their kids access the Retiro at a time when it is supposed to be closed to avoid prostitutes, drug addicts, illegal immigrants, and other 'undesirables' conquering the space.[26] Already during the production and dissemination period of *Taxi* the Retiro was heavily policed, but Saura's film does not even mention the parallels between the policemen's and the fictional taxi drivers' 'cleaning' operations, both with the aim to re-occupy attractive space in the center of Madrid, albeit with different methods and agendas.

3.1.5 Concluding Remarks

As examples of European cinema of the 1990s, *Letters from Alou* and *Taxi* undermine the city authorities' claim of harmonious coexistence and transcultural interaction in Madrid by pointing out severe integration problems, including legal boundaries, patterns of economic exploitation, hierarchical culture constructs, and racism. Most of these obstacles can be regarded as 'neocolonial' because of their structural links to key concepts from colonial discourse, an aspect that is ignored in city council narratives, whereas it is explicit in many films (e.g., *Letters from Alou, Things I Left in Havana,* and *Poniente*) and implicit in others (*Taxi, Bwana,* and *Salt Water*). The construction of space in city narrative and film not only helps us understand such cultural-historical allusions, but it allows us to approach the shortcomings in city council and cinematic discourse that lead to unacknowledged neocolonial subtexts in both cases. As such, cracks in the city authorities' argumentation in 'esMadrid.com' and 'investinmadrid.com' reveal that their concept of a 'melting pot' (aimed at 'selling' Madrid to tourists and investors in what is now a fierce international interurban competition for economic capital) does not imply political interest in ethnic mixing and instead enhances the continuity of cultural separatism. *Letters from Alou* criticizes neocolonial discrimination, strict separation, and open exploitation of illegal immigrants as cheap labor without individual rights, but in its framing of Alou as an example of a pre-civilized corporal world it follows a key concept of colonial stereotyping. *Taxi* reviews the attraction of biological racism for common people in a contemporary metropolis. This is explicitly linked to Spain's relatively recent fascist past and is founded in much older patterns of cultural and racial discrimination. However, in its objectification of Moroccans and black Africans as helpless victims in desperate need of patriarchal protection by strong whites, colonial power hierarchies are re-established along the lines of Las Casas's agenda.

Unlike *Taxi*, most of the above-named films stress migrants' chances at shaping their own future in Spain—assuming they decide to fight for it. Hyperactive Alou is a good role model as he rejects the neocolonial spaces offered to him and continues his quest for a 'home'. This is not to be imagined in the traditional sense as geographically fixed (either somewhere in Africa or on a Spanish plantation) but as a place that can be anywhere as long as it facilitates a life with human dignity. Cuban Nena is a good example with her refusal to take on the unpaid shop assistant role and the arranged marriage in Madrid, and her boyfriend Igor confirms the need for resistance with his swearing on 'the damn fatherland' ('la cochina madre patria'). In opposition to cosmopolitan images of Madrid, the films do not raise expectations regarding success in integration but stress instead the difficulties, especially for those with low economic and cultural capital who have never been invited to Madrid or to any other place in Spain—like Alou, Ombasi, and Adbembi. However, the problem starts if and when the focus on mechanisms of exclusion becomes so strong that the films ignore common patterns of acculturation (see Hofstede 2001: 426) and embodiment (Thomas 2007: 41f.), which is certainly the case in *Letters from Alou* and *Taxi*. Similarly problematic seems the cinematic preference for the 'mise-en-scène' of failed cross-cultural relationships, with which films like *Susanna*, *Two for Tea*, *In July*, and even Iglesias' widely celebrated *Un franco, 14 pesetas* (2006) connect to colonial fears of cultural/racial contagion and intermixing, a tendency explored in Spanish cinema by Flesler (2004)[27] and in German cinema by Rings (2008). Also, the migrant-protagonists' return to their country of origin as the only imaginable 'home' and 'correct place to be' provides a traditional monocultural solution advocated even by productions like *Salt Water*, *Solino,* and *Princesses*, despite their own focus on transcultural friendships and spaces. In short, there is evidence that the insistence on clearly definable cultural borders, and especially the perception of individual cultures as essentially different and geographically fixed, continues to shape most of European cinema of the 1990s and with it the perspective of its viewers on migration and diaspora. All this can be summarized as a return to binary patterns of thought that ultimately support the neocolonial structures the films set out to de-construct.

3.2 Assimilation Tendencies in Gurinder Chadha's *Bend It Like Beckham*

3.2.1 Preliminary Remarks

Gurinder Chadha, the director and co-scriptwriter of *Bend It Like Beckham* (with her husband Paul Mayeda Berges and Guljit Bindra), could probably best be described as one of the leading British-Asian film directors. Although born in Nairobi (Kenya), her Punjabi parents moved to Southall, London, when she was only two years of age, and it is her life as a woman with Indian background in London that marks her output. This includes documentaries like *I'm British but...* (1989), *Nice Arrangement* (1990), and *Acting Our Age* (1991) as well as full-length fictional movies such as *Bhaji on the Beach* (1993), *Bend It Like Beckham* (2002), and *Bride and Prejudice* (2004). Whereas the first fictional movies are centered on 'East-West' encounters, *Angus, Thongs and Perfect Snogging* (2008) explores British migration to New Zealand, before Chadha returns to the Indian diaspora in London with *It's a Wonderful Afterlife* (2010), an extremely simplistic comedy that has received very negative reviews and was a major box office flop.

Chadha's biggest commercial success to date remains *Bend It Like Beckham*, a film that at a first glance follows the traditional pattern of generational conflicts within the British-Asian diaspora: a young second-generation British-Indian woman (Jess, played by Parminder Nagra) clashes with family traditions when pursuing her personal ambitions as a footballer. However, the film setting in Hounslow (Southall, London), near the area where Chadha grew up, and the numerous links to her own autobiography enable the director to present a differentiated picture of a diverse community. Chadha herself goes so far as to link the success to that aspect: 'in Britain it's the most successful British-financed British movie ever [...] because it's very culturally specific to Hounslow, to West London, and it talks about a world which is really mixed without going on about it' (Fischer 2003).

Whatever the reasons for its international popularity, the movie follows in the footsteps of Damian O'Donnell's *East is East* (1999) in the way that it rejects the art-house design of most European migrant films of the 1980s and 1990s. In its combination of light-hearted comedy and an exploration of 'identity, belonging and Britishness',[28] Chadha's *Bend It Like Beckham* was—just like *East is East*—marketed extensively for a British audience. It is for the entertainment and critical reflection of this audience that Chadha wanted to shoot the film 'from the point of view of someone who is Indian and English at the same time' (Fischer 2003), meaning Jess, but obviously referring to the director herself as well. As an account of a young woman of Indian origin who refuses to cook and serve others in her search for an alternative way of life, *Bend It Like Beckham* is based on biographical evidence, starting with a rebellious character that Chadha describes as follows:

> I refused to wear Indian clothes, and I would always get out of cooking. [...] Whenever guests came, the men would sit at the table, and the women would have to serve them, and I would sit at the table as well. [...] At the same time, I was extremely outspoken, and I used to say, well mum, look, I'm not cooking, you know, it's oppressive. You don't even understand.
>
> (Fischer 2003)

Jess is similarly skeptical as regards traditional agendas, and she is also very outspoken, when it comes to defending her football interests that develop during the film. At the beginning, the audience gets to know the protagonist as somebody occasionally playing football with boys in the park. However, this gets more serious when Jules, a white middle class English girl (played by now famous Keira Knightly) invites Jess to join the local women's soccer team, the Hounslow Harriers trained by Joe, an Irish coach who always wanted to play professional football but was held back by a knee injury. He now tries to help Jess and Jules fulfill their dream of a professional career in the US, an idea of which Jess's parents strongly disapprove when they discover the secret football activities of their daughter. However, when Jess's father realizes how important the football career has become for his daughter, he appears much more tolerant, and with his new personal attitude comes a change in the behavior of the whole family who now allows Jess to join Jules on her journey to the US.

As the title suggests, Jess's role model is not Guru Nanak, whose portrait is prominently placed in her parents' living room, but rather the former British football icon David Beckham, whose posters cover the walls of her bedroom. The parallel montage of Mrs. Bhamra appealing to Guru Nanak when Jess's exam results arrive and Jess seeking guidance from Beckham stresses this difference between older generations' beliefs and younger generations' orientation. In this sense, the title can be understood in both a literal and a metaphorical sense: Jess wants to be able to bend balls like Beckham, but in order to pursue her big dream on the football pitch she must first learn how to bend the social norms that govern her life. It certainly is about 'bending' norms rather than breaking them, because Jess does not want to completely alienate the family she loves. The cultural and generational conflict is enriched by explorations of gender images (women in a masculine sport), ethnic discrimination (against both 'Paki' Jess and Irish Joe) and sexual orientation (heterosexual norms and homosexual fears) in a coming-of-age film that combines key aspects of drama, comedy, and a short love story.

The $5 million film that grossed up to $350 million worldwide in its first year alone[29], an astounding amount to which one has to add the extensive video and DVD rental, streaming and purchase from the last six years, has in particular been received as an 'amusing comedy' and a 'feel-good' movie (Elley 2002: 32) or, in short 'a well-made audience-pleaser' (Chaudhury 2003, see also Rotten Tomatoes 2014). However, some critics have stated that the film has the 'capacity to provoke thought and discussion on [...] cultural differences and identity' (Raschke 2004: 126), including 'cultural dichotomies' (Berghahn 2013: 126). Algeo's claim to use it for the enhancement of critical analysis in cultural geography classes (2007: 133) correlates with Sandhu's impression that the film addresses key aspects in the life of South Asian women in the diaspora, especially when inter-generational and inter-ethnic conflicts in sport are at stake. This seems to be the case with Sandhu herself who, a second-generation Sikh woman living in Canada, recognizes herself and her family in the movie ('I had never seen myself being so accurately reflected in popular culture before', 2005: 7), but also—and perhaps even more—with the participants of her study, a tendency that seems to connect with Chadha's own experiences.

Considering that the film has been criticized repeatedly as a stereotypical 'mise-en-scène' of Indian culture, a perspective well represented by Elley when he summarizes Chadha's work as a 'gallery of broadly played stereotypes' (2002: 32), this chapter will explore how far *Bend It Like Beckham* supports popular monocultural constructs of British-Indian relations and to what degree its transcultural elements are able to break with the Othering of traditional hegemonic narrative.

3.2.2 A Protagonist Between Cultures?

There is no doubt that Jess combines aspects from both cultures, Indian or—to be more precise—Sikh traditions maintained by her parents and partially her sister Pinky, and English customs and preferences associated with young women's independence and a celebration of football for which Jules and her father are given as examples. Algeo is right in criticizing current research on *Bend It Like Beckham* for its radical marginalization or complete ignorance of the Bhamra family's Sikh background (2007: 133), which links up to Chadha's family tradition. This gap in research is surprising, as the film indicates this dimension very clearly. First, there is a painting of the Golden Temple of Amritsar prominently placed in the living room near Guru Nanak's portrait, and a gold model of that temple sits on the shelf close to the bar area. Also, Mr. Bhamra's turban can hardly be overlooked, and the fact that—during his older daughter's engagement ceremony—he gives her fiancée the traditional gift of a 'kara'-bracelet reminds critical viewers of the 'five K' practices that are 'symbolic of maintaining proper spiritual order' in a Sikh household (Algeo 2007: 135).

In addition, cultural boundaries are drawn by food, e.g., when Mrs. Bhamra—the guardian of the family's cultural heritage—repeatedly

Figure 3.2.2.1 Guru Nanak's blessing in *Bend It Like Beckham*.

forces Jess to help prepare traditional food from the Punjabi region most British Sikhs originate from. This attitude is closely linked to her perception of young Indian women as future wives for Indian men, as one of her statements suggests: 'what kind of family would want a daughter-in-law who can kick a football around all day but can't make round chapattis?' A comparable mechanism of 'Othering' via food is visible when Jules's mother, Paula Paxton, talks to Jess about the 'lovely curry' she made the other night. The overarching interest in entertaining a wider audience does not allow elaborating on these aspects, but they are present, and Chadha herself highlights food as a 'great codifier of culture' (Fischer 2003).

Similarly, the average viewer does not have to be familiar with the details of recent English football history in order to follow the film, but a basic knowledge of Beckham's ability to 'bend the ball', his 'metrosexual' appearance, and the cross-generational and cross-class popularity of football are helpful for an analysis of the 'Englishness' portrayed. Football is the key topic that unites Jules and her father Frank Paxton from the very beginning of the movie and toward the end even manages to bridge the generational difference between Jules and her mother. Highly symbolic is the scene in which Frank explains offside rules to his wife Paula, because this is done with the help of international food, including Japanese teriyaki sauce and 'posh French mustard', which he moves forward and backward on the table. The English middle-class family is here characterized as a harmonious group thanks to the unifying power of football, and international food reflects Paula's open-mindedness vis-à-vis other cultures.

Jess is from the very beginning of the film situated between the two camps: On the one hand, she loves her parents and does not want to disappoint them or ruin her sister's wedding. In order to please them she wears traditional dresses and serves guests when required, and—toward the end—she is even prepared to give up on Joe with the remark: 'letting me go is a big step for my mum and dad. I don't know how they'd survive if I told them about you too'. On the other hand, she cannot accept the future role her parents have reserved for her, which implies studying to become a solicitor but then ultimately marrying an Indian man to fulfill the traditional role of a housewife, for which purpose she has to learn how to cook Punjabi food. On her search for an alternative life, Jess discovers football, and she is determined to develop her skills further, despite her parent's disapproval of female football and her own desire to maintain good relations with them, which force her to hide everything related to it. Consequently, we see her in numerous carnevalesque situations: sometimes carrying platters of samosas and wearing the 'salwar kamiz'[30] in traditional parties at home, but then again pursuing her football interests in professional outfit, which for her mother means running around 'half-naked' in front of men. The construction of filmic space stresses this position 'in-between' by framing the traditional Punjabi family predominantly indoors, the British footballers mainly outdoors, and Jess as highly mobile individual either constantly on the move between these places or addressing her football dreams in her parents' garden.

One example is the traditional wedding party for her sister Pinky at the Bhamra family home, at which Jess appears at first dancing in the very center, but then has to stop because she gets dizzy from constantly turning around at increasingly higher speed in the middle of the living room filled up with cheering relatives in traditional dresses. By taking her perspective and turning around with her, the camera highlights her growing lack of orientation in the middle of this place with quickly blurring images of the party guests. When we see her shortly afterward in the front garden talking to Joe, who has just encouraged Mr. Bhamra to allow her daughter to take part in the tournament, she is very self-confident again. All this highlights that her place is not in the middle of the claustrophobic traditional family environment but outside, albeit close by, because Jess would like to combine collective tradition and individual dream, which leads back to the title of the film. *Bend It Like Beckham* is about bending traditional norms, not about breaking them, because that is likely to result in a family break-up.

Support for such a transcultural life-style comes from both ethnic backgrounds. Pinky helps Jess to cover up most football activities in front of her parents, and Joe tries to convince Mr. Bhamra of the need to let go of Jess so that she can develop her talent. That support allows her to engage in a quest for her own British-Asian identity vis-à-vis homogenous, separatist, and essentialist culture concepts cultivated by her parents and Jules's mother and might lead Berghahn to the statement that *Bend It Like Beckham* 'mitigates cultural dichotomies' and 'reduces Otherness' (2013: 126f.). In her comments on *Bhaji on the Beach*, Malik describes such British-Asianness as follows:

> We do not get the sense that any one culture has 'crossed over' or been assimilated, but that a new form of cultural identity is emerging. This hybrid identity is 'British-Asianness', a fluid evolving identity, which cannot be reduced to any one thing. (1996: 213)

A hybrid position can also be claimed for George's children in *East is East*, Bohm's Turkish-German protagonist in *Yasemin* (1988), and Hüseyin's children in Samdereli's *Almanya* (2010). In all cases, cultural boundaries are transgressed, and it is usually second-generation migrants who select more or less consciously what aspects of each cultural background are acceptable and preferable for them. Also, *East is East* and *Yasemin* are—with *Bend It Like Beckham*—good examples of the frequently resulting generational conflict in European migrant cinema, in which the role of the guardian of 'oriental' traditions tends to be associated with the first generation, and most children appear as 'rebels'.[31] Finally, *Yasmin* and *Bend It Like Beckham* exemplify a significant group of films, in which sport facilitates that rebellion by providing youngsters with new identity constructs.

Although male children also rebel (see Casim in Loach's *Ae Fond Kiss* 2004, and Tariq in *East is East*), the resistance of young women against the cultural heritage of sexism seems to be of particular interest for directors of European migrant cinema. Reasons for this are likely that its transcultural gender dimension engages more viewers and sells better and that young women are often in a weaker position to develop their views within the framework of the traditional patriarchal norms of their parents' societies. Certainly, in Philippe Faucon's *Samia* (2000), *Yasemin* and *Bend It Like Beckham*, both father and mother try to make their daughters follow traditional patterns of 'coming of age', although with different degrees of stubbornness and directness, which in Bohm's and Chadha's work significantly change in the course of the story. In addition, there is in all of these films an element of 'machismo' that governs the behavior of many younger males and makes them support the patriarchal hierarchies implemented by the first generation. Samia's eldest brother and Yasemin's cousin are good examples of that tendency, but the tall Indian male at Pinky's wedding who wants to 'conquer' as many women as possible, including Jess, fits into the same category.

Like Samia and Yasemin, Jess does not want to confirm fully to her parents' cultural expectations but rather wishes to be part of life in the host culture, which she has accepted as part of her own. However, the degree of 'deterritorialization' and 'territorialization' of cultural ground varies a lot. Depending on family relations, contacts in the host culture, and the message the director wishes to disseminate, the 'life-style model' proposed can lead to one of two things: A blurring of boundaries can occur in a transcultural identity construct in which hybridity is key, or there can be a simple shift of boundaries, within which a new monocultural, traditional multicultural, or traditional intercultural construct is being created by assimilating particular features and embedding others (very selected forms of hybridity) into larger container cultures (see the discussion in 1.2).

3.2.3 New Anglo-American Boundaries

Football has crossed cultural and gender boundaries, and world championships for both men and women could be given as examples for their global dimension, which *Bend It Like Beckham* stresses with references to women football in Britain, Germany, and—above all—the US as a model to follow. Even more important seems to be the ethnic mix of professional football teams, to which the Hounslow Harriers fully subscribe when they nominate a black girl as team captain, an Irish man as coach, and British-Asian Jess as attacker. In this sense, football in the film helps to connect people, but how far does it support transcultural dialogue and individual search for new hybrid identities? What kind of cultural choice does it facilitate, and does that choice imply a major victory of human agency over collective structures, as Huggan (2006) would hope for? In parallel, we might want to ask the same questions for cricket, which is the other sport highlighted in the film. Mr. Bhamra originally wanted to join an English cricket team, and his bitterness caused by rejection is very significant in his disapproval of Jess joining an English football team.

First, it is worth noting that England played a major role in the development of both sports. The Football Association founded in 1863 in London is the oldest national football association, which still hosts all professional football clubs in England and is ultimately responsible for the appointment of managers to national teams (men and women). Cricket, on the other hand, is first documented as being played in England, and since the 18th century it has been portrayed as the English national sport. Originally, neither cricket nor football was particularly associated with India, but the expansion of the British Empire led to a strong assimilation of cricket by Indian elites during colonial rule and can be considered as part of the 'mimicry' mechanisms Bhabha outlines in his *Location of Culture* (1994). In the meantime, India has become famous for cricket too (since 1926 it is a member of the Imperial and then International Cricket Conference, ICC), and Mr. Bhamra's strong interest should be seen in the context of this colonial heritage. His daughter Jess carries on his tendencies when she aims for very much the same: admission by an English sport club to play professionally 'for England'. This is stressed right at the beginning of the film in her daydream sequence, in which she plays with Beckham for Manchester United against the Belgian football club Anderlecht; later it becomes a reality when she plays for the Hounslow Harriers against a German team in Hamburg. Not by coincidence, her role model is David Beckham, the captain of the English national team at the time of the movie's filming.

In other words, neither young Mr. Bhamra nor Jess is an individual who is consciously aiming at a life that combines British and Indian cultures on equal footing. It is fair to say that their main objective is to become part of the British host culture. In both cases it has to be understood that the sport they are obsessed with stands for a way of life they want to achieve. Cricket can be associated with English upper class traditions that many British still want to follow (in particular if they have never been part of the upper class). Football is the more popular sport that seems to nurture old dreams of individual fame and wealth regardless of one's humble origins, which ties in to the success stories of former working class footballers like David Beckham and Wayne Rooney. It is not surprising that Mr. Bhamra who worked for the British colonial elite in East Africa tends to see his way of life embodied in cricket, whereas his daughter—a second-generation migrant raised in Hounslow—who is familiar with her and other South Asians being 'othered' as 'Pakis' affiliates more with British working class heroes. It is obvious that both descendants of colonized subjects would like the members of the former colonial center in which they have decided to stay to respect them. This dimension is not elaborated upon in detail because the film is aimed at entertaining a British mass audience, but racism toward South Asian migrants from the former colonies is highlighted when another footballer calls Jess a 'Paki' and when Mr. Bhamra talks about English cricket players who 'threw' him 'out of the club like a dog'. In both cases, the former colonial subject feels extremely humiliated: Jess assaults the other player and gets sent off the football pitch for it, and Mr. Bhamra 'vows' to never play cricket again.

It is worth remembering that the Bhamra family—like Chadha's parents—appears as 'twice migrants' in the sense that they migrated from India to Kenya first, before finally coming to Britain. Chadha was born in Nairobi, the capital and the largest city of Kenya, and Mr. Bhamra mentions to Joe as an explanation of his disapproval of Jess's football activities that he was 'Nairobi's best fast bowler' and still did not get a chance to play in an English club. Once again, there is a clear link to colonial history as it was the British East Africa Company that recruited substantial numbers of Sikhs for the construction of the Ugandan railroad, and they tended to form part of a new middle class in colonial East Africa:

> Europeans dominated administration, Indians filled positions in white-collar support, construction, and infrastructure development, and black Africans were relegated to manual labor. (Algeo 2007: 136)

This loyal position at the side of the colonial master caused a mass exodus of Indians after Kenyan independence in 1963; that makes the exclusion of Mr. Bhamra from an English cricket club 'back' in the British 'fatherland' all the more humiliating. From his perspective, it must seem that he and fellow Indians were good enough to help stabilize the British Empire and to lose their positions with the British when they were deprived of their privileges during 'decolonization', but they were not good enough for a life alongside the white man.

Consequently, neither young Mr. Bhamra nor Jess starts from notions of 'interlocking interdependence of cultures' (Antor 2010: 12) in their identity search, but from different ideas of Englishness, be it traditional-aristocratic or contemporary-popular, which both characters regard as the lead culture for all ethnicities to follow. Admittedly, during major parts of the film, Mr. Bhamra explicitly rejects all forms of Englishness because of his rejection by the English (cricket players). As soon as he understands that everybody has to 'fight' for his rights against occasional demonstrations of racism, the viewer sees him in the final sequence playing cricket publicly in front of the house, while an ice-cream van, a nostalgic symbol of traditional English culture, passes by. This interpretation is enhanced by the 'mise-en-scène' of all of the major English characters who seem to be extremely tolerant, open-minded, and 'transcultural' in the best sense of the concept. Most do not perceive any cultural or biological differences in their interaction with Jess but instead value her talent or character, as a good football player (Jules's perception), Jules's friend (Mr. Paxton's perception), or a loveable team mate. The Hounslow Harriers appear to be a team without prejudice or envy. On the few occasions, on which cultural differences are noted, it is either in a positive way (e.g., when Jules's mother associates 'respect for elders' with Indian culture and wants Jess to teach that to her daughter), or the negative aspect can be revised on the spot.[32]

Behind these constructs, the US seems to be the ultimate paradise for female football and the highly dynamic and emancipated contemporary lifestyle Jess and Jules stand for. In particular, the world power and, as such, successor of the European empires, is presented as the model to follow when it comes to equal opportunities in the competitive life football represents, and in this respect the new way of life appears to be ultimately an American one. All this is reminiscent of Ritzer's strong critique of the McDonaldization of societies that follow increasingly the four key concepts exemplified by the well-known fast-food chain: efficiency, predictability, control, and calculability (Ritzer 2011: 13f.). No doubt Jess has fully signed up for these norms, as she wants to be assessed according to her performance on the football pitch; her job is to shoot goals or to help Jules shoot them, and it is the final score that counts. She supports the capitalist cult around football heroes like Beckham by purchasing his posters and football shirts, and she is able to set an example in school. At least her father deducts from her A-level results that she can become a 'fine top-class solicitor'. In this respect, English and American ways of life appear to be compatible, although Northern Americans are leading the way in emancipation from outdated norms, and they have more resources to support new players in the field. The emigration of top talents like Jess and Jules resembles the famous brain drain from Europe to the US, and Joe knows only too well about the mechanics of money when uttering that he will recruit the two into a yet-to-be established professional English team 'if he can afford it'. However, it is not all about money as Joe's intonation suggests. Just like in Hollywood robinsonades, such as *Cast Away* (Zemeckis 2000) and *The Beach* (Boyle 2000), the end of this British movie reflects 'a popular mythology of the US as the metaphoric center of the world, the place to which the rest of the world flees in search for a better life' (Weaver-Hightower 2006: 304). If, however, instead of cultural dialogue and negotiations of identity constructs, *Bend It Like Beckham* offers predominantly an imagined Anglo-American West as a superior model to follow, it might not be wrong to return to Edward Said's exploration of the traditional dichotomy between the 'West and Rest' (1995[1978]: 20) Stuart Hall has summarized as follows:

> This 'West and the Rest' discourse greatly influenced Enlightenment thinking [...]. In Enlightenment discourse, the West was the model, the prototype and the measure of social progress. It was western progress, civilization, rationality and development that were celebrated. And yet [...] without the Rest (or its internal 'Others') the West would not have been able to recognize and represent itself as the summit of human history. The figure of 'the Other', banished to the edge of the conceptual world and constructed as the absolute opposite, the negation, of everything the West stood for, reappeared at the very center of the discourse of civilization, refinement, modernity and development in the West. 'The Other' was the 'dark' side—forgotten, repressed and denied; the reverse image of Enlightenment and modernity'. (1992: 312ff.)

Taking into account that *Bend It Like Beckham* has been designed as a comedy for common entertainment, it is not surprising that the Indian Other does not appear as 'the absolute opposite' and 'the negation of everything the West stands for'. There is, however, no doubt that the traditional Indian alternatives to Jess's Western life-style are being stressed in their exotic, stagnant, and either grotesque-funny or simply oppressive difference to Anglo-American liberalism, and all this highlights again that Welsch's assumption of increasing transculturality via globalization (1999: 198) is far too simplistic. The early scene, in which Jess and Jules effortlessly overtake two traditionally dressed, elderly, quite big and ridiculously slow Indian women during their jogging in the park, has in all its humor a clear symbolic message to deliver: The winners in contemporary society are those who fully adapt to the new Western way of life. If, however, individual choice for traditional British-Asians is limited to a possibility of assimilation and success or 'being left behind' if they continue to stick to their absurd traditions, it is no surprise that ultimately most filmic characters show at least a willingness to sign up to the West. Examples are the traditional British-Asian ladies jogging, Mr. Bhamra changing his mind, and even Mrs. Bhamra and some of the aunts happily accepting Jess's decision to play professional football in the US.

It is extremely unfortunate that *Bend It Like Beckham* ignores not only the increasing criticism regarding 'western' capitalist concepts, which has become particularly strong in the context of decolonization, environmentalism, and new US xenophobia and human rights abuses following the 9/11 attacks (roughly half a year before the launch of Chadha's film).[33] It also fails to develop the potential within the film. Not long after the discussion of the A-level results, in which Mrs. Bhamra's prayers to Guru Nanak are portrayed as something to laugh about (note the bird's eye perspective on the traditionally dressed Mrs. Bhamra and the impatience of Jess and Mr. Bhamra), the camera homes in on Jess in her bedroom talking to a poster of David Beckham. Although there might be some irony in the parallel montage, there is this time no bird's eye perspective, and nobody impatiently watches the clock or asks Jess 'to hurry up', because confessing hopes and fears to posters of a rich football star are apparently no laughing matter in the rational civilized West.

3.2.4 The Guardians of Monocultural Space

Throughout major parts of the film, Mr. and Mrs. Bhamra are the main obstacles for Jess's personal and professional development, in one instance an existential threat for Pinky, and—indirectly—also a problem for Jules, because she needs somebody like Jess to help her score the goals and advance her career. Although the Bhamra family respects patriarchal hierarchy, Mrs. Bhamra is in charge of safeguarding moral traditions in the household on a day-to-day basis. Consequently, most conflicts tend to involve her in the very first instance, which makes Jess's mother a personification of an often grotesquely funny stereotypization of traditional Indian identity characterized by the superstitious belief in Guru Nanak as well as obsessions with cooking abilities and monocultural marriage. The latter is marked by deep racism, and Jess provides a good summary of that dilemma when she explains the family norms for dating men: 'White? No. Black? Definitely not. Muslim? Eh-eh (the sound is accompanied by a gesture of a finger slicing her throat).' Overall, but particularly in this context, Mrs. Bhamra gets support from Jess's aunts whose conversation at the engagement ceremony is dominated by racist comments that prolong the colonial construct of the Other's virility and enhance the boundaries of the 'closed' culture (Benessaieh 2010: 13): 'it's only our men that have a big engine and full MOT, eh?' Even Pinky rejects inter-ethnic marriage by arguing that Indian men have everything an Indian woman can possibly look for and by tying the knot with an Indian man herself. Next to food and choice of partners, clothes are key expressions of the identity concept portrayed, and whereas dynamic Jess changes effortlessly from a 'salwar kamiz' into a football outfit, her mother and her aunts appear during the whole film in their traditional dress as essential, never-changing homogenous and culturally separatist characters. The dream sequence right at the beginning of the film clearly introduces her mother as hopelessly 'backwards' (complaining about her daughter's outfit when everybody else celebrates her as a new football star). One of the last scenes confirms the conservative link to Pinky and the aunts when they together form the imaginative wall around which Jess tries to bend the ball in order to achieve a goal in the decisive match. The *Nessun Dorma* theme from Puccini's opera Turandot, which accompanies her free kick, summarizes these familiar challenges in a humorous way by comparing them to the numerous obstacles Calif had to overcome in order to fulfil his dream (princess Turandot).

Figure 3.2.4.1 The traditional wall.

In contrast, Mr. Bhamra appears far less funny and—due to his own background—more understanding with regard to Jess's 'sport as a life-style' attitude, but he tends to remain similarly out of touch with Jess's hopes and desires. As a more or less traditional Sikh with beard and 'kesh' (uncut hair hidden by his turban), he cannot take Jess's admiration of Beckham, 'the bold man' on the posters in her room, too seriously. Preparing Jess as a future wife and mother is not really a hot topic for him, as he wants her to become a 'top class solicitor' first, an objective in which he mistakenly equates his own desires for socio-economic advancement with his daughter's aims. Problems arise when Jess appears to bring shame to the family: She supposedly kisses a blond guy at a bus stop (this turns out to be a hug for Jules); she repeatedly makes her family think that she has given up on football; and she buys football shoes with the money her mother gave her to buy new shoes for Pinky's wedding. However, Mr. Bhamra is open enough to learn for himself: He watches Jess play football for the Hounslow Harriers and changes his attitude when he realizes that his daughter is extremely unhappy. The latter is particularly obvious at the end of the film, as he then even allows her to leave Pinky's wedding so that she may take part in the football match that matters so much to her. Faced with his wife's disapproval, he makes his personal preference very clear: 'making two daughters happy on the same day. What more can a father ask for?' Mr. Bhamra is not a unique example in contemporary migrant cinema: there are clear parallels to Yasemin's father in the first part of Bohm's popular movie 14 years earlier (1988). However, the patriarch in *Yasemin* ultimately returns to oppressive patterns, whereas most other 'father figures' maintain their position as guardians of outdated traditions all the way through, be it George Khan in *East is East* or—more violently—Samia's eldest brother acting as a father replacement in Faucon's *Samia* (2000).

Unfortunately, the development of Mr. Bhamra's culture concept, from monocultural island allegories of superior Sikh customs (vis-à-vis an immoral and disloyal English society) to an attitude that embraces notions of individual happiness, comes with a gross ignorance of the factors impacting on Jess's supposedly free and independent decision for football. The star cult in football is never explored in its grotesque capitalist or cultural-imperialist dimensions, and there is no reflection on the conservation of the cultural binaries the film sets out to destabilize. From Mrs. Bhamra's 'either/or' mentality in favor of an imagined authentic Indian culture, the movie shifts—on the basis of Mr. Bhamra's benevolence—toward Jess's 'either/or' in support of an Anglo-American way of life as model for all to follow. Although Chan is mistaken when arguing that Jess is so trapped by Indian food that she 'does not have the ability to cast off curry and spices' (2005: 15), the importance of Punjabi food for the framing of traditional identities cannot be overlooked. Just like Chadha's childhood memories, the movie leaves no space to imagine a young girl equally enjoying key aspects of two cultures, e.g., by cooking or eating Punjabi dinner with the same pleasure as playing football in a professional team. Not by coincidence, Jess does not like Punjabi food, traditional dresses are a nuisance for her, and Guru Nanak appears as a superstitious relict from pre-modern times, whereas talking to Beckham posters for advice seems to be rational and modern. With her emigration to the assumed center of an Anglo-American way of life, Jess confirms her early rejection of traditional Indian culture in favor of what she regards as 'progress' for all, not only the younger generation of Jules and herself but also their parents. The latter want their children to be happy, and everybody suffers from the cultural retreat as Mr. Bhamra acknowledges when arguing that he made a mistake by 'accepting life, accepting situations'.

Although Sandhu's idea of constant negotiations of identity in the film are based on Jess's wish to achieve this new life 'without damaging her relationship with her parents' (2005: 12), it should be noted that the protagonist's interest in maintaining good family relations can hardly be described as an exclusive feature of Indian culture. On the contrary, the film establishes numerous parallels between the Bhamras and the Paxtons. Jess is quite comparable to Jules in the way she does not take 'no for an answer'. Mrs. Bhamra and Mrs. Paxton both regard marriage as the ultimate aim in the life of a young girl, and women football as a childish game that distracts them from achieving that aim. Consequently, the first portrayal of Jules and her mother reveals a conflict while shopping: Jules is interested in a sports bra, whereas her mother wants her to buy a model that makes her breasts look bigger. On the other hand, Mr. Bhamra and Mr. Paxton share a strong interest in sports and in the personal well-being of their daughters, whereas their major difference could be linked to Mr. Bhamra's past experience of discrimination. Taking all of this into account, Jess's humorous hide-and-seek of her football activities can hardly be regarded as the negotiation of a new identity in-between Asian family traditions and competitive Britishness. Rather, it appears as a less than convincing attempt to temporarily hide cultural assimilation attempts in the presence of non-integrated authoritative parents. That is yet another feature that crosses cultural boundaries.

3.2.5 Concluding Remarks

Considering that the retreat of Jess's family, and in particular her mother and aunts, into monocultural constructs seems incompatible with the collective well-being, the film ultimately recommends throwing off the shackles of what has been portrayed as Indian cultural heritage in the wider sense and traditional Sikhism in particular in order to fully embrace Anglo-American lead culture. When Mr. Bhamra motivates Jess at the very end 'to fight' and 'to win' he does not make any reference to her Indian background but focuses on the competitive football career his daughter seems to have chosen completely of her own free will. Although benevolent Mr. Bhamra reveals here a different attitude than the stubborn and violent George Khan from *East is East* and Yasemin's father Yusuf in the second half of Bohm's film, the key message of incompatibility and culture clash is very much the same. As Chadha supports her messages with the metaphorical use of food as markers of cultural difference, it is no coincidence that eight-year-old Jess burns her upper leg while trying to make herself some beans on toast. From Mrs. Bhamra's perspective a good Sikh woman from the Punjabi region cooks and eats Punjabi food (not beans on toast) and marries another Sikh (not an Irish guy). The problem with Chadha's film is that it fights this dichotomy with another binary construct by ignoring any valid hybrid construct in-between. You are either trapped in traditional Indian customs and cannot even prepare beans on toast without seriously injuring yourself, or you are geared up for an Anglo-American way of life marked by the capitalist cult of football heroes and do not want to cook Punjabi food, dress up traditionally or pray to Guru Nanak, because it simply does not fit. There is no hybrid dish in the whole film, and international food seems to be acceptable in a genuinely English family only, not in a British-Asian household. Whereas some of George Khan's children combine mosque visits with the carrying of a Christian cross during Easter processions and hamburger eating at home, for Jess it is an 'either/or', and the cultural spaces are clearly highlighted. The claustrophobic collective space at home is traditional Indian, whereas open public spaces (like the football pitch) tend to be free from those traditions. However, the supposedly free spaces seem to be advancing into traditional places, and Jess's room is a good example. In this dynamic conquest, some temporary individual mixtures are imaginable, but they tend to appear very limited, fragile, and ridiculously funny in their slow adaptation of Western norms and customs (see the two Indian women jogging in traditional dresses in the park). This stresses again the incompatibility of South Asian and Anglo-American cultures.

Unlike George Khan or Yusuf, Mr. and Mrs. Bhamra are ultimately depicted as nice examples of first-generation British-Asian migrants, but they seem so likeable precisely because they manage to throw off the shackles of Indian traditions when it gets too critical. Instead of preserving their cultural heritage (or what they perceive as such) at all costs, e.g., with the use of violence as Mr. Khan and Yusuf, they either openly admit their 'mistakes' (Mr. Bhamra) or simply surrender to the collective will (Mrs. Bhamra).

The backwardness of traditional migrant culture means that the 'saviors' in films like *Yasemin* and *Bend It Like Beckham* tend to come from the host culture or its hemisphere. In *Yasemin*, this is mirrored in the narrative structure of a traditional knight's tale, in which contemporary German knight Jan has to rescue his beloved Turkish-German girl on his modern horse (his motor bike) from the inhuman Turkish kidnappers that want to deport her to Turkey. Jess, on the other hand, can rely on English Jules and on Irish Joe, who repeatedly confronts Mr. Bhamra and facilitates Jess's and Jules's trip to the US with which the film ends. In both contexts, Western saviors show enormous tolerance and good will in their encounters with the other culture. Jan tries to learn Turkish with the help of a dictionary, and Joe demonstrates full understanding for Jess's family, even after Mr. Bhamra's repeated rejection of their football activities and the refusal to discuss his opinion. Instead of openly criticizing the Other's self-enclosure, Joe outlines to Jess: 'you are lucky to have a family that cares so much about you'. In other words, the monocultural 'island concept' of first-generation British-Indian characters is met by seemingly never-ending cultural openness from British characters, which renders obsolete the traditional multicultural option of separatist coexistence proposed by Jess's parents as well as George Khan.

It is here that films like Loach's *Ae Fond Kiss* fill a gap in European migrant cinema. In contrast to most other productions, the film highlights the monocultural vision of conservative Irish Catholicism via the 'mise-en-scène' of an Irish priest (Father David) who cannot accept Roisin's affair with Casim, a Pakistani Muslim. Marriage would be acceptable but only if the Muslim converts to Catholicism, and the particular problem for the young couple is that Roisin's job as a teacher in a Catholic school depends on Father David's good will to sign a document of good conduct. Roisin rejects Father David's suggestion to either leave her Muslim boyfriend or force him to embrace Catholicism, and she consequently loses her job. Unfortunately, there are not many films that dare to present monocultural European vision as an obstacle for inter-ethnic relations. With its internalized Orientalism, *Bend It Like Beckham* prolongs a more traditional Othering, for which Tevfik Baser's films could be referenced, but also—in a more humorous way—*My Big Fat Greek Wedding* (Zwick 2002).

3.3 From Principles of Coexistence and Limited Interaction before German Unification to Transcultural Exchange in Fatih Akın's *The Edge of Heaven*

3.3.1 Preliminary Remarks

This chapter explores key aspects of identity construction in Turkish-German migrant cinema before and after German Unification with a particular focus on Fatih Akın's work and *The Edge of Heaven* (2007) as case studies. Akın is probably the most popular and certainly one of the most acclaimed Turkish-German directors, screenwriters, and producers: Only a few years after his experimental shorts, *Sensin... You're the One!* (1995) and *Weed* (1996), he was awarded the Bronze Leopard at the Locarno Film Festival for his first feature film *Short Sharp Shock* (1998). This was followed by the Golden Bear for *Head-On* (2004), more than 20 awards for *The Edge of Heaven*, the special award of the jury at the Venice International Film Festival for *Soul Kitchen* (2009), and the Federal Cross of Germany (Bundesverdienstkreuz 2010), as well as the Peter-Weiss-Award (2012) for his work as a whole. The Federal Cross was awarded because Akın shows very explicitly 'the life and the problems of Germans with Turkish background' (Der Bundespräsident 2010), but how exactly he portrays Turkish-German identity construction will have to be further explored in this chapter.

The *Edge of Heaven* has been selected for in-depth analysis because of its sustained conceptual commitment to transcultural dialogue and exchange. Together with *Head-On* and *The Cut* (2014), the film forms part of Akın's 'love, death and devil' trilogy, which has been praised as 'his most ambitious and most widely celebrated feature-length work' (Isenberg 2011: 56), although *The Cut* was more convincing in its humanitarian message than in plot or montage and is in this respect comparable to Nava's *Bordertown*. How much *The Edge of Heaven* should be categorized as a 'far more ambitious [...] film' than *Head-On* (Ide 2008: 9) depends on one's perspective. However, Gramling is right in arguing that the former 'broadens the trilingual resolution' of the latter (2010: 366). I would suggest that it considers a far wider range of Turkish-Germanness than all other Akın films, which tend to marginalize mainstream diaspora in their focus on exotic Others and will be examined more closely in 3.3.2. In this context, one should avoid generalizations of Akın's films as work favoring 'a hybrid character [...] that resists all notions of fixed identity' (Isenberg 2011: 61) and appears 'decidedly multi-ethnic and polyphonic' (Gueneli 2014: 352). However, in all of his films, there is an attempt to explore individual agency within dynamic open spheres of cultural backgrounds, and *The Edge of Heaven* has a particularly strong transcultural agenda, which should be regarded as an alternative to closed sphere concepts shaping most Turkish-German films before Unification.

Drawing on interpretations of Fassbinder's and Sanders-Brahm's films, I argue that substantial inspiration for contemporary German migrant cinema, including Fatih Akın's productions, comes from so-called New German

Cinema, which most scholars date from 1962 ('Oberhausener Manifest') to either 1982 (*Fassbinder's Death*) or 1987 (*Wim Wenders's Wings of Desire*). This cinema includes films on the life of guest workers in Germany, such as *Katzelmacher* (1969), *Fear Eats the Soul* (1974)[34] and *Shirin's Wedding* (1975). Some connections between contemporary migrant cinema and New German Cinema have already been noted,[35] but there remains room for improvement when it comes to the analysis of such links. Göktürk's interpretation of both streams as part of a 'cinema of duty', which 'ties' film-makers dependent on German funding 'to sorrowful stories about being lost between two cultures' (2002: 250), appears to be an over-simplification. Although funding tendencies should not be underestimated, her comments neither address the enormous diversity and fundamental social critique of the New German Cinema (mainly funded from the same sources as 1980s and 1990s migrant cinema), nor the economic alternatives open to migrant directors,[36] regardless of their socio-cultural background and experiences, which can be traced back to the films.

There are, however, astonishing similarities in the construction of outsider protagonists, to which guest workers and other migrants in pre-unified Germany tend to belong. In line with most New German films, Tevfik Baser's *40 Square Meters of Germany* (1985) and *Farewell to a False Paradise* (1988) feature outsider-protagonists in profound isolation, lack of communication, personal impotence, failure, and existential fear, who are trapped in an often existential inner fight between rebellion and subordination. All of these characteristics have been explored as key aspects of New German Cinema protagonists first by Elsaesser (1989 and 1994: 283ff.), and I suggest applying them to contemporary migrant cinema as well. Worth considering is also the special combination of Brecht-inspired alienation techniques and Hollywood melodrama techniques, which shape outsider protagonists in films like *Fear Eats the Soul* and *The Marriage of Maria Braun* (1979). This combination helps Fassbinder gain international recognition, it increases his popularity well beyond the boundaries of art cinema circles, and it ultimately guides viewers' perceptions of Baser's female outsiders Turna and Elif, although they clearly do not gain the socio-cultural depth that Ali, Emma, and Maria Braun offer. Whereas Fassbinder's protagonists critically interrogate the capitalist foundations of Western industrialized societies, Baser's outsiders lead viewers predominantly to an enclosed, separatist, and essentialist notion of Turkish culture artificially established and maintained in Germany by so-called guest workers.

Particularly in *40 Square Meters of Germany*, first-generation Turkish migrants and Germans coexist more than interact, and the cultural separation seems to be a consequence of extreme patriarchal and inhuman behavior from the Turkish side. This perspective is represented by Dursun, a guest worker who cultivates the image of a 'pure' Turkish culture in need of protection against corrupting German influences. This (re-)construction of a cultural hierarchy, within which an imagined archaic Turkey occupies the moral high ground and contemporary Germany becomes a symbol of modern sin, leads Dursun to lock his new wife Turna into the small flat (40 square meters) where she has to stay until her husband's death nearly a year later. *Farewell to a False Paradise* (1988) reveals at first a similarly separatist view of the two cultures, within which Turkey remains the male-oriented inhuman culture that brutally suppresses its women. However, unlike Turna, Elif kills her husband when he tries to rape her, and her sentence (manslaughter) takes her to a German prison, which gives her space for personal development by protecting her from (Turkish) death threats, and by enhancing cultural exchange between Elif and female German inmates. In particular, Elif's new German surroundings seem to offer alternatives to Turna's female enclosure and mistreatment in Turkish diasporic family structures, although it remains 'a false paradise' due to its temporary nature. It is worth asking how far the astonishing intercultural solidarity of women in jail and the evil portrayal of Turkish diaspora can be accepted as believable constructs (see *FILMDIENST* 1989: 271), but it should be stressed that in the same year as *Farewell to a False Paradise* a very similar notion of traditional interculturality is developed further in Bohm's *Yasemin*.

Bohm was already well known for his participation in the New German Cinema, in particular as an actor in films by Fassbinder and Alexander Kluge, as director of *North Sea Is Dead Sea* (1976), and co-founder of the 'Filmverlag der Autoren', a key production company for many New German films. However, wide-spread national and international recognition only followed *Yasemin*, which won the German Film Prize in Gold and was extensively used in German as a foreign language class. At the center of the film is the young Turkish-German Yasemin, who presents a very playful and uncomplicated way of dealing with non-corresponding socio-cultural norms. Her carnevalesque role play, which is well reflected in clothing (for school she shortens her skirt and gets rid of the long pullover) and dancing (from individualist Western disco style to more collective traditional Turkish dance), mirrors a hyphenated identity that develops particularly well in border areas. Examples are school and especially the judo club, which provides her with a similar Third Space (Bhabha 1994) for identity construction and cultural exchange as football many years later in Chadha's *Bend It Like Beckham* (2002) and Panahi's *Offside* (2006).[37]

Unfortunately, in the second half of the film, Bohm's movie mirrors the cultural hierarchy adopted by most Western films about migration including *Bend It Like Beckham* and O'Donnell's *East is East* (1999),[38] when it reconstructs the alarmed Turkish community as the only obstacle to Jan's and Yasemin's relationship. This includes the sudden transformation of the friendly Turkish father figure into a criminal, whose desire to kidnap and deport his daughter to Turkey opens parallels to Dursun's portrayal in *40 Square Meters of Germany*. In Bohm's film, the solution is an adventurous rescue operation by Western-liberal hero Jan who manages to free his girlfriend from the Oriental criminals. Yasemin is therefore allowed to keep a position between Turna's subordination and Elif's violent rebellion, but the extreme hostility of the Turkish environment is likely to force her into assimilation with the friendly German surrounding, which would mean that her attempt at Third Space construction has failed.

Göktürk summarizes this rescue operation with the statement 'Turkish women—especially the young and beautiful—can only be liberated by saving them from their repressive men' (2002: 251), which is reminiscent of Spivak's famous phrase about 'white men [having to save] brown women from the terror of brown men' in a colonial context (1999: 206f.). From this postcolonial perspective, I argue that the romantic love story between Jan and Yasemin follows neo-colonial hierarchies that re-construct the superiority of Western liberalism over Oriental barbarism and justifies Western intervention in favor of the victims of that barbarism. However, precisely because of these connotations, *Yasemin* links up far less to traditional 'Romeo and Juliet' narratives[39] than to modern editions of medieval knight stories featuring the romantic love of an Occidental hero for an Oriental princess under threat. The numerous elements that support such an interpretation include Jan's presentation outside of Yasemin's window resembling 'Minnesang' traditions, and Yasemin's rescue on the back of Jan's motorbike, which mirrors the traditional image of an aristocratic lady being rescued on the back of a horse.

As examples of German migrant cinema before Unification, *40 Square Meters of Germany*, *Farewell to a False Paradise,* and *Yasemin* highlight that there is no evidence for a radical shift from monoculturality to transculturality as Göktürk implies when arguing that the sheer 'mobility of migrants [...] opens up [...] a "third space" of transnational translation' (2002: 248). Instead, traditional identity concepts based on ethnic membership and binary oppositions between Turkish migrants and German 'hosts' seem to have survived mass migration. The films stress that Herder-inspired concepts of culture are not limited to host culture perspectives, because they include migrants' perceptions of the Self and the Other. However, most directors tend to concentrate either on host culture discrimination or on minority culture discrimination, and the shift from one viewpoint to the next does not seem to occur before the middle of the 1970s. I argue that until then, representatives of a German 'folk culture' tend to be portrayed as main obstacles for a peaceful life together (see *Katzelmacher* and *Fear Eats the Soul*), whereas later on—for example in Baser's work—the directors' interest shifts to xenophobia, racism, and self-enclosure by Turkish migrants. This paradigmatic change appears to be a response to socio-political developments. After sharply increasing the numbers of guest-workers,[40] German xenophobia reaches culminating points in the context of two recessions (1966/67 and 1973), which correlate with hostile articles in the print-media of the time[41] and with an exploration of German hostility in Fassbinder's *Katzelmacher* (1969) and *Fear Eats the Soul* (1974). However, as soon as the 'Anwerbestopp' is achieved (1973), the oil crisis has come to an end (1974), and there is evidence that most guest workers will stay in Germany, politicians and film makers concentrate on potential problems of integration arising from the migrants' cultural background.

3.3.2 Potential and Limits of Cultural Exchange in Akın's Films

After only a short period of celebrations, German Unification was quickly overshadowed by debates about increasing immigration, rising nationalism, and growing xenophobia, which culminated in anti-racist attacks[42] and marked the historical context of cinematic productions especially within the recession years from 1991 to early 1994. Whereas children's literature substantially drew on these developments,[43] cinema has preferred to marginalize them. How far this can be linked to censorship by the 'Freiwillige Selbstkontrolle' and German funding bodies or even to direct political pressure remains unclear, but some directors and critics have highlighted political concerns as a main reason.[44] Also, the acceptance of national taboos were not new,[45] and it would correlate with the fact that, due to relatively high production costs and the dependence on comparably few distribution channels, politically undesirable films were easier to suppress than literature. In this context, it is perhaps not surprising that the most popular production featuring Turkish diaspora in the period of growing neo-Nazi activity after Unification was Doris Dörrie's light-hearted comedy *Happy Birthday, Turk/Happy Birthday, Türke* (1992). This was followed by Sinan Çetin's drama *Berlin in Berlin* (1993), which managed to explore the failure of peaceful multicultural co-existence in a period of right-wing extremism without major reference to that extremism.

However, in the second half of the 1990s, German migrant cinema achieved significant attention again, largely due to a second generation of migrants successfully completing film studies degrees and leaving college with a major interest in exploring their environment. These included Thomas Arslan and Fatih Akın, who started their cinematic careers with *Geschwister – Kardesler* (1997) and *Short Sharp Shock* (1998). In the next decades, Akın managed to become the most popular Turkish-German director, and received numerous awards for his collage-style productions that stand out with a rather emotional use of film quotations as well as frequent changes of perspectives, moods, and locations (see Löser 2007: 5). A good example is his first long feature film *Short Sharp Shock*, which combines 'the gangster film aesthetic à la Martin Scorsese's *Mean Streets*' (Göktürk 2002: 254) with an exploration of ghettoized marginality already successfully elaborated in Mathieu Kassovitz's *La Haine* (1995) and then continued in Ariel Zeïtoun's *Yamakasi* (2001) and Aladag's *Rage* (2006). Akın's film offers a psychographic profile of the transcultural friendship between Gabriel, a second-generation Turk who is looking for a different life after his time in jail, Costa, a second-generation Greek who lives from car robbery and other petty crime, and Bobby, a little criminal obsessed with becoming a well-known gangster.

The extreme poles are marked by Gabriel's wish for social integration through a regular job and Bobby's drive for leadership in an underworld inspired by gangster movies. In these very different quests for happiness,

Turkish, Greek, Serbian, and/or German cultural backgrounds are far less important than differences in personal life experiences (e.g., Gabriel's time in jail, Costa's success in petty crime) and the impact of cinema and TV on individuals. The latter is of particular importance when it becomes clear that Bobby's interest in Mafia films with Al Pacino goes far beyond the interest of his friends in action films. By joining the local Albanian Mafia, Bobby not only desperately attempts to follow the example of Pacino's character (Tony Montana) from *Scarface* but destroys his own life and the life of his friends. Akın's interest in the life philosophies of young outsider-protagonists, who manage to blur the boundaries of their cultural heritage when they are amongst themselves links *Short Sharp Shock* to *La Haine* and *Yamakasi*. However, Akın's film goes further in his exploration of individual agency, rather than individual reactions or collective culture-based agency, and he also indicates quite self-evident personal alternatives to the traditional binary of pluricultural ghetto versus white center that governs the French productions. Instead of permanent confrontations with national police or politicians from the power center, *Short Sharp Shock* offers potential bridges via Turkish-German relationships that start embedding the three protagonists into their German surrounding.

However, there is unfortunately no elaboration on the roles of the German Others in the development of the protagonists' characters. Although Gabriel's sister Ceyda dumps Costa in order to start a serious relationship with German Sven, and Gabriel starts an affair with Bobby's German girlfriend, Alice, these German characters remain excluded from the serious decision-making processes. One example is provided by Ceyda and Gabriel because they change to Turkish language in Alice's presence when the existential question of vendetta for Bobby's murder comes up. Another example is Ceyda's incapacity to protect her boyfriend from her brother's assault. Just like in *La Haine*, *Yamakasi*, and Arslan's *Dealer*, Akın's underdogs remain in their enclosed community, and in this respect similar to Fassbinder's outsider protagonists in isolation and incommunication from mainstream society. Whereas one could argue that this is a consequence of their strong loyalty toward ghetto-friends, which means they can always count on ghetto-solidarity and are never as isolated as Jorgos in *Katzelmacher* or Ali in *Fear Eats the Soul*, it is clear that this loyalty is misguided because it ruins Bobby's, Costa's and Gabriel's lives. This implies that their option for active rebellion and suppression of fear, which is very different froms Jorgos's and Ali's tendency to passive subordination, ends in a comparable display of personal impotence and failure. Although there is always a rather vague hope for Ali's stomach ulcer to be cured and for Gabriel's dream of a new life in Turkey to come true, the vicious cycles of (self-) exclusion remain in place.

I argue that such portrayals can be linked back to the ghetto culture concept proudly presented in Feridun Zaimoğlu's *Kanak Sprak* (1999[1995]), which has inspired many directors, including Lars Becker whose *Kanak*

Attack (2000) is based on Zaimoğlu's script. The 24 testimonial narratives selected and introduced in *Kanak Sprak* draw on a concept that defines second- and third-generation German Turks as part of a new oppositional 'wog' ('Kanak') culture, rather than as people 'in-between' with the potential to bridge traditional differences. When describing his interviewees as part of a 'league of the doomed' ('Liga der Verdammten') that has to resist 'claims on cultural hegemony' ('kulturhegemoniale Ansprüche'), Zaimoğlu refers to individual self-portrayals such as Akay's:

> We are all nigger here; we have our ghetto, we carry it everywhere, [...] our sweat is nigger, our life is nigger, the golden necklaces are nigger, our noses and our faces and our own style is so bloody nigger, that we scratch our skin like nuts, and by doing that we get it: in order to be a nigger you do not need the stale dark skin but you need to be different, to live differently'. (Zaimoğlu 1999: 17, 25)[46]

However, the parallels that Zaimoğlu establishes between his interviewees and the North American black-consciousness movement are as misleading as his attempts to construct 'wog'-mentality as a foundation for the creation of new emancipatory identities. Whereas black-consciousness has been a movement across the traditional boundaries of age, gender, and class, Zaimoğlu's interviewees are predominantly young males (13–33 years old), most of whom live from 'petty crime', casual work, and/or unemployment money. The fact that Zaimoğlu explicitly excludes the absolute majority of Turks in regular employment as well as Turkish-German intellectuals might make some sense with regard to his interest in allowing 'wogs' to speak, an aim that films like *Dealer*, *Short Sharp Shock* and *Kanak Attack* share. It allows neither for such voices to be placed at the same level as the black-consciousness movement nor for them to be misjudged as representative of Turkish-German diaspora.[47]

Assuming Spivak (1999) is right in her assessment that subalterns cannot speak but are frequently misrepresented as autonomous speakers, e.g., by privileged writers like Zaimoğlu, one should question how far his 'free adaptation'[48] of individual voices from the Turkish–German precariat can realistically represent that collective. Perhaps it can only represent a grossly distorted and romanticized version of it. Even more problematic is the fact that Zaimoğlu and his interviewees are not developing a new culture concept but are going back to monocultural perspectives, within which a very diverse community is reduced to a culture of 'wogs'. This essentialist and homogenous vision, which remains completely subordinated to male perspectives when labelling women as 'pussy', 'blowjob giver', and/or 'filly' ('Loch', 'Blaskapelle', 'Stute': 125, 126, 23), is certainly as wrong and dangerous in its paradigm of exclusion as the nationalist racism in mainstream society that Zaimoğlu and his interviewees criticize. In *Koppstoff* the author amends a female dimension in order to correct the correlation of traditional gender and culture construct in *Kanak Sprak* but he fails to deconstruct the artificial ethnic and class boundaries erected in his earlier work.

As criminal migrant milieus in Buck's *Tough Enough* (2006), Tasma's *Fracture* (2010), Naber's *The Albanian* (2010), and Monzón's *El Niño* (2014) illustrate, the ghetto-concept that informs *Short Sharp Shock, Kanak Sprak, Kanak Attack, Ghettokids,* and *Rage* continues to inspire European directors. The inspiration may be due to the assumption that melodramatic stories of exoticized criminal underdogs are easier to sell to a mainstream audience than stories of integrated, educated, and hard-working people who are more representative for mass migration to Europe. Although it is desirable for contemporary European cinema to include less educated, unemployed, and/or otherwise particularly challenging people with migrant background as active subjects trying to negotiate their positions, the portrayal of diasporas as criminal 'wog-cultures' remains grossly misleading and in its exclusion of Others as hegemonic as the heavily criticized majority culture. At least in this respect, *Short Sharp Shock* remains a positive exception to the new ghetto-mainstream-fiction, because it does not marginalize conflictive notions within the culture portrayed. This way it allows for the ghetto to be considered as another 'imagined community' (Anderson 1991) and might ultimately lead critical viewers to develop a more differentiated perspective outside the binary of occidental center and oriental ghetto periphery.

Akın's later films vary between an even stricter separation of cultures and a more open approach. This study regards *In July* (1999) and *Solino* (2002) as examples of a more separatist approach despite the transcultural dimensions opened up in the first part of each film. *In July* begins with a hint at a potential relationship between dreamy teaching assistant Daniel from Hamburg, who is admired by Juli, and a Turkish girl named Melek ('angel'), who has a Turkish boyfriend. Not knowing about him, Daniel follows Melek to Istanbul by car, and this is the main topic of a film that combines road movie, fairy tale, and comedy. Akın re-constructs clichés for the purpose of deconstruction,[49] but overall he fails to explore non-German identities in any greater depth. Melek remains framed in Daniel's gaze as an exotic-erotic object of desire, and there is no serious attempt to elaborate her or other exotic females (e.g., Luna) as self-determined (rather than instinct- or male-driven) individuals. The film ends on a monocultural note that is in line with traditional nationalist superiority constructs: The Turkish couple Melek–İsa remains together and the two Germans, Juli and Daniel, find true love together. Jones summarizes:

> Daniel's quest remains thoroughly restorative. He does not become a European cosmopolitan, and there is no suggestion of any relationship across cultures with any of their potential tensions. [...] Where *Short Sharp Shock* leaves problems of identity conflict, *In July* circumvents them completely. (2003: 89)

Similarly restorative is Akın's *Solino* (2002), which tells the story of an Italian guest worker family opening up the first 'Pizzeria' in Duisburg. A rather grey, cold, and anonymous Duisburg is here contrasted with the family's small picturesque native town called Solino that reminds the viewer of 'Bella Italia' images from German films of the 1960s and 1970s, hence the pizzeria's name. As in most migrant films, the first generation appears to concentrate on its culture of origin, with Rosa—the mother—refusing intercultural contact and finally returning to her village as a fatally ill and worn out woman. Her husband Romano has affairs with German women, but there is no evidence of serious relationships, and his driving force remains his greed. Consequently, it is up to the two children, Gigi and Giancarlo, to open up to their German environment. Their mutual interest in the German neighbor Jo and Gigi's exchange with the owner of a photo shop are examples of this. Ultimately, the two brothers mirror their parents by either going back to their cultural roots or ending up isolated. Gigi returns to Solino to help his mother and to start a new life with Ada, an Italian girl from the village, whereas his egocentric brother Giancarlo, who is to blame for Gigi losing both Jo and his career as film maker, becomes a frustrated and lonely outsider, just like his father Romano. In contrast to *Kanak Attack, Short Sharp Shock,* and *Rage*, films like *In July, Solino,* and *Kiss Me Kismet* (Holtz 2006) might destabilize socio-economic boundaries, either by refusing to elaborate on backgrounds (see Melek and İsa) or by concentrating on characters with average capital. However, they highlight a strong sense of cultural belonging that leads to ethnically pure relationships (*In July, Solino*) or to an extremely rigid form of mental 'ghettoization', which proves to be a major obstacle for mixed relationships (*Kiss Me Kismet*).

On the other hand, Akın's *Head-On* (2003) and *The Edge of Heaven* (2007) offer a considerably more transcultural 'mise en scène' of protagonists, which includes plot and character development 'outside of the opposition of own and other cultures', as Welsch would expect it (1997: 69). In *Head-On*, it is not a coincidence that Turkish-German protagonists Sibel and Cahit are introduced by suicide attempts rather than by violence against members of a different culture. Sibel cuts her wrists as a symbol of rebellion against the patriarchy at home, which suppresses her individualism, whereas alcoholic junk-boy Cahit drives his car full speed against a wall—hence the title of the film—in order to escape his own misery caused by the death of his beloved first wife and his decline ever since. As such, the film concentrates on human destinies that are not bound to a particular culture. Although Sibel could be regarded as a victim of her Turkish family, her wish to escape parental tutelage is universal, and there is no German hero like Jan from Bohm's *Yasemin* around to 'rescue' her. Finally, Sibel seems at this stage a far too extreme character for successful integration into a liberal-bourgeois environment, be it of German, Turkish, or any other origin. Instead, both Cahit and Sibel reflect mentalities that are

86   *Migrants in Europe*

incompatible with 'bourgeois deliberation' and 'emotional safeguarding',[50] and precisely because of their mentalities they get together without any interest in a binding relationship.

The transcultural orientation of the film is furthermore stressed by Sibel's rejection of the capitalist alternative offered by her sister, the business woman Selma in Istanbul. Unlike *Shirin's Wedding*, *40 Square Meters of Germany*, and *Solino*, *Head-On* predominantly associates capitalist alternatives not with a German but rather a new Turkish way of life. All this destabilizes the stereotypical binary of a modern progressive Germany facing a traditional stagnant Turkey. It also opens the viewers' mind to the ambiguity of contemporary Turkey between tradition (Sibel's parents) and modernity (Sibel's cousin Selma), which had already been explored very convincingly in Arslan's *A Fine Day* (2001; compare Deniz's mother and sister), and which remains a hot topic in Turkey itself (see Kutlug Ataman's *2 Girls* 2005 and *Kuzu* 2014). Even more so, *The Edge of Heaven* concentrates on transcultural themes and finally blurs the underdog ghetto-boundaries to which Cahit and Sibel had subscribed.

3.3.3 *Transcultural Possibilities in* The Edge of Heaven

Death as a recurrent theme of the second part of Akın's latest trilogy subdivides *The Edge of Heaven* explicitly into three parts ('Yeter's Death', 'Lotte's Death', and 'The Edge of Heaven'), but it also links the stories of the six protagonists by bringing strangers together (Meza 2008: 9). In particular, its unpredictability and ubiquity, which accidentally and suddenly ends the lives of the Turkish and German key characters, forces the remaining protagonists to start a quest for their own identity, which blurs the cultural, generational, educational, and political boundaries that separate them.

This is particularly obvious in the case of Ali Aksu, a first generation Turkish migrant living in Bremen, and Nejat Aksu, his second-generation son who works as a professor of German literature in Hamburg. Although they are portrayed as estranged individuals from the very beginning of the film, and the distance grows substantially after Ali kills Turkish prostitute Yeter accidentally, Nejat ultimately reflects on that relationship and on his own life and follows his father to his Turkish village. The film ends with him waiting for Ali to return from a boat trip. Similarly, Susanne Staub, who at first rejected her daughter's lesbian relationship with Kurdish Ayten, changes her attitude after Lotte's death. In the last part of the film, we see her continuing her daughter's fight for Ayten, while both mourn the loss of a loved one. The two groups are connected by a personal link (Yeter is Ayten's mother) and by spatial proximities that they ignore: For example, when Nejat gives one of his lectures, Ayten sleeps in the back of the lecture hall. In another scene, Nejat and Yeter are in a train together, while Ayten and Lotte pass by car and, ultimately, Nejat has a brief conversation with Ayten in Istanbul without either of them becoming aware of their connection.

Figure 3.3.3.1 Ayten and Lotte in *The Edge of Heaven*.

Gueneli has explored this interconnectedness very convincingly as result of conscious soundscape construction, which is particularly explicit in the heterogeneity of music and dialogue that help to (re-)create a particularly 'diverse and multi-ethnic European space' in the film (2014: 351). One example is the creation of a musical leitmotif by multiplication of Kazim Kuyuncu's *Ben Seni Sevduğumi (That I love you)*, for which Akın's collaborator DJ Shantel breaks the song up into different tracks with a focus on one instrument each and then links it to different key scenes of the film (ibid.: 340, 341). Another example is ethnic and cultural blending within one song, for example in Bullard's *Bach on the Banjo*, which connects classic German Bach with Irish and American folk music, enhances the hybridity of Nejats bookshop, and 'helps break essentialist and elitist conceptions of culture and cultural master narratives' (ibid.: 344). All this is further developed by links to similarly hybrid dialogues and other voices, for which two examples should suffice.

In the first part of the film, Nejat accompanies his father to the races, but the English name of the horse that Ali has put his money on highlights his lack of foreign language knowledge as well as the mental distance between a highly educated son and his working class father:

NEJAT: [Trying to repeat his father's words] *Of loof sunsine?*
ALI: *Dördüncü yarış, beşinci at.* (The fifth horse in the fourth heat.)
NEJAT: [Reading the newspaper] Sunshine of life, *mı*? (Do you mean Sunshine of Life?)
ALI: Ne demek bu? (What does that mean?)
NEJAT: *Sonne des Lebens, Hayatin güneşi.* (Sunshine of Life.)

Gramling uses this scene to elaborate on 'conversational repairs, corrections, creative re-appropriations, and deferrals' (2010: 368), which happen frequently in the film. However, their importance as symbols of omnipresent misunderstanding is particularly obvious when they shape the private conversation between father and son, who are supposed to know each other. This illustration of the 'patent unlikelihood that any two of the film's characters [...] will arrive at the same signifieds' is for Gramlin a confirmation of 'the semiodiverse conception of multilingualism', which locates *The Edge of Heaven* 'on the other side of monolingualism' and facilitates the exploration of 'the frictions and nuances of multiple language use' (ibid.: 368, 353, 371). However, I would argue that it is primarily an excellent example of a transcultural deficiency that Fassbinder's outsider protagonists highlighted through their lack of communication, isolation, and loneliness. In this context, it might not be a coincidence that Akın chose the same name for his portrayal of a first-generation male Turkish migrant in Germany as the New German Cinema director for a comparable guest worker protagonist in *Fear Eats the Soul* roughly 35 years earlier. If *Head-On* can be categorized as 'the tale [...] of Ali's children', as Isenberg suggests (2011: 58), then the naming of Nejat's father and the integration of Fassbinder's muse Hanna Schygulla as Susanne in *The Edge of Heaven* is reminiscent of such inspiration as well. In particular, Fassbinder's and Akın's 'guest workers' remain similarly lonely in Germany: The former appears objectified in the German surrounding, and the latter clashes repeatedly with both Nejat and Yeter; his son lives in a different city, and Yeter's company has to be purchased at a price that is well above his monthly retirement pension (3000 euros/month).[51] Furthermore, both characters share a personal impotence, which is mirrored in sexual as well as social terms[52] and highlights that change depends very much on the support they get. After severe crisis of their closest personal relationships (Fassbinder's Ali leaves Emmi temporarily, and Nejat ignores his father after Yeter's death), both films end with a strong statement of solidarity.[53] All of this provides some hope for reconciliation and a better future together, but ultimately the films refuse to offer a traditional happy ending, which seems to suggest that transcultural opportunities do not develop 'automatically'. Instead, they very much depend on the willingness of all individuals involved to fight constantly for them and, even then, there is no guarantee of success. However, against the threat of increasing incommunication, isolation, and loneliness, Emmi and Nejat find alternatives that are worth fighting for. At the same time, such intertextuality highlights cinematic developments, in which the ethnic background of directors might not be crucial for formal and thematic choice anymore. It is surprising that Huber ignores not only the symbolic role of soundscapes and the function of multilingualism, but the intertextual link to Fassbinder when he summarizes *The Edge of Heaven* in opposition to Seidl's *Import Export* as 'German-Turkish mix-and-match of buzzwords [...] heavy handedly constructed connections [...] and sensationally stupid symbolism' (2007).

A more positive example of transculturality is the connection of German and Arabic in the second part of *The Edge of Heaven*. When Susanne and Nejat talk about men going to the mosque in German language, we hear simultaneously an Arabic prayer, and this acoustic link is further elaborated when Nejat explains to Susanne the meaning of Bayram, the Turkish Feast of the Sacrifice. In this case, the Quran's story of Ibrahim's consent to sacrifice his own son Ishmael reminds Susanne of Abraham's willingness to kill his son Isaac as told in the Book of Genesis. This helps her to consider parallels in religious mythifications from Judaism and Christianity to Islam. Gueneli is right in assuming that this 'new sound of Europe', which links West and East of the continent, creates a polyphony that promotes European diversity (ibid.: 353, 352). Similarly, Gramling is convincing in his interpretation of 'the fragmented, often aphasic call-and-response between generations, languages, texts, and media' as a reflection of 'structures, toward which the multilingual characters in the film take up subversive, pragmatic stances' (2014: 369). However, neither the film studies scholar nor the linguist recognizes that Akın goes ultimately far beyond notions of ethnic diversity and multilingualism in his (re-)construction of a transcultural space in-between 'the West and the Rest' (Said 1995: 20), or the North-South divide. Instead of isolating and opposing sounds, which would allow the (re-)creation of monocultural, traditional multicultural or, at best, traditional intercultural contexts (see 1.1), Akın highlights parallels and solidarity initiatives that lead to new highly dynamic, interconnected, and transitory bonds (see Benessaieh 2010: 11), with Lotte and Ayten followed by Susanne and Ayten as prime examples.

These bonds are based on affect, shared personal feelings, and 'transcultural memory' (Moses/Rothberg 2014) in so far as Lotte's and Ayten's affection opens the way for an alternative (cross-cultural lesbian) romantic love, before Susanne's and Ayten's joint memory of existential loss and mourning following Lotte's death leads to the construction of an alternative (single mother cross-cultural patchwork) family. It also means a new role and sense of life for Susanne, which Stewart summarizes as 'Susanne's rebirth' (2014: 212), and which is mirrored in the 'mise-en-scène': Instead of observing changes in her own German house with silence or laconic comments from a sofa or a chair, the camera shows her in direct exchange with Nejat and Ayten in Istanbul. When Susanne takes over Yeter's and Ayten Lotte's role, the film suggests a break with traditional ethnic, political, and generational boundaries. This could be regarded as a contemporary variation on Fassbinder's break with ethnic and age-related boundaries in *Fear Eats the Soul* exemplified by the marriage of German Emmi and a much-younger Turkish Ali, who are similarly driven by affection. Both films can be categorized as melodramas (see Rings 2000, Stewart 2014), and they stress through these key relationships the importance of affects for individual and interpersonal change. After Lotte's death, her mother travels to Istanbul and mourns in her hotel room but then longs to stay in Lotte's former room in Nejat's house, visits Ayten in prison and—in contrast to her strong rejection of the rebellious Kurdish activist before—expresses the wish to support her: 'Listen, I want to help you. This is what she [Lotte] wanted, and this is what I want now.'

Figure 3.3.3.2 Susanne and Ayten in Nejat's bookshop.

Similarly, Emmi changes her behavior toward Ali after he has left her, because she experiences now the loss of the partner that she desperately wants to have back: 'You don't have to say anything. Just come back. I need you Ali. I need you so much!'

Affect is particularly visible in the loss of control that all protagonists experience at some stage in *The Edge of Heaven* and that can lead to chain reactions. The most dramatic chain of events in the first part of the film leads to Yeter's death: When Ali gets so drunk that he starts humiliating Yeter by ordering her to give him a blow job in the garden, she starts pushing him away with the intent to leave him for good; this provokes Ali to slap her. However, when he recognizes that he has killed her accidentally with this one slap, Ali breaks down, remains on his knees, and bursts into tears. Through a long shot of this emotional performance the camera allows viewers to get access to Ali's affects, which leads to a more differentiated assessment of his action. His reduction of Yeter to a commodity could lead to his rejection as 'patriarchal ("wannabe") capitalist' (Breger 2014: 75), and his killing of Yeter has to lead to a jail sentence. However, the mourning scene also invites us to consider the desperation and limited culpability of the old drunk, who did not mean to kill the woman he desired so much. Similarly, Lotte's death in the second part of the film is a result of a chain reaction: After street children run away with her bag and Ayten's pistol in it, Lotte pursues them and takes them to task, which makes one of the children use the pistol he is holding in his hand and shoot her. In its third part, the film suggests to regard these tragedies as a result of very unfortunate spontaneous reactions, rather than pre-meditated murder. This in itself is not self-understood, as highly educated Nejat confirms when he refuses to visit his father in prison because he regards him as a murderer. In addition, the viewer is encouraged to explore the affirmative side of effects, in particular by Susanne's successful attempt to understand 'the other side of Ayten', which includes her humanism that Lotte appreciated so much. Rather than following a politics of hatred 'of the half-different and partially familiar' (Gilroy 1999), in which case Susanne could have easily blamed the death of her daughter on the Kurdish Other, she opts for reconciliation. All of that reminds us of Gilroy's defense of a 'utopia of tolerance, peace and mutual regard' based on human solidarity (2004: 2), which will be further developed by Marcel and Idrissa in Kaurismäki's *Le Havre*.

This brings us back to the original title of the film, 'Auf der anderen Seite', which means literally 'On the Other Side' and has been very poorly transferred into English and Italian as 'The Edge of Heaven' and 'Ai confini del paradiso', whereas the French 'De l'autre coté' comes closest in so far that it leaves the spatial dimension intact. Notions of another world are misleading because Akın's film is not suggesting we search for 'the other side' in 'heaven' or any other imagined afterlife, and there is no proposal to wait for rewards in that second life by sacrifice in this world. Instead, we are encouraged to explore and understand in the here and now the Other in the Self, especially at a personal level and on the basis of transcultural memory and affect, with the expectation to act on it and develop the necessary solidarity in order to improve our lives together. *The Edge of Heaven* addresses here Gilroy's notion of 'conviviality' (2004) by drawing on shared memories and affect as starting point for a new 'openness' (Massumi, in: Zournazi 2003). This helps to further develop notions of human interconnectedness and prepares the ground for new transcultural solidarity tendencies in European cinema with Kaurismäki's *Le Havre* (2011) and Bochert's *Krüger aus Almanya* (2015) as more recent examples.

3.3.4 Reconstructing Boundaries

The Edge of Heaven marks a departure from the portrayal of second-generation migrants as small-time ghetto criminals in *Short Sharp Shock* and the reconstruction of the exotic Turkish-German Other as an erotic object of desire in *In July*. However, the film also reconstructs national identity constructs and some traditional stereotypes that remain in tension with the transcultural tendencies elaborated so far.

In particular, *The Edge of Heaven* remains framed by traditional Kemalist and contemporary Islamist discourses, within which the suppression of ethnic minorities, political opposition, and human rights activists in Turkey is discredited as part of the flourishing fantasies of radical Kurdish fighters and foreigners. Turkey's human rights record improved in the second half of the 20th century when there were strong interests in joining the EU. However, it remains difficult to overlook the clash between the film's positive framing of the Turkish penal system and the high number of severe human rights violations condemned by the European Court of Human Rights (ECHR), Amnesty International (AI), and Human Rights Watch (HRW). Overall, *The Edge of Heaven* presents Turkish police as merely reacting to the aggressive stance of Kurdish radicals, and it portrays the jail in which Ayten is held not only as a place in which detainees are treated with utmost fairness and respect, but as a space that gives rebels an opportunity for reflection, remorse, and reconciliation. Interestingly enough, the only threat for Ayten comes from other political activists in jail who put her under pressure to hand over the pistol that she picked up from a persecuted policeman before her arrest and even threaten to kill her.

In one scene, the camera frames Ayten and another woman from the resistance group in a window facing the peaceful courtyard, in which inmates are playing volleyball while two female guards remain respectfully in the background. The medium shot shows Ayten facing the camera, which allows viewers to more easily identify with her, while the other woman is filmed from the side staring at Ayten and threatening her: 'Don't muck me about, or I kill you' ('Verarsch mich nicht, oder ich töte dich'). The scene is crucial as it leads directly to Lotte's death, because Ayten instructs her to retrieve the pistol from the hiding place, and the weapon could be interpreted as a symbol of hatred and death. I would, however, disagree with Cha's assessment that the pistol mirrors Ayten's hatred (2010: 142), because the hatred in this scene comes from a more radical activist who interrupts the volleyball game to remind Ayten of 'the group's' expectations. On Ayten's release from prison, the same extremist sees her off by spitting into her face and labelling her as 'traitor' ('Verräterin') for using her 'right to remorse'.

In contrast, from 1999 to 2008, i.e., in the production and dissemination period of Akın's film, the main threat for human rights activists in Turkey emanates clearly from the Turkish police, Turkish military, and a corrupt penal system. Not by coincidence, the ECHR found Turkey in that period guilty of nearly 1700 cases of human rights violations (ECHR 2009), and the situation has deteriorated since with Erdoğan's brutal suppression of the Gezi street protests, ongoing persecution of opposition journalists, radical internet censorship, and unequal treatment of Kurdish minorities (HRW 2014). Ayten draws attention to such violations of basic rights, especially when she summarizes the aims of her resistance group in Susanne's kitchen ('one hundred percent human rights, and freedom of speech and social education'), but her 'mise-en-scéne' as radical, her remorse, and the lack of supportive evidence in the film suggests that there is a lot of activist fantasy involved. This includes a scene in which Ayten's 'comrades' are being arrested and the detained Kurdish activists call out their own names out of fear that the police might want to make them 'disappear', whereas the applause of neighbors and the treatment of prisoners shown in jail does not corroborate such ideas. Similarly, Lotte's complaints about Turkish law are being destabilized by her portrayal as a rather immature, if not naïve rebel[54] who is in love with Ayten. Finally, the few other hints at a problematic Turkish human rights history, which includes the note on Ayten's Alawite father being killed in 1978, are not elaborated. All this is in line with the treatment of Kurdish-Turkish difference as a taboo, which again mirrors Turkish national discourse and leads Naiboğlu to the conclusion that Akın follows 'the nationalist reductivist process' in his assertion of 'sameness' (2010: 91).

Whether Akın decided on such an uncritical portrayal of Turkey in 2007, because this facilitated his economic and symbolic success in his parents' country, remains to be discussed. It is, however, worth stressing that such a marginalization of human rights violations is in itself a strong political statement that allows for a categorization of *The Edge of Heaven* as a political film far beyond the boundaries of 'implicit dialogicity' highlighted by Breger (2014: 73). In this context, it is unfortunate that *The Cut* (2014) has received such overwhelmingly negative reviews, because its exploration of the Armenian genocide shortly before its 100th anniversary on April 24, 2015, should be considered as a courageous artistic intervention against its century-long ignorance by Turkish governments. Despite its melodramatic excess and other shortfalls, the film highlights Akın's growing self-awareness of the need to fight monocultural identity construction and help re-establish the multidirectional memory that governmental forces continue to suppress rigorously in 21st century Turkey,[55] and there is some evidence that Fassbinder's *Fear Eats the Soul* facilitated such socio-critical development.[56]

Fear Eats the Soul might have also given Akın inspiration regarding the reconstruction of stereotypes for the purpose of deconstruction in *The Edge of Heaven*. Beyond the stereotypically Turkish portrayal of Kurdish fighters and their sympathizers as naïve radicals, the film tries to avoid traditional culture, gender, age, and education-related dichotomies. If Ali shows excessive emotion and Nejat too little, then it is in Susanne's and Lotte's case the other way around. These differences seem to draw on individual backgrounds and desires more than on collective characteristics. The lesbian relationship between Ayten and Lotte is another example of personal desire overcoming social imagination and regulation, in this case especially the heterosexual norm that shaped all of Akın's earlier films, but also the cultural horizons indicated by Ayten's Kurdish activism against human rights violations in Turkey and Lotte's skepticism vis-à-vis German mentalities. Finally, the transcultural bond offered by Susanne suggests a dissolution of temporal boundaries with Ayten taking over Lotte's place, as she remains deeply connected.[57] There are weaknesses in these constructs, which include their melodramatic staging, but it is worth stressing that none of Akın's protagonists opts for assimilation in the way that Chadha's Jess in *Bend It Like Beckham* does. Instead, they are able and willing to negotiate a Third Space in-between (Bhabha 1994), be it Lotte and Ayten in Germany or Susanne and Ayten in Turkey. In this context, I follow Silvey's and Hillman's analysis that the blurring of boundaries repositions 'Turks and Turkish Germans as constitutive of German culture and vice versa' (2010: 99), and I disagree with Tezcan's résumé that 'Turks remain Turks and Germans remain Germans' in the film.[58]

Unfortunately, there is evidence for the interpretation of Akın's Germany as 'the dull world of books' and 'restricted life' vis-à-vis portrayals of Turkey as 'the living landscape of the soul, which triggers a maelstrom of images and movements' (Cha 2010: 140). Admittedly, books appear to be key for all characters, including Nejat and Susanne, Lotte in her attempt to free Ayten, and Ali in his desire to come closer to his son by reading the book he recommended (Selim Özdoğan's *The Blacksmith's Daughter/Die Tochter des Schmieds*). There is, however, a mismatch in the portrayal of passive immobile readers versus active life-affirming subjects with the latter being linked to a romanticized version of Turkey.

This binary is highlighted in the clash between Susanne and her daughter at home. When Lotte and Ayten enter, Susanne is reading the newspaper on the sofa, and she remains there staring at the newcomer without trying to get directly involved, although her daughter has just decided that her new friend may stay as long as she wishes and may take from the kitchen whatever she wants. At a later stage, we see Susanne challenging the situation, but in both scenes she remains seated—drinking coffee or pitting cherries for a cake. When Susanne tells her daughter that she does not even know Ayten, Lotte blames her passivity and personal distance very explicitly on the national character ('This is German, mama'/'Das ist deutsch, Mama'), and this has to be assessed in the context of a comparable emotionless performance of Nejat in Germany. For example, when he makes references to Goethe's anti-revolutionary perspective in a scene that is frequently repeated in the film, the fake Goethe quote might help to subvert German Leitkultur, as Gueneli suggests (2014: 344), but it also enhances the reconstruction of national clichés with regard to content (against revolutionary action) and form of presentation (a dull lecture).

On the other hand, a romanticized version of traditional Turkey stands for mobility, change, and reflection. Not by coincidence, the Hamburg nightclub plays Turkish music when Lotte and Ayten have their first kiss, and the remote petrol station, at which Nejat stops on the way to see his father, has been carefully selected to mirror Akın's exotic vision of Turkey,[59] just like the idyllic village in which Nejat's search ends. In this context, I suggest putting Breger's viewpoint of a geographically detached Nejat into perspective (2014: 77). The German-Turkish professor might have come to Istanbul in order to find Ayten, and teaching might not be his calling, as he himself states to his cousin, but it is not a coincidence that he spontaneously decides to purchase the small German bookshop in Istanbul. After all, this nostalgic shop in the center of a nostalgic Turkey provides him with an environment in which he is able to develop his affects, because it combines the cognitive orientation from German literature with an emotionally charged collective cityscape. In this sense, the Turkish-German literature professor is coming home at the end of the film, but his home is a space in-between Turkey and Germany. Although this is very much in line with transcultural identity concepts, it is unfortunate that Akın decided to draw on the stereotypical binary of Northern European indifference vis-à-vis Southern European solidarity in order to make this statement.

3.3.5 Concluding Remarks

In its exploration of images of migration to Germany before and after Unification, this chapter has explored shifts from portrayals of discrimination (*Katzelmacher*, *Fear Eats the Soul*) and first- generation migrant self-enclosure (*40 Square Meters of Germany*, *Farewell to a False Paradise*) to patterns of (self-) exclusion affecting second-generation diaspora (*Short Sharp Shock*, *Kanak Attack*). As the vast majority of first generation migrants had very low economic and cultural capital, it is understandable that directors of the first two (pre-Unification) groups concentrated on that collective. In contrast, it remains unfortunate that the third (post-Unification) group tends to settle for unemployed and small-time criminals with migrant background, because they are clearly not representative of their generation. However, overall Turkish, German, and Turkish–German cinema mirror quite closely the socio-historical tendencies portrayed in the mass media of their time, with paradigmatic changes in the middle of the 1970s (focus on integration after ban on recruitment/'Anwerbestopp' and oil crisis) and the second half of the 1990s (shaped by new nationalism, racism, and recession following German Unification).

Twenty-first century films like *A Fine Day* and *The Edge of Heaven* could be regarded as prime examples of a fourth group, in which transcultural tendencies remain in the foreground and offer a more differentiated portrayal of Turkish-German life in Germany. *The Edge of Heaven* is the more popular film, and it is particularly interesting due to the 'subversive, pragmatic stances' of multilingual protagonists (Gramling 2014: 369), and the polyphony, which Gueneli has explored as the 'new sound of Europe' (2014: 353, 352). I suggest building on these interpretations but take them further, because Akın goes far beyond notions of ethnic diversity and multilingualism in his (re-)construction of a transcultural space in-between traditional West-East and North-South divides. Instead of isolating and opposing sounds, languages, and cultures, *The Edge of Heaven* concentrates on individual parallels and cultural interconnectedness based on shared human affects and multidirectional memories that break with postmodern tendencies to indifference, isolation, and incommunication and lead to transcultural bonds. In particular, the film suggests considering negative as well as affirmative sides of affects, which are exemplified by two accidental deaths in the first parts of the film followed by Susanne's affection for Ayten's humanism that leads to reconciliation and the foundation of a substitute family.

There is a need to reconsider misleading transfers of the German title ('Auf der anderen Seite' meaning literally 'On the Other Side') into other languages. The French 'De l'autre coté' comes closest in so far as it draws on spatial connotations that help to explore cross-culturality and the dissolution of boundaries between Susanne and Ayten. The religious nuances in 'The Edge of Heaven' and 'Ai confini del paradiso' are not convincing because Akın neither suggests searching for 'the other side' in an imagined afterlife, nor proposes waiting for rewards in that second life through sacrifice in this world. Instead, viewers are encouraged to explore and understand in the here and now the Other in the Self, especially at a personal level and on the basis of transcultural memory and affect, with the expectation to act on it. All this addresses Gilroy's notion of 'conviviality' (2004) and prepares the ground for new transcultural solidarity tendencies in European cinema with Kaurismäki's *Le Havre* (2011), Kahane's *Blindgänger* (2015), and Bochert's *Krüger aus Almanya* (2015) as more recent examples.

Unfortunately, *The Edge of Heaven* remains very much in line with Turkish governmental discourse, when it dissolves the suppression of ethnic minorities, political opposition, and human rights activists in Turkey as flourishing fantasies of radical Kurdish fighters and foreign tourists. Although Akın tries hard to avoid nurturing stereotypes, there is evidence that the stereotypical North-South divide, with Northern Europeans exemplifying indifference vis-à-vis Southern Europeans standing for solidarity, has survived all attempts at deconstruction. Finally, we consider the parallel continuity of the 'Kanaken' cult, which enhances a monocultural or at best traditional multicultural perceptions of diasporas. There is no evidence that the transcultural orientation proposed by *A Fine Day* and *The Edge of Heaven* is representative for contemporary European migrant cinema, be it as a consequence of large-scale migration or because of directors with migrant backgrounds gaining ground in cinema and on TV.

In this respect, the impact Göktürk expected from the sheer 'mobility of migrants' on 'Third Space' construction (2002: 248) remains limited. Generalizations of Turkish-Germans as 'cosmopolitan, syncretic, rhizomatic, and transnational' (Kaya 2007: 483, Mennel 2010: 43) are simply unconvincing, and there continues to be a cinematic preference for more exotic and melodramatic monocultural, traditional multicultural, or traditional intercultural clashes, which can be observed from Baser's *40 Square Meters of Germany* and Bohm's *Yasemin* to Akın's earlier work and well beyond. All this correlates with a global mass media environment shaped by melodramatic excess, within which directors tend to assume that the dramatic elaboration of culture, gender, age, and education-related clashes are more consumer appealing than transcultural explorations and consequently more profitable in economic, social, and symbolic terms. However, some producers, scriptwriters, and directors seem to become increasingly aware of their postcolonial responsibilities and question the likely impact of their selections accordingly.

3.4 New Solidarity in Aki Kaurismäki's *Le Havre*

3.4.1 Preliminary Remarks

Written and directed by Finnish auteur Aki Kaurismäki and co-produced by Sputnik and Pandora Filmproduktion, *Le Havre* does not easily fit into traditional categorizations of French cinema. It corresponds, however, to our definition of French migrant cinema due to its focus on contemporary migration to France. Moreover, it can be considered an excellent example of new transcultural French cinema insofar as the abundance of references to France's cultural history, Sarkozy's conservative politics, and the film's European cast, production, and scriptwriting teams join forces to explore a key aspect of Europe's postcolonial heritage in highly original ways.

The blurring of boundaries starts with the cinematic landscape. Although the film is set in very specific locations of Le Havre in Northern France (Gare SNCF, Port, Quartier Saint-François, Impasse Réal, Seine-Maritime), the plot could take place in almost any European seaport. It is based on the story of an unsuccessful writer and now aging shoe shiner Marcel Marx (played by French stage actor André Wilms), who hides illegal African child refugee Idrissa from the national police and then helps him to continue his journey to England so that he can be reunited with his mother. None of this would have been possible without neighborhood support. The friendly baker Yvette; the singer 'Little Bob', who is a first generation migrant; Italian-born Roberto Piazza, played here by himself; and even the at first rather distant grocer help out and, at the end, show their solidarity by organizing a concert that pays for Idrissa's trip to London. However, in particular, it is a film about the encounter, alliance, and shared humanity of two 'losers of our society' (Tageszeitung 2014: 17): an aging white European shoe shiner and a young black African refugee. Rascaroli summarizes this transcultural microcosm as 'an example of a certain tendency of 21st century European art cinema to speak about the entire continent from a specific location' (2013: 328).

At the same time, *Le Havre* travels through different periods of French film history by linking Jean Renoir's appeal to solidarity from *Life Belongs to Us* and *The Crime of Monsieur Lange* (both 1936) with Robert Bresson's 'clipped, sometimes elliptical editing, inexpressive acting, emphatic use of off-screen space and visual synecdoche' (Quandt 2011: 75). All of this is particularly explicit in Bresson's *The Devil, Probably* (1977), which might have inspired the use of documentary footage in *Le Havre* (ibid.: 76). However, Kaurismäki could have also regarded it as an excellent reference point for a critical interrogation of continuities in human ethnocentrism and egocentrism ranging from ecological despoliation in *The Devil, Probably* to the humanitarian crisis and demolition of the French refugee camp 'The Jungle' in *Le Havre*. Furthermore, there is an homage to Jean-Pierre Melville's film noir crime dramas, such as *Doulos: The Finger Man* (1962), *The Samurai* (1967), and *The Red Circle* (1969), right at the beginning of *Le Havre*, when ruthless killers in trench coats shoot their greased-hair Italian victim in front

98 Migrants in Europe

of the protagonist. Following this style, the investigation is then led by an inspector with black trench coat, black hat and black gloves, who manages to stop another shooting, albeit this time by a French policemen who aims at Idrissa, which establishes a parallel montage with mechanical killing mentality as a link between the contemporary underworld and the police. Also, there are references to Melville's classic French Resistance movie *Army of Shadows* (1969) (Taubin 2011: 56), to which we will return in the next chapter. Finally, Kaurismäki mentions inspiration from Vittorio de Sica and Cesare Zavattini as 'background' for the development of his neo-realist style in *Le Havre*, which leads to 'a Marcel Carné or Jacques Becker tone' (Bagh 2011: 40).

Considering this particularly rich intertextual background, the excellent choice of protagonists, and Kaurismäki's internationally recognized experience in the filmic exploration of society's losers,[60] it might come as no surprise that *Le Havre* was listed as one of the top 5 in the Cannes Film Festival 2011 (see Taubin 2011: 57). It also won the International Federation of Film Critics (FIPRESCI) prize for best film, and it received extremely favorable reviews. Taubin finishes her discussion of the Cannes Film Festival with an unrestricted praise of the well-placed *Le Havre* ('Sometimes critics get things right', 2011: 59), Hoberman regards the film as a 'comeback' for Kaurismäki (2011), and Palomo celebrates it as 'an indisputable master piece' ('una obra maestra incontestable' 2015). However, the academic debate concentrates so far on the film's intertextuality (see above), challenges in defining its genre,[61] Kaurismäki's film style (Sáez-González 2012), and funding issues (Paden 2015), whereas transcultural concepts behind the protagonists' solidarity constructs remain unexplored. This chapter aims to reduce that gap in research.

3.4.2 Outsider-Protagonists Between Cultures

In his analysis of Claire Denis's *Beau Travail* (1999), Elsaesser remarks that Europe 'has turned obsessively towards the past, towards commemoration and collective nostalgia' (2012: 708). This turn is particularly obvious in German governmental initiatives to commemorate National Socialist crimes sometimes on a weekly basis, but it is similarly explicit in French initiatives to further enhance knowledge of the Holocaust, which includes Nicolas Sarkozy's ultimately unsuccessful proposal to oblige schoolchildren to get to know a Jewish child killed in the Holocaust.[62] One could argue that these are well-meant initiatives. However, it should be stressed that they represent efforts to reconstruct a particular national memory, which tends to divert attention from contemporary forms of marginalization and discrimination as well as the misery and death of current Others, who might be Palestinian civilians bombed by Israeli forces or refugees dying in attempts to cross the Mediterranean.[63] In such a context, films like Philippe Lioret's *Welcome* (2009), Romain Goupil's *Hands Up* (2010), and Kaurismäki's *Le Havre* 'call for an enlargement of one's own memory, [...] a multidirectional memory [...], which is constructed by an interlacing of different events and temporal strata'. Instead of asking for 'the adoption of the memory of a dead child', these films prefer to elaborate on the need for care of 'a living child' (Fevry 2014: 240, 254), which is enhanced by references to similar needs and a similar lack of support in the past. Such an attempt to (re-) construct and disseminate multidirectional memories does not come with the suggestion to ignore the Holocaust or any other crime against humanity. There is, however, the recommendation to focus on the present and explore contemporary injustice in the socio-political, economic, and cultural context of 20th and 21st century European history, rather than start from and remain in the past.

In this context, aging Marcel's care for the child refugee Idrissa could be interpreted as spontaneous and affect-based adoption of the Other, not only into the private space of Marcel and Arletty's home, but into the neighborhood community. This is in line with the ethics of affect developed in *The Edge of Heaven*, and it highlights affects as 'ways of connecting to others' (Massumi, in: Zournazi 2003), which are not discursively controlled.

Figure 3.4.2.1 Marcel and Idrissa in *Le Havre*.

Marcel and Arletty mirror contemporary France and Europe in many ways: If there were ever glorious times, they are gone now. Marcel and Arletty are old, they have no children, which reminds us of ongoing demographic trends, and—above all—they tend to live in the past. The interior design of their home, the neighborhood, the music played in the bar, and nearly all objects are dated, although there is no focus on a specific epoch. Instead, Kaurismäki mixes and links different periods of time, which reflects his interest in multidirectional memories, rather than governmental 'prescriptions' of one particular memory that leaves little room for others. Rascaroli summarizes the historical dimension in the film as follows:

> Jukeboxes, clocks and record players, cars and buses, LPs and Bakelite telephones, sweet boxes, furniture, pinball machines—the vast majority of the objects in *Le Havre* are dated from the 1930s to the 1970s. (2013: 334)

This time frame is in line with most of the cinematic references outlined above, which stresses the need for solidarity at either end, from Renoir's hope for working-class solidarity in *Life Belongs to Us* and *The Crime of Monsieur Lange* in the 1930s to Bresson's appeal to jointly intervene against ecological despoliation in *The Devil, Probably* in the 1970s. The references are enhanced by links to Renoir's poetic realism and Bresson's ascetic style. These include the blending of comedy and tragedy, particularly characteristic of Renoir's work, shapes Kaurismäki's shots and montage from the very beginning to the very end of the film,[64] and should be interpreted as a reflection of socio-cultural hybridity in *Le Havre*. There are no fixed boundaries between 'good' and 'bad' or 'real' and 'imagined', because every character has the ability to change (see grocer and Monet). First impressions and categorizations might be wrong (Marcel continues to classify Monet as persecutor, when he has long changed sides). However, everything is possible as long as there is hope and a strong will, which Kaurismäki mirrors in Marcel and Arletty's loving relationship as well as scenes of neighborhood solidarity (Arletty recovers from her illness, and Idrissa is likely to reach England). Furthermore, the permanent tension between comedy and tragedy as well as inexpressive acting, which is typical for Bresson's work, allows the viewer to maintain a critical distance and reduces the melodramatic elements of the film.

The 1970s were the times of Little Bob's success as a rock star in the city of Le Havre. His appearance in the film as a local musician who becomes a key representative of the neighborhood solidarity movement when he gives his charity concert for Idrissa adds as much importance to the time frame as the music he plays. In particular, his rock music should be regarded as an alternative to 'small-town puritanism' and, more broadly, an attempt 'to resolve collectively experienced problems arising from contradictions in the social structure' by helping to create a form of 'collective identity [...] outside that ascribed by class, education and occupation'.[65] While avoiding the term 'counter culture', Little Bob describes in one interview rock as 'made of people who moan, who grumble, who express what they think, whatever their language is'.[66] So it is no coincidence that his concert in *Le Havre* marks the climax of the small-scale collective solidarity movement he leads with Marcel as representatives of socio-economically marginalized white French communities. His song 'Libero', which is then played in full, connects directly to their fight for Idrissa's freedom to choose his own destiny, because 'Libero means free' (Little Bob, in: Marie 2009). The reference to his Italian father Libero Piazza reminds us of the singer's own migrant background and his link to multi-ethnic France: 'France is the country that welcomed me, that adopted me, that's where I have my fans, my friends' (ibid.). I argue that Kaurismäki's Little Bob requests the same right of 'adoption' for Idrissa through the charity concert, and that the social rebellion expressed via the concert goes well beyond the notion of 'working-class solidarity', with which Hoberman and Bagh (both 2011) attempt to summarize its key message. Instead, the extremely heterogeneous group that includes aging artist Little Bob, unsuccessful writer Marcel, house wife Arletty, baker Yvette, a nameless grocer, and black African child Idrissa blurs traditional class, gender, and ethnic boundaries in its critical interrogation of French law, monocultural racism, and neo-colonial tendencies in contemporary Europe.

Most obvious is the film's support of renegotiations of the French Penal Code after the criticism of article L622-1 in Lioret's *Welcome* and subsequent mass-media coverage and protests against it.[67] Simon, the middle-aged swimming instructor in *Welcome,* risks 5 years imprisonment and a 30,000 euro fine for helping Bilal to cross the Channel. The trans-class, trans-gender and above all, transcultural alliance in *Le Havre* could face the same penalty for a very similar 'crime' due to an article that aims to punish 'any person who will have, by direct or indirect aid, facilitated or attempted to facilitate the entry, circulation or irregular stay of a foreigner in France'.[68] Not by coincidence, the political authorities in *Le Havre* are represented by French Police, who treats illegal immigrants as criminals (one policeman might have shot Idrissa had the inspector not intervened) in its fruitless attempt to defend national (and with it, European) boundaries.

Lioret indicates parallels between contemporary French Law and the German National Socialist Penal Code in occupied France.[69] In the same spirit, Kaurismäki establishes a link to the Vichy government by references to Melville's *Army of the Shadows* (1969)[70] with popular stars of French cinema Lino Ventura and Simone Signoret in key roles that portrayed the blurring of class and gender boundaries as a pre-requisite to efficiently fight German occupation troops in the 1940s. The underdog alliance in *Le Havre* takes this request for solidarity in a hostile environment one step further by including transcultural efforts to protect human dignity and fight traditional binaries of exclusion that lead to history repeating itself. At the same time, they remain as anonymous as the Resistance in the 1940s, and their main motivation can be linked to an honor-based desire for freedom,[71] although notions of 'honor' and 'freedom' have changed significantly. In particular, there is now a much more critical distance to patriotic leitmotifs, which allows *Le Havre* to blur nationalist boundaries that were not negotiable for French Resistance dramas of the 1950s and 1960s. In this context, I argue that Arletty's miraculous recovery from cancer and inspector Monet's similarly surprising decision not to pursue Idrissa further could be read as a parallel montage, which invites a critical interrogation of traditional boundaries. The name of Marcel's wife refers to the French star Arletty, famous for her role as seductive Garance in Marcel Carné's *Children of Paradise* (1945) and for her liaison with German officer Hans-Jürgen Soehring in occupied France. For this she was shaved, imprisoned, made a social outcast, and excluded from acting until 1949. If French nationalists categorized her liaison as moral treason, which *Le Havre* appears to reflect metaphorically via Arletty's cancer, then her recovery in the film suggests that it is about time to overcome the simplistic binary. Very similarly, Monet's radical change from persecutor to protector, who ultimately helps to hide the child refugee from arrest and deportation, highlights that the nationalist mentality, which he has been asked to represent, remains an inhuman construct.

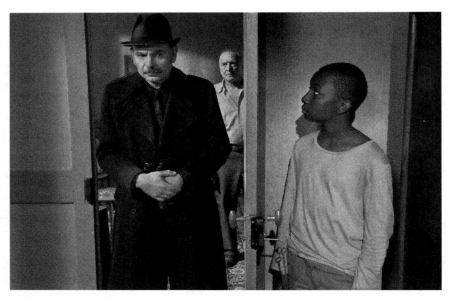

Figure 3.4.2.2 Inspector Monet's investigation.

Welcome's intervention against article L622-1 led to a wider discussion that ultimately resulted in important amendments made by law 2012-1560, which excludes humanitarian actions from prosecution.[72] This highlights again the potential impact of European cinema after the change in law following the denunciation of discrimination of French-African soldiers during and after World War II in Bouchareb's *Days of Glory*.[73] However, the exceptions listed in article L622-4, which allow for a temporary humanitarian supply of food, accommodation, and medical assistance,[74] do not cover a concert organized to pay smugglers to bring a refugee to London. Consequently, *Le Havre*'s outsider-protagonists remain criminals from a French legal perspective, which is a viewpoint that neither Kaurismäki nor Lioret supports. Also, legal reforms in one European country do not necessarily imply a turning point within the European Union, as recent British governmental proposals to punish landlords with up to five years in prison for renting out properties to illegal migrants confirm (Grice 2015).

Little Bob's concert for Idrissa could also be regarded as an ironic subversion of monocultural perspectives, in which rock appears as barbarian and non-European. One example is provided by John Tyndall, leader of the *National Front* in the 1970s and co-founder of the *British National Party* (1982), who commented in the early 1960s on the Beatles as follows:

> I had heard that their brand of music was thoroughly British [...] But having sampled a few bars of it, I became convinced that this 'music' was certainly not native to Britain, nor to Europe nor to anywhere in the world where civilisation exists. As these effeminate oddities gyrated their underdeveloped bodies about the stage, looking for all the world like the members of a primitive African tribe [...] Is this not the age [...] in which the cultural values of historic Europe have been relegated to the poorhouse to be replaced by the ravings of the new 'nigger symphony'. (Brake 2013: 82)

Tyndall might have regarded Little Bob as yet another 'effeminate oddity', but there can be no doubt that the musician and his underdog friends defend civilized Europe in *Le Havre*, although their definition of civilization is in a transcultural sense inclusive, rather than monoculturally exclusive. In particular, they value the European humanist tradition with its focus on the individual, a child refugee in this case. They intervene to protect Idrissa's rights for free movement and family reunification, which links up to basic principles defended by the *European Convention on Human Rights* (ECHR) and the *European Court of Human Rights* in Strasbourg. It is difficult to imagine a more European agenda, but it remains unclear far Tyndall, the National Front, and the BNP can be regarded as part of this tradition.

Finally, the opposition between 'outdated' outsider-protagonists and a modern police force, a contrast that is stressed by the use of current police uniforms and weapons, draws viewers' attention to socio-economic and political shifts in contemporary European history. In particular, there is a substantial change from inclusive national welfare systems, strong unions, and solidarity movements culminating in the 1968 attempt at a cultural revolution to the more neo-liberal present-day Europe characterized by sharply reduced welfare systems, weaker unions, and less socio-political organization. This shift had both local and global consequences, which have been a hot topic for postcolonial research. Wilkin criticizes especially the neo-liberal aim 'to overturn the limited gains made by working people throughout the world-system in the post-war period' (1996: 231), which Lazarus summarizes as a 'savage restructuring of class and social relations [...] in the interest of capital' (2012: 7). This 'assault upon ideas of collectivism', which narrows 'the public space within which political action can take place' and excludes 'those who do not have the necessary forms of private power' (Wilkin 1996: 232), is mirrored by a foreign policy that Lazarus describes as 'the reassertion of imperial dominance' (2012: 9). Both Wilkin and Lazarus condemn here a socio-political and economic shift toward a lack of solidarity they date from the 1970s and that has a substantial impact on cultural relations both within and beyond national boundaries. *Le Havre* criticizes this neo-liberal tendency with its selection of an impoverished white French citizen and an even poorer African child refugee as protagonists, joining forces within a marginalized neighborhood. Rascaroli summarizes Marcel's, Arletty's, and their friends' outsider status as follows:

> Old objects represent them in that they are salvaged remnants of previous epochs, unwanted leftovers, used by people who, by chance or necessity, are extraneous to the logic of consumerist society. […] they are […] poor things, though undeniably linked to an oppositional – and somewhat romantic – aesthetics of reusability and sustainability. (2013: 335)

In his optimistic fairy tale, Kaurismäki wants these outsiders to concentrate on what they have in common with the illegal African migrant, such as their exclusion from consumerist society, but also their marginalization in public policies and governmental representation. None of them can expect significant support from local, national or supra-national institutions, such as the city council of Le Havre, the French government, or the European Commission. If anything, they all have to live in fear of being criminalized and chased by police at any moment, in which they show basic solidarity with each other. However, this solidarity for people in need appears to be key, not only to avoid the Other's deportation, but to better understand the precarious existence of the Self with a view to dissolving the simplistic binary. Kaurismäki suggests establishing a new 'Resistance' against ongoing mechanisms of exclusion, suppression, and even assisted elimination that remind him of Vichy France. The aim is to recognize and overcome the shared heritage of isolation, incommunication, and personal impotence that links *Le Havre*'s outcasts to outsider-protagonists of Nouvelle Vague as well as New German Cinema. The historical parallel helps us understand that this solidarity, which is essential to 'experience' the Other (see Epstein on transculturality, 2009: 340), does not have to be developed from scratch. It is a fundamental part of European tradition, from its humanism in the 15th and 16th centuries and French revolutionary ideals of 'liberté', 'fraternité', and 'egalité' in the 18th century to postcolonial and transcultural perspectives in the 21st century.

3.4.3 Monocultural Characters and Ongoing Marginalisation

In the opening scene, the camera moves from gangsters killing one of their own to French police getting ready to chase the criminals. What starts as inspector Monet's investigation into the mafia murder, however, soon develops into a persecution of illegal migrants trapped in a shipping container. Not by coincidence the special forces that arrive to arrest them following orders from the Ministry of the Interior prepare their automatic weapons before opening the container as if they are about to go into battle. Monet is not convinced that the use of special forces is appropriate ('Is this necessary?'). Thus he has an intermediating role, in which he stops one member of the unit from shooting Idrissa. However, his leadership in the successful persecution and his outfit are reminiscent of the gangsters introduced shortly before (similar trench coat, hat, gloves) and of Hitler's SS as presented in French Resistance dramas (fully dressed in black, presenting lack of emotions). Considering the supporting role of Vichy police for the SS, which included the persecution of Jews on behalf of the National Socialist regime, it could be argued that Monet is being (re-) constructed in these scenes as an arch-enemy trying to implement a monocultural vision of France, within which there is no space for the Other. Although Marcel does not link Monet explicitly to Vichy France, he regards him as main opponent in his attempt to provide Idrissa with humanitarian aid, and so does the small solidarity movement. The anonymity of the prefect, integrated only as a nameless voice from the officer that gives Monet the orders to search for the fugitive, as well as the repeated 'mise-en-scène' of a 'spy' in the neighborhood, who keeps phoning the police to help them catch Idrissa, further support the impression of an authoritarian regime at work. Suffering and persecution of the French under the National Socialist Vichy regime and contemporary migrants' suffering and persecution by French and other European police forces are this way linked to facilitate the recognition of shared memories of monocultural suppression, which Moses and Rothberg outline as essential for the development of an 'ethics of transcultural memory' (2014: 29).

I argue that the (re-)construction of Monet as representative of 'dark forces' from the past in the first half of the film predominantly serves the purpose of deconstruction in the second half. Although Monet knows very well that Marcel is hiding the child, he neither requests an interrogation at the police station nor orders a search of his home. Instead, he opts for a thorough but informal investigation of Marcel's background. The protagonist misinterprets this as the collection of proof for his arrest, but he should read it as the basis for deciding what kind of support Marcel deserves. After all, Monet risks his career, a jail sentence, and a fine when he warns the protagonist of the spy's activities and the police search before directly misleading 'the course of justice' with his lie to a fellow-policeman about the vault of the French fisherman's ship being empty when in fact Idrissa is hiding in it.

Admittedly, the mysterious inspector remains the exception that confirms the rule. While he uses his skills to critically interrogate French law and its implementation, the rest of the police continue to mechanically fulfill orders, from the special forces member who aims at the child refugee at the beginning of the film to the policeman who insists on inspecting the vault at its very end. The mechanics of their behavior draw on an internalized belief in authority[75] that correlates with the strict hierarchy of the force and a conditioning that makes them react to orders, rather than examine them.

All of this reminds viewers of the control mechanisms and actual policing in Aldous Huxley's *Brave New World* (1931), George Orwell's *1984* (1948), and Joseph Kessel's *Army of the Shadows* (1943), which was then adapted by Melville for his 1969 film with the same title. Not completely dissimilar to Huxley, Orwell, and Kessel, Kaurismäki stresses the mechanical continuity of *Le Havre*'s repressive police system, which is enhanced by the prefect and the neighborhood spy remaining in place with the support of privileged classes. An example of the latter is the shoe shop owner, who explicitly categorizes Marcel as 'terroriste' and drives him away from his entrance, simply because his work as a shoe-shiner goes against mainstream consumerism and could therefore potentially reduce his profits.

Finally, the captain of the small French boat who brings Idrissa to British waters indicates that English police might be worse than their French counterpart, when he mentions the high risk of ship confiscation for the British captain taking the child refugee on board. In a context, in which the guardians of monocultural space will keep doing their very best to arrest and deport so-called illegal migrants, Marcel's and Monet's interventions have to be regarded as a very individual, temporary limited, and coincidental solution to the challenges of migration to Europe. In particular, viewers cannot assume that Idrissa will be able to live a modest life with his mother in London, i.e., in the capital of a country in which landlords might now face up to five years in jail for renting accommodations to migrants like them.

The happy end of Kaurismäki's narrative should, however, also be questioned with regard to the limits of migrant agency portrayed. The challenge starts with the director's choice of a well-educated, obedient, and largely passive black child as an example for African migrants trying to reach Europe. This choice is as demographically misleading as it is problematic from a postcolonial point of view. It correlates with European colonial perspectives, within which colonizers are presented as cognitively superior adults vis-à-vis the instinct-led colonized in need of patriarchal protection by the white man. Without any doubt, Marcel's superiority is enhanced by the presentation of Idrissa as a child in desperate need of protection, e.g., when he hides from the police under a pier in the water, and Marcel is portrayed as the one person able and willing to provide that protection. All of this opens up direct parallels to *Welcome* and *Hands Up*, which similarly concentrate on white French adults protecting helpless child refugees, but it also links up to comparable portrayals between adults, for which Paz's intervention on behalf of an older black salesman in Saura's *Taxi* remains an excellent example (see 3.1). In *Le Havre*, the hierarchy is stressed when Marcel insists that the boy must obey him in every situation,[76] and his instructions, which often concentrate on the need for Idrissa to hide in the house, further enhance the child's position as an object, rather than subject of his own destiny. Finally, when Marcel has to temporarily leave the child with Yvette, he gives her—rather than Idrissa—very detailed instructions that stress the need to take a shower, put on new clothes and stay in the house ('Ne laisse pas sortir le garçon').

During their first conversation in the living room, Idrissa comments on the strong hierarchy by calling Marcel 'mon génerale', but his passivity and Marcel's success in the face of powerful opponents and extremely limited financial resources justify his authority.

Le Havre also establishes a parallel between Idrissa and Marcel's dog Laïka. Not only does the dog usually go wherever Idrissa goes, which means for Yvette that she has to take care of both while Marcel goes to Calais, but the protagonist's care for the two of them is comparable.[77] Overall, they remain at a similar level: In some scenes, Idrissa holds Laïka's leash and guides him, whereas in others the dog takes the initiative and the child follows him or Laïka leads Marcel to the child's hiding place. When the spy grabs Idrissa's arm to force him to wait for the police, the two appear similarly helpless, because they can object but, ultimately Chang has to intervene so that they can leave. With this parallel construction, Kaurismäki might have attempted to stress the lack of human dignity experienced by Idrissa as a refugee, but he failed to elaborate on his agency, which means that Marcel and other white French characters have to become 'makers of history' for the child and his mother, who represent illegal mass migration to Europe.[78] Although the director makes it clear that Marcel's Europe does not show major progress, Idrissa's passivity combined with his lack of initiative and ideas to take his destiny in his own hands confirm traditional European self-portrayals.

All of this could be compared to films like Nakache's and Toledano's *Samba* (2014), which presents a more balanced view of agency in its portrayal of the black African protagonist of the same name who manages to survive in Paris for more than 10 years without support from the French host society and with only minor aid from a relative. When he ultimately receives help from the French social worker Alice, it becomes clear that she needs him as much as he needs her. Nakache and Toledano also fight colonial stereotypes by refusing to define Samba in corporal and/or emotional concepts,[79] which are still strong in Claire Denis's portrayal of Protée in *Chocolat* (1988) and in Uribe's framing of Ombasi in *Bwana* (1996).[80] Idrissa's main strengths are running away (from the special unit inspecting the shipping container and from the police called by the spy), hiding (under the pier and in Laïka's corner of Marcel's house), and educated manners (received from his father, a teacher). Samba, on the other hand, manages overall very well on his own and, when he accepts help, he tends to give something back. There is of course the age difference worth considering between Idrissa, a boy of about 12 years, and Samba, a man in his thirties. However, most contemporary directors give child protagonists substantially more agency than Kaurismäki does, and it was the director's decision to represent contemporary African migrants to Europe by a 12 year old.

The portrayal of women, who tend to be reduced to traditional support roles for the male protagonist, is similarly disappointing. Marcel is presented as the only breadwinner in the small household; Arletty cooks dinner for

108 *Migrants in Europe*

her husband, serves him, and then waits next to the table for him to finish the main course, so that she can bring desert. Similarly, the baker Yvette and the pub owner Claire tend to react to Marcel's requests, rather than work proactively to help Idrissa reach London. Yvette hides Idrissa in her own home, and Claire helps the protagonist escape from police surveillance by letting him out through the backdoor of her pub, but in both cases Marcel has to ask for it. There are attempts to deconstruct gender stereotypes, for example when Arletty administers Marcel's income and when she categorizes him as her 'big child'. Also, the exaggeration of her servant role at the beginning of the film was probably meant to draw attention to the grotesque nature of traditional gender roles. However, agency in this migration story remains predominantly white and male, and this is enhanced in the second part of the film when Arletty's illness increases her passivity to the degree that she no longer knows what happens in her own home. Similarly, Yvette's interest in providing Marcel and Idrissa with bread corresponds to stereotypical gender images. This support is dwarfed by the male grocer, who not only gives away substantially more provisions but, at the end of the film in a scene that reminds us of Tati's absurd humor, the camera zooms in on him bringing Idrissa out of danger in his pushcart, while the police stand by, watch him, and search his shop. Finally, the police seem to be male only, including proactive inspector Monet, and the same applies to refugees who show some initiative. In this context, women remain predominantly passive and reactive beings in opposition to active and proactive men, who reappear as 'makers of history'—albeit only at a local level led by marginalized artists like Marcel and Little Bob, with whom Kaurismäki might be able to empathize most easily.

3.4.4 Concluding Remarks

Le Havre's exploration of basic human solidarity and the numerous obstacles are strong statements for the need to transform transcultural capabilities and empirically measurable tendencies into sociopolitical and legal frameworks that 'have to be established by socio-political institutions', as Schachtner highlights in her discussion of 'culture flows and virtual publics' (2015: 240). In particular, Kaurismäki's film supports and strengthens the appeal from *Welcome* and *Hands Up* to revise article L622-1 of the French Penal Code.

In many ways comparable to *Welcome*, *Le Havre* succeeds in its transcultural message due to its intertextual depth, which reminds viewers of historical parallels in monocultural suppression, especially under the Vichy regime, but it does not force them to follow a similarly fixed alternative viewpoint. Instead, the continuous mix of comedy and tragedy as well as inexpressive acting help to gain critical distance, allow for some freedom in interpretation, and avoid the simple inversion of popular right-wing rhetoric. Frequent errors in the stereotypical categorization of Others, highlighted by Marcel's unshakable but misleading perception of Monet as a main opponent, further enhanced by unconvincing negative portrayals of the grocer in the first half of the film, contribute to the creation of a space 'in-between' traditional binaries. All of this facilitates the integration of Others, be it of the same culture, albeit a different class (Monet, grocer), or of a different ethnicity (Idrissa). There is also an attempt to overcome gender boundaries, because Marcel's success would be difficult to imagine without Yvette's and Claire's support, and the blurring of age boundaries is mirrored in the joint fight of a 70 year old and a 12 year old. Overall, the small-scale solidarity movement brought together and headed by Marcel could in this regard be summarized as trans-class, trans-gender, trans-age and transcultural, or simply transcultural in its wider sense.

However, in questions of agency, *Le Havre* still follows traditional patterns with its presentation of white men as makers of local history and women in support roles. The representation of contemporary mass migration from Africa to Europe by a rather passive 12-year-old child is not only demographically misleading, but—above all—an example for the continuity of neocolonial patterns of thought. All this reminds us of Echevarría's unfortunate portrayal of female Indians and the black slave Esteban as passive and reactive beings in *Cabeza de Vaca*, the lack of female agency in *Letters from Alou*, and the lack of migrant agency in *Taxi*. Although this highlights again the difficulties in overcoming traditional boundaries, it does not discredit the socio-political and cultural criticism of contemporary migrant cinema and its contribution to establishing the framework for a transcultural society.

Notes

1. See our discussion in chapter 1.1, which builds on the line of argumentation established by Welsch (1997/1999), Huggan (2006), Antor (2006/2010), and Benessaieh (2010/2012).
2. For an overview of 'capital' linked to professions and jobs see Bourdieu 1998: 19 and 1987: 212f.
3. See Madrid Destino 2014, 'Plan your trip'—'Other cultures', and 'Discover Madrid'—'Choose your Madrid').
4. See Empresa Municipal 2008, 'Always'—'Explore Madrid'. Applying Urban's differentiation between 'space' and 'place' (2007: 50f.), the text might want to portray Madrid as a highly dynamic open 'space', within which migrants could establish clear borderlines to subjectively define their own 'place' in society.
5. These are predominantly new EU members from the East of Europe, i.e., 198,000 Romanians, 29,000 Bulgarians, and 21,000 Poles (see INE 2014). Due to the economic crisis in Spain, the number of foreign nationals—including Eastern Europeans—has decreased in the last years, but out of a total population of just under 6,500,000 inhabitants in Madrid, around 960,000 are of foreign origin (ibid.).
6. According to the 'Observatorio', the percentage of foreign residents among the total population of the city of Madrid increased from 1% in 1986 to nearly 16% in 2005 (2005: 5), before it dropped slightly to under 14% in 2014 (INE 2014).

110 *Migrants in Europe*

7. Before its closure, the 'Observatorio de las Migraciones y de la Convivencia Intercultural de la Ciuddad de Madrid' was able to record nearly 40% foreign residents in San Cristóbal/Villaverde as opposed to 2% in Fuencarral/El Pardo (2005: 5). A study by García Ballesteros and Jiménez Blasco confirms a concentration of foreign population in southern districts such as Villaverde, Carabanchel, and Usera, which are characterized by old working class neighborhoods from the 1960s and 1970s and within which small ethnic business has developed particularly well (2012: 91–96).
8. See Madrid Destino 2014, 'Discover Madrid'—'Neighborhoods'.
9. See Madrid Destino 2014, 'Plan your trip'—'Other cultures'. The term 'cross-breeding' tends to be used for animals and plants.
10. See Madrid Destino 2014, 'Discover Madrid'—'Madrid Neighborhoods'—'Lavapiés'.
11. Not by coincidence, the website on Madrid's 'Top 10' attractions starts with a long list of museums headed by Prado (general admission €14) and Thyssen-Bornemisza (€10) (see Madrid Destino 2014, 'Discover Madrid'—'At a glance'—'Madrid Top 10'). Following complaints about high prices for admission to cultural heritage, Madrid city council now offers the Madrid Card, but this alternative could easily lead to higher expenditure as its most economical 24 hour version is €47. Madrid city council also uses its website to promote 'official guided tours' and 'tourist busses', and its 'Luxury Madrid' website helps marketing four and five star restaurants, five star hotels, and luxury shopping opportunities (see Madrid Destino 2014, 'Discover Madrid'—'Choose your Madrid'—'Luxury Madrid').
12. See Santaolalla for details on viewers' feedback (2007: 468f.).
13. See Invest in Madrid (2014) 'Business location'—'Key facts'—'Business Environment': 'The salary cost of Madrid is below that of Copenhagen, Dublin, Brussels, London, Munich, Berlin, Amsterdam, Paris, or Milan (2011). In 2012, labor costs in Spain were practically half those in Belgium'.
14. Deveny also applies Nacify's 'Accented Cinema' theory to *Letters from Alou*, but this leads mainly to confirmations of the film's multilingualism and the 'film letter' framework (2012: 26–27), which confirms my questioning of this theory for our case study analysis in Chapter 1.3.
15. See also Saïd's experience in *Poniente* when trying to rent a flat in the village.
16. See Görling (2007: 153f.) for claustrophobia in Tevfik Baser's films.
17. Although the film might superficially support Görling's romantic notion of love as an entity without boundaries (2004: 45), the socio-economic components of the relationship should not be ignored. For a fruitful discussion of equality and dignity from a legal perspective, see Gómez Jiménez (2014).
18. In a parallel to the Mercedes logo in *Jamón, jamón*, in which Raúl pulls out the car and which Fouz-Hernández (2005: 197f.) explores as an example of global consumerism, I suggest reading the pears picked by cheap labor on a fruit plantation in *Letters from Alou* as symbols of forced colonial work.
19. Drawing on Said's discussion of 'Orientalism' as a hegemonic representation of non-occidental cultures (1978: 2f., 45f.) and Bhabha's notion of mimicry in colonial discourse (1994: 86f.), I regard this behavior as example of internalized Orientalism. This is comparable to Baser's framing of traditional Turkish culture as backwards, stagnant, and barbarian in *40 Square Meters of Germany* and *Farewell to a False Paradise* (see Rings 2008: 12f.).

20. See Young on the duality of colonial discourse between desire and rejection (1995: 90–117); Santaolalla (2007: 469f.) outlines Alou's erotic features but does not recognize the link to colonial imagery.
21. 'Son los que roban vuestros trabajos y violan a vuestras mujeres'.
22. An early example of Spanish discourse governed by such dichotomies is Sepúlveda's portrayal of the conquest of America as a 'bellum iustum' based on the categorization of indigenous population as human-flesh eating barbarians that need to be forced to accept Christian values (see Rings 2005: 58f.). Spanish fascism under Franco, the direct model for Calero's 'cleaning' of Madrid, draws for its historical re-construction on a comparable dichotomy. With the notion of fascist Spain as the leader of a new crusade against pagans, Franco constructs a historical legitimation by linking crusades, re-conquest, conquest, and Spanish civil war.
23. This does not necessarily imply that violent racists are easier to persecute in a rural setting—as films like Hüseyin's *Anita and Me* indicate, but Bollaín's *Flowers of Another World* seems to argue along these lines.
24. See in this context also the scene of Calero throwing away Paz's lighter, which comes with the inscription 'Fight for peace' ('Lucha por la paz') and which he finds in Dani's possession.
25. Most tourist brochures stress the role of Philipp II, who considerably enlarged the royal retreat while his colonial enterprise enhanced Spain's development to a global power. Philipp IV commissioned famous architects to further expand and enrich the park with prestigious buildings and a major lake when Spanish territory reached its maximum expansion.
26. See Fraser (2006: 27). Particularly problematic is his attempt to categorize the taxi drivers' assaults as traditional class conflict, because the heterogeneous group of taxi drivers and skinheads cannot be summarized as middle class, and 'underclass'-belonging is not a pre-requisite for the fascists to attack black people (see assault of the African diplomat).
27. I question Flesler's interpretation of *Letters from Alou*, which differs from the other films in her analysis due to Rosa's successful marriage to Mulai and Carmen's love for Alou, but I agree with her that the end of *Poniente* meets monocultural expectations, although this has little to do with Adbembi's premature comments about Curro (see Flesler 2004: 107). Instead, I regard the continuity of the Spanish relationship (Curro and Lucía) in the context of the break-up of the Spanish-Moroccan friendship (Curro and Adbembi) and Adbembi's return 'home' as challenging.
28. Malik describes *East Is East* as 'between the style of a Northern "kitchen sink" 1960s drama, a 1970s slapstick farce and a modern social realist interrogation into identity, belonging and Britishness' (2002: 96).
29. Silicone team (2003: 15), although estimates range from $150 million (Bend It Networks 2014) to $350 million worldwide. Whatever calculation is applied, it appears to be the 'UK highest grossing British-financed, British-distributed film' prior to Slumdog Millionaire (ibid.).
30. This is a traditional dress consisting of trousers and a long tunic with a scarf that can be placed over the shoulder or over the head. See Algeo 2007: 136.
31. There are only very few exceptions to that pattern like Prasad's *My Son the Fanatic* (1997), in which the generational conflict is reversed.
32. This is the case with Joe, who is at first skeptical of Jess's talent, which seems to correlate with the fact that he has 'never seen South Asian women playing

112   *Migrants in Europe*

football'. However, he is prepared to let her play and, once he recognizes her talent, has no problem in revising his pre-judgment.
33. For a summary see Mishra (2014).
34. The English title is a misinterpretation of the German original, which uses grammatically incorrect German infinitive construction and no article, to reconstruct—for the purpose of deconstruction—German stereotypes of the guest worker's inability to communicate.
35. See Göktürk (2000: 332 and 2002: 249ff.); also Rendi (2006: 82).
36. Şerif Gören produced his *Polizei* (1988) in Turkey, and Sinan Çetin got private sponsorship for *Berlin in Berlin* (1993).
37. Particularly fruitful could be an exploration of the potential and limits of transculturality in sport films, as the blurring of class, gender, and/or race boundaries in boxing has been a major topic in Germany, including Züli Aladag's *Elefantenherz* (2002), Catharina Deus's *Die Boxerin* (2005), and Uwe Boll's *Max Schmeling* (2010), as well as in the Hollywood *Rocky* films with Sylvester Stallone.
38. One important exception to the rule is Ken Loach's *Ae Fond Kiss* (2004). Paul Laverty's script impressively depicts here the cultural divide between second-generation Pakistani Casim and Irish Catholic teacher Roisin by exploring different culture concepts rather than blaming conflicts exclusively on 'Oriental' fundamentalism.
39. See Göktürk (2002: 251) for such a link.
40. This is a consequence of the economic boom and the radical stop of immigration from East Germany after the erection of the Berlin Wall (1961).
41. See for example the *Der Spiegel* article from July 30, 1973: 'The Turks are Coming – Every Man for Himself' ('Die Türken kommen - rette sich wer kann').
42. Examples are the assaults by skinheads against guest workers and asylum seekers in Hoyerswerda in 1991 and more than 14 different neo-Nazi attacks in 1992, particularly in East Germany.
43. See the exploration of skinhead milieus in Marie Hagemann's *Schwarzer, Wolf, Skin* (1993) and Ingo Hasselbach's *Die Abrechnung. Ein Neonazi steigt aus* (1993).
44. See Mansour Ghadarkhah, the director of *Eye for an Eye* (*Auge um Auge* 1992), who claims that his film about the fear of asylum seekers after Hoyerswerda was prevented from entering the Berlinale for political reasons. Whatever the main argument for excluding *Eye for an Eye* might have been, it can be assumed that explorations of East German racism in cinema of the early 1990s might not have received major support from the public engineers of German Unification.
45. In feature films, the Holocaust was first widely explored on German screen by the New German cinema and then by the American series *Holocaust* in the late 1970s, which means a 20 to 30 year delay in the cinematic discussion.
46. 'Wir sind hier allesamt nigger; wir haben unser ghetto, wir schleppen's überall hin, [...]unser schweiß ist nigger, unser leben ist nigger, die goldketten sind nigger, unsere zinken und unsere fressen und unser eigner stil ist so verdammt nigger, dass wir wie blöde an unserer Haut kratzen, und dabei kapieren wir, dass zum nigger nicht die olle pechhaut gehört, aber zum nigger gehört ne ganze menge anderssein und andres leben' (ibid. 25).
47. Even less convincing are Zaimoğlu's arguments for the exclusion: His categorization of integration efforts as 'mutation to the nice colleague "Ali", who one takes occasionally to the favourite pub after knocking-off time' ('Mutation

zum netten Kollegen "Ali", den man mal nach Feierabend zum Stammlokal mitnimmt') is clearly as debatable as his opinion about the intellectuals' lack of a 'social powder keg' ('gesellschaftliche Sprengkraft' (ibid. 18).
48. The term 'Nachdichtung' is used by Zaimoğlu himself (1999: 18).
49. Probably the most obvious example is the portrayal of Melek's Turkish-German boyfriend İsa as a dark-clothed dangerous criminal who attacks desperate Daniel and hides a corpse in the boot of his car. Only much later, in the interrogation set up by an apparently merciless Turkish border patrol, the film reveals that İsa is just trying to fulfill the final wish of an uncle who died in Germany but wanted to be buried in Turkish soil, a new situation to which the border police reacts by celebrating the family hero.
50. 'Bürgerliches Kalkül' and 'emotionale Absicherungen'; Lederle (2004: 29).
51. He is also considerably older than Fassbinder's Ali (judging from the age gap it could be Fassbinder's protagonist grown old), and the fact that he has to pay a woman to live with him stresses his despair.
52. Sexual impotence is highlighted in *Fear Eats the Soul* when Ali reject's the young Turkish woman's approach in the guest worker pub with the comment 'cock broken' ('Schwanz kaputt'), and *The Edge of Heaven* makes it a key topic in the first encounter between Ali and Yeter when the short dialogue ('Can you still get it up at your age? – God willing.'/'Kriegst du ihn in deinem Alter noch hoch? – So Gott will.') is followed by a blow job. In both films, sexual impotence accompanies social impotence, which culminates in Fassbinder's Ali suffering racist discrimination and objectification, whereas Akın's Ali has to serve a jail sentence for killing Yeter and is then deported back to Turkey.
53. In *Fear Eats the Soul* Emmi promises to fight her husband's illness, and *The Edge of Heaven* finishes with Nejat waiting for his father in his Turkish birthplace to return from the sea.
54. Lotte continues to live in Hotel Mum and appears to depend in all her actions on her mother's financial support.
55. Whereas Akın uses the term 'genocide' in an interview with Greuling (2014), which is in line with US and Vatican perspectives on the topic, Turkish president Erdoğan continues to fight such perspectives, for example in April 2015 by summoning the Vatican's ambassador in a show of protest.
56. Two years after *The Edge of Heaven*, Akın drew international attention to the minaret ban in Switzerland by an open letter, in which he highlighted his inspiration from Fassbinder: 'My only explanation for the Swiss referendum [that led to the minaret ban] is fear. Fear is the source of all evil. *Fear Eats the Soul* is the title of a film by Rainer Werner Fassbinder. Maybe fear has eaten too many souls in Switzerland already' (Akın 2009).
57. The connection between Lotte and Ayten is very well visualized in the doubling of the ferry scene, in which one girl after another crosses the Bosporus, and with it the divide between East and West, albeit in different directions: In the first setting Lotte is on the ferry in the direction of Eastern Istanbul and facing the camera; in the second scene Ayten is on her way to Western Istanbul facing the ferry's wake (see Silvey/Hillman 2010: 111–112).
58. 'Türken [bleiben] Türken und Deutsche Deutsche'; Tezcan (2010: 68).
59. See Göktürk for the selection and refurbishment of an abandoned petrol station close to the current motorway with numerous modern petrol stations (2010: 26). Whereas Göktürk regards this 'mise-en-scène' as 'affective production of the

114   *Migrants in Europe*

glocal' ('affektive Produktion des Glokalen', ibid.), I would categorize it as reconstruction of stereotypical perspectives on Turkey as exotic and collective space.

60. The so-called Working-class Trilogy (also known as Proletariat Trilogy), which includes *Shadows in* Paradise 1986, *Ariel* 1988, and *The Match Factory Girl* 1990, as well as the Finland Trilogy (with *Drifting Clouds* 1996, *The Man Without a Past* 2002, and *Lights in the Dusk* 2006) have 'losers' as protagonists. Kaurismäki describes Nikander, the protagonist from *Shadows in Paradise*, as a 'loser character' (Romney 1997: 13), and the Finland Trilolgy is also known as Loser Trilogy (Wilson 2009).
61. For Hoberman, *Le Havre* is predominantly a 'warmhearted comedy' (2011), whereas Sáez González discusses it as a 'melodrama' (2012: 124) and Kaurismäki as 'optimistic fairy tale' (Bagh 2011: 40).
62. For an introduction see Aridj's summary of Sarkozy's statements (2008) and Fevry's discussion (2014: 252–254).
63. The same applies to forms of nostalgia highlighted by films like Nakache and Toledano's *Samba* (2014), which starts with a 1930s style high-society white French wedding party in an upper-class restaurant before the camera moves into the dishwasher section of the kitchen staffed exclusively by black people and then to the back entrance of the restaurant with black and Asian staff enjoying a cigarette break.
64. At the beginning, the camera shows Marcel and Chang waiting for customers at the train station and follows their perspective (i.e., looking down on the shoes of arriving passengers), which has a humorous undertone that is enhanced by the slightly grotesque presentation of the first customer (out-of-date Italian mafioso style). However, shortly afterwards, that customer gets ruthlessly killed, before Marcel suggests focusing on the positive side of the tragedy: 'Luckily, he had time to pay'/'Heureusement, il a payé'.
65. See Brake's youth subculture analysis (2013: 147, VII).
66. This includes his own music, on which he comments: 'There is always some kind of rebellion on each record' (Marie 2009).
67. See for example Sparks (2009), Phillips (2010), and Vincent (2012).
68. See Legifrance (2015): 'toute personne qui aura, par aide directe ou indirecte, facilité ou tenté de faciliter l'entrée, la circulation ou le séjour irréguliers, d'un étranger en France sera punie d'un emprisonnement de cinq ans et d'une amende de 30 000 Euros'.
69. In his interview with Lemercier (2009), Lioret mentions similarities between house searches by National Socialists in the 1940s and French police in the 21st century.
70. After preparing viewers for the homage to Melville by exaggerating references to his film noir work, Kaurismäki indicates his familiarity with *Army of the Shadows* via Marcel's statement 'Money moves in the shadows'. This comment shortly after the mechanical killing of the Mafioso, who carried a valuable case, could be interpreted as a criticism of the shift from a fascist apparatus to mechanics in neo-liberal capitalism. The latter is mirrored by emotionless persecution (of Idrissa and other refugees), humiliation (of Marcel when pushed back by a policeman in his own house) and destruction (see documentary on eviction of 'The Jungle' as film in the film).
71. The North American and French trailers of *Army of the Shadows* stress 'honor' and the anonymity of outsider work—summarized by the question 'who are

they?' ('qui sont-ils ?')—as key aspects for Melville's protagonists (Melville 1969).
72. Following major media interest and mass protests, Law 2012–1560 was finally ratified in December 2012 in order to protect people with humanitarian interests from persecution ('pour en exclure les actions humanitaires et désintéressées'; Legifrance 2015).
73. The media debate enhanced by *Days of Glory* culminated in President Jacques Chirac adjusting their pensions to those of French veterans.
74. Article L622-4 lists as activities excluded from punishment 'des prestations de restauration, d'hébergement ou de soins médicaux destinées à assurer des conditions de vie dignes et décentes à l'étranger', whereas the pre-2012 wording of article L622-1 remains the same.
75. Not by coincidence, the policeman in the boat scene backs down only when Monet asks him if he wants to question his authority.
76. For example, when Marcel returns from Calais, he tells Idrissa that his grandfather wanted him to obey ('notamment obéir').
77. At the beginning of the film, Marcel feeds the dog, then Idrissa. He also talks to both of them in a similar way, with Marcel giving orders and the dog and/or boy obeying.
78. Blaut further elaborates on European self-portrayals in colonial discourse: 'The world has a permanent geographical centre and permanent periphery: an Inside and an Outside. Inside leads, Outside lags. Inside innovates, Outside imitates' (1993: 1).
79. Samba does not dance; he usually keeps his cloths on, and he tends to control his sexual instincts in particular in the context of Walid's obsession with women.
80. Denis's in many respects outstanding postcolonial film remains shaped by a female gaze that highlights black African Protée as a sex object, e.g., in the shower scene, in which Isaach De Bankolé presents his naked body to the viewer. Similarly, Uribe presents his protagonist Ombasi (Emilio Buale) as a (half-)naked sex object, not only in Dori's dreams but in numerous other situations in the water and on the beach.

Filmography

Akın, Fatih (1995): *Sensin... You're the One!/Sensin – Du bist es!* Germany: Wüste Filmproduktion.
Akın, Fatih (1996): *Weed/Getürkt*. Germany: Wüste Filmproduktion.
Akın, Fatih (1998): *Short Sharp Shock/kurz und schmerzlos*. Germany: Wüste Filmproduktion.
Akın, Fatih (1999): *In July/Im Juli*. Germany: Wüste Filmproduktion.
Akın, Fatih (2002): *Solino*. Germany: Wüste Filmproduktion.
Akın, Fatih (2003): *Head-On/Gegen die Wand*. Germany: Wüste Filmproduktion.
Akın, Fatih (2005): *Crossing the Bridge – The Sound of Istanbul*. Germany: corazón international/intervista digital media/NDR.
Akın, Fatih (2007): *The Edge of Heaven/Auf der anderen Seite*. Germany/Turkey: Anka Film.
Akın, Fatih (2009): *Soul Kitchen*. Germany, France, Italy: CNC, Corazón International, Dorje Film.

116 *Migrants in Europe*

Akın, Fatih (2014): *The Cut*. Germany et al.: Bombero International, Pyramide Productions, Corazón International.
Aladag, Züli (2002): *Elefantenherz*. Germany: Westdeutscher Rundfunk.
Aladag, Züli (2006): *Rage/Wut*. Germany: Colonia Media Filmproduktions GmbH.
Alakus, Buket (2001): *Anam*. Germany: Wüste Filmproduktion.
Armendáriz, Montxo (1990): *Letters from Alou/Las cartas de Alou*. Spain: Elías Querejeta Producciones Cinematográficas S.L., Televisión Española (TVE).
Arslan, Thomas (1997): *Geschwister – Kardesler*. Germany: ZDF/Trans-Film.
Arslan, Thomas (1998): *Dealer*. Germany: Trans-Film.
Arslan, Thomas (2001): *A Fine Day/Der schöne Tag*. Germany: Pickpocket Filmproduktion/zero-film/ZDF.
Ataman, Kutlug (2005): *2 Girls/Zwei Mädchen aus Istanbul* (iki genç kız). Turkey: mitosfilm.
Ataman, Kutlug (2014): *Kuzu*. Turkey, Germany: Institute for the Readjustment of Clocks, Detailfilm.
Baser, Tefvik (1985): *40 Square Meters of Germany/40 Quadratmeter Deutschland*. Germany: Letterbox Filmproduktion.
Baser, Tefvik (1988): *Farewell to a False Paradise/Abschied vom falschen Paradies*. Germany: Letterbox Filmproduktion/ZDF.
Becker, Lars (2000): *Kanak Attack*. Germany: Becker & Häberle Filmproduktion GmbH.
Bochert, Marc-Andreas (2015): *Krüger aus Almanya*. Germany: Provobis.
Bohm, Hark (1976): *North Sea Is Dead Sea/Nordsee ist Mordsee*. German Federal Republic: Hamburger Kino-Kompanie.
Bohm, Hark (1988): *Yasemin*. Germany: Hamburger Kino Kompanie/ZDF.
Boll, Uwe (2010): *Max Schmeling*. Germany, Croatia: Boll Kino Beteiligungs GmbH & Co. KG, Herold Productions, Jadran Film.
Bollaín, Iciar (1999): *Flowers from Another World/Flores de otro mundo*. Spain: Producciones La Iguana.
Bouchareb, Rachid (2006): *Days of Glory/Indigènes*. Algeria, France: Tessalit Productions, Kiss Films, France 2 Cinéma.
Boyle, Danny (2000): *The Beach*. US, UK: Figment Films.
Bresson, Robert (1959): *Pickpocket*. France: Agnès Delahaie Productions.
Bresson, Robert (1969): *Mouchette*. France: Argos-Films, Parc Film.
Bresson, Robert (1977): *The Devil, Probably/Le diable probablement*. France/.
Bresson, Robert (1983): *Money/L'argent*. France/Switzerland: Marion's Films, France 3, EOS Films.
Bresson, Robert (1983): *Money/L'argent*. France/Switzerland: Marion's Films/France 3/EOS Films.
Buck, Detlev (2006): *Tough Enough/Knallhart*. Germany: Boje Buck Produktion.
Carné, Marcel (1945): *Children of Paradise/Les Enfants du Paradis*. France: Société Nouvelle Pathé Cinéma.
Çetin, Sinan (1993): *Berlin in Berlin*. Turkey/Germany: Plato Film Production.
Chadha, Gurinder (2002): *Bend It Like Beckham*. Great Britain: Kintop Pictures.
Chadha, Gurindher (1989): *I'm British but...* UK: Channel Four.
Chadha, Gurindher (1990): *Nice Arrangement*. UK: Umbi Films.
Chadha, Gurindher (1991): *Acting Our Age*. UK: Umbi Films.
Chadha, Gurindher (2002): *Bend It Like Beckham*. UK, Germany, US: Kintop Pictures.
Chadha, Gurindher (2004): *Bride and Prejudice*. UK, US: Pathé Pictures International.

Migrants in Europe 117

Chadha, Gurindher (2008): *Angus, Thongs and Perfect Snogging*. US: Goldcrest Pictures.
Chadha, Gurindher (2010): *It's a Wonderful Afterlife*. US: Goldcrest Pictures.
Chavarrí, Antonio (1996): *Susanna*. Spain: Oberón Cinematográfica.
Danquart, Pepe (1993): *Fare Dodger/Schwarzfahrer*. Germany: Trans-Film.
Denis, Claire (1988): *Chocolat*. France, West Germany, Cameroon: Caroline Productions, Cerito Films, Cinémanuel.
Denis, Claire (2008): *35 Shots of Rum/35 rhums*. France, Germany: Soudaine Compagnie, Pandora Filmproduktion.
Deus, Catharina (2005): *Die Boxerin*. Germany: Credofilm.
Dörrie, Doris (1992): *Happy Birthday, Türke*. Germany: Cobra Film GmbH.
Echevarría, Nicolás (1990): *Cabeza de Vaca*. Mexico, Spain, US, UK: Producciones Iguana.
Echevarría, Nicolás (1991): *Cabeza de Vaca*. Mexico, Spain, US, UK: Producciones Iguana.
Fassbinder, Rainer Werner (1969): *Katzelmacher*. Germany: Antitheater-X-Film.
Fassbinder, Rainer Werner (1974): *Fear Eats the Soul/Angst essen Seele auf*. Germany: Filmverlag der Autoren.
Fassbinder, Rainer Werner (1979): *The Marriage of Maria Braun/Die Ehe der Maria Braun*. German Federal Republic: Albatros-Filmproduktion/Trio-Film/Westdeutscher Rundfunk
Faucon, Philippe (2000): *Samia*. France: Canal+.
Gardela, Isabel (2000): *Two for Tea/Tomándote*. Spain: Kilimanjaro Productions.
Ghadarkhah, Mansour (1992): *Auge um Auge*. Germany: Roya Film.
Gören, Şerif (1988): *Polizei*. Turkey/Germany: Penta Films.
Goupil, Romain (2010): *Hands Up/Les mains en l'air*. France: Les Films du Losange, France 3 Cinéma, France Télévision.
Gutiérrez Aragón, Manuel (1997): *Things I Left in Havana/Cosas que dejé en la Habana*. Spain: Alta Films, Argentina Video Home, Primer Plano Film Group.
Gutiérrez, Chus (2002): *Poniente*. Spain: Amboto Audiovisual.
Haneke, Michael (2000): *Code Unknown/Code inconnu*. France, Germany: Canal+, Bavaria Film.
Holtz, Stefan (2006): *Kiss Me Kismet/Meine verrückte türkische Hochzeit*. Germany: Rat Pack Filmproduktion GmbH.
Hüseyin, Metin (2002): *Anita and Me*. UK: BBC.
Iglesias, Carlos (2006): *Un franco, 14 pesetas*. Spain: Adivina Producciones.
Jamal, Ahmed A. (1983): *Majdhar*. UK: Retake Film.
Kahane, Peter (2015): *The Blind Flyers/Blindgänger*. Germany: Polyphon.
Kassovitz, Mathieu (1995): *La Haine/La haine*. France: Productions Lazennec/Sept Cinéma/Studio Canal+.
Kaurismäki, Aki (1986): *Shadows in Paradise/Varjoja paratiisissa*. Finland: Villealfa Filmproduction.
Kaurismäki, Aki (1988): *Ariel*. Finland: Finnish Film Foundation, Villealfa Filmproduction.
Kaurismäki, Aki (1990): *The Match Factory Girl/Tulitikkutehtaan tyttö*. Finland, Sweden: Esselte Video, Finnkino, Svenska Filminstitutet.
Kaurismäki, Aki (1996): *Drifting Clouds/Kauas pilvet karkaavat*. Finland: Sputnik.
Kaurismäki, Aki (2002): *The Man without a Past/Mies vailla menneisyyttä*. Finland, Germany, France: Bavaria Film, Pandora Filmproduktion, Pyramide Productions.

118 Migrants in Europe

Kaurismäki, Aki (2006): *Lights in the Dusk/Laitakaupungin valot*. Finland, Germany, France: Sputnik.
Kaurismäki, Aki (2011): *Le Havre*. Finland, France, Germany: Sputnik, Pyramide Productions, Pandora Filmproduktion.
León de Aranoa, Fernando (2005): *Princesses/Princesas*. Spain: Reposado Producciones.
Lioret, Philippe (2009): *Welcome*. France: Nord-Ouest Productions, Studio 37, France 3 Cinéma.
Loach, Ken (2004): *Ae Fond Kiss*. Great Britain/Belgium/Germany/Italy/Spain: Bianca Film.
Luna, Bigas (1992): *Jamon Jamon/Jamón, jamón*. Spain: Lolafilms, Ovídeo.
Melville, Jean-Pierre (1962): *Doulos: The Finger Man/Le Doulos*. France: Compagnia Cinematografica Champion, Rome Paris Films.
Melville, Jean-Pierre (1967): *The Samurai/Le Samouraï*. France, Italy: Compagnie Industrielle et Commerciale Cinématographique (CICC), Fida Cinematografica.
Melville, Jean-Pierre (1969): *The Army of Shadows/L'armée des ombres*. France, Italy: Les Films Corona, Fono Roma.
Melville, Jean-Pierre (1969): *The Red Circle/Le cercle rouge*. France: Euro International Film, Les Films Corona, Selenia Cinematografica.
Monzón, Daniel (2014): *El Niño*. Spain: Telecinco Cinema, Ikiru Films, Vaca Films.
Naber, Johannes (2010): *The Albanian/Der Albaner*. Germany, Albania: ARTE.
Nakache, Olivier; Eric Toledano (2014): *Samba*. France: Quad Productions, Ten Films, Gaumont.
Nava, Gregory (1995): *My Family*. US: American Playhouse, American Zoetrope, Majestic Films International.
Nava, Gregory (2006): *Bordertown*. US: Möbius Entertainment, El Norte Productions, Nuyorican Productions.
O'Donnel, Damien (1999): *East Is East*. Great Britain: FilmFour.
Panahi, Jafar (2006): *Offside*. Iran: Jafar Panahi Film Productions.
Prasad, Udayan (1997): *My Son the Fanatic*. UK, France: Arts Council of England.
Pérez Rosado, Pedro (2005): *Salt Water/Agua con sal*. Spain: Wanda Visión.
Renoir, Jean (1936): *The Crime of Monsieur Lange/Le crime de Monsieur Lange*. France: Films Obéron.
Renoir, Jean et al. (1936): *Life Belongs to Us/La vie est à nous*. France: Collective Films, Parti Communiste Français.
Samdereli, Yasmin (2011): *Almanya – Willkommen in Deutschland*. Germany: Roxy Film, Infa Film.
Sanders-Brahms, Helma (1976): *Shirin's Wedding/Shirins Hochzeit*. German Federal Republic: Westdeutscher Rundfunk.
Saura, Carlos (1996): *Taxi*. Spain: Canal+.
Scorcese, Martin (1973): *Mean Streets*. US: Warner Bros./Taplin-Perry-Scorsese Productions.
Seidl, Ulrich (2007): *Import/Export*. Austria, France, Germany: Ulrich Seidl Filmproduktion GmbH, Pronto Film, Société Parisienne de Production.
Smith, Peter K. (1974): *A Private Enterprise*. UK: BFI.
Tasma, Alain (2010): *Fracture*. France: ACSE, CNC.
Tykwer, Tom (1998): *Run Lola Run/Lola Rennt*. United Germany: X Filme Creative Pool/Westdeutscher Rundfunk/ARTE/Filmstiftung NRW/FilmFernsehFonds Bayern/ Bundesministerium des Innern/Filmförderung in Berlin-Brandenburg.
Uribe, Imanol (1996): *Bwana*. Spain: Aurum.

Wenders, Wim (1987): *Wings of Desire/Der Himmel über Berlin*. German Federal Republic/France: Road Movies Filmproduktion GmbH/Argos-Films/ Westdeutscher Rundfunk.
Zemeckis, Robert (2000): *Cast Away*. US: Twentieth Century Fox, DreamWorks.
Zeïtoun, Ariel (2001): *Yamakasi – Les samouraïs des temps modernes*. France: Leeloo Productions, TF1 Films Productions, Canal+, Digital City.
Zeïtoun, Ariel (2001): *Yamakasi – Les samouraïs des temps modernes*. France: Leeloo Productions/TF1 Films Productions/Canal+/Digital City.
Zwick, Joel (2002): *My Big Fat Greek Wedding*. US, Canada: Gold Circle Films.
Zübert, Christian (2011): *Three Quarter Moon/Dreiviertelmond*. Germany: BR, ARTE.

Bibliography

Akın, Fatih (2009): 'Offener Brief', in: *Migazin*, December 4, 2009 (http://www.migazin.de/ 2009/12/04/fatih-akın-boykottiert-filmpremiere-in-der-schweiz) (last accessed July 28, 2015).
Algeo, Katie (2007): 'Teaching Cultural Geography with "Bend It Like Beckham"', in: *The Journal of Geography* 106/3, pp. 133–143.
Anderson, Benedict (1991[1983]): *Imagined Communities*. London: Verso Books.
Antor, Heinz (2006): 'Multikulturalismus, Interkulturalität und Transkulturalität. Perspektiven für interdisziplinäre Forschung und Lehre', in: Antor, Heinz (ed.): *Inter- und Transkulturelle Studien: Theoretische Grundlagen und interdisziplinäre Praxis*. Heidelberg: Winter, pp. 25–39.
Antor, Heinz (2010): 'From Postcolonialism and Interculturalism to the Ethics of Transculturalism in the Age of Globalization', in: Antor, Heinz; Matthias Merkl; Klaus Stierstorfer; Laurenz Volkmann (eds.): *From Interculturalism to Transculturalism: Mediating Encounters in Cosmopolitan Contexts*. Heidelberg: Universitätsverlag Winter, pp. 1–14.
Appiah, Kwame Anthony (2007): *Cosmopolitanism: Ethics in a World of Strangers*. New York: Norton.
Aridj, Jamila (2008): 'Shoah: Sarkozy veut raviver le devoir de mémoire', in: *Le Point.fr*, February 14, 2008 (http://www.lepoint.fr/actualites-politique/2008-02-14/shoah-sarkozy-veut-raviver-le-devoir-de-memoire/917/0/223440) (last accessed July 27, 2015).
Bagh, Peter (2011): 'Common People', in: *Film Comment* 47/5, pp. 38–42.
Ballesteros, Isolina (2015): *Immigration Cinema in the New Europe*. Chicago: University of Chicago Press.
Bend It Networks (2014): *Executive Summary: 'Bend It Like Beckham'. The Stage Show* (http://tonyhussain.co.uk/wp-content/uploads/2014/11/BEND-IT-STAGE_Tax.-Executive-Summary-copy.pdf) (last accessed July 27, 2015).
Benessaieh, Afef (2010): 'Multiculturalism, Interculturality, Transculturality', in: Benessaieh, Afef (ed.): *Transcultural Americas/Amériques transculturelles*. Ottawa: Ottawa University Press, pp. 11–38.
Benessaieh, Afef (2012): 'Après Bouchard-Taylor: multiculturalisme, interculturalisme et transculturalisme au Québec', in: Imbert, Patrick; Brigitte Fontille (eds.): *Trans, multi, interculturalité, trans, multi, interdisciplinarité*. Québec: Laval, 2012, pp. 81–98.
Berghahn, Daniela (2013): *Far-Flung Families in Film. The Diasporic Family in Contemporary European Cinema*. Edingburgh: Edingburgh University Press.

Bhabha, Homi (1994): *The Location of Culture*. New York: Routledge.
Bianchini, Franco (2006): 'European Urban Mindscapes: Concepts, Cultural Representations and Policy Applications', in: Weiss-Sussex, Godela; Franco Bianchini (eds.): *Urban Mindscapes of Europe*. Amsterdam, New York: Rodopi, pp. 13–31.
Blaut, James M. (1993): *The Coloniser's Model of the World: Geographical Diffusionism and Eurocentric History*. New York: The Guilford Press.
Bourdieu, Pierre (1987): *Die feinen Unterschiede. Kritik der gesellschaftlichen Urteilskraft*. Translated by Bernd Schwibs and Achim Russer. Frankfurt/Main: Suhrkamp.
Bourdieu, Pierre (1998): *Praktische Vernunft: Zur Theorie des Handelns*. Translated by Hella Beister. Frankfurt/Main: Suhrkamp.
Brake, Michael (2013[1980]): *The Sociology of Youth Culture and Youth Subcultures*. London: Routledge.
Breger, Claudia (2014): 'Configuring Affect: Complex World Making in Fatih Akın's "Auf der anderen Seite" ("The Edge of Heaven")', in: *Cinema Journal* 54/1, pp. 65–87.
Bundespräsidialamt (2010): 'Ordensverleihungen zum Tag der deutschen Einheit', in: *Der Bundespräsident* (http://www.bundespraesident.de/SharedDocs/Berichte/DE/Reisen-und-Termine/1010/101004-deutsche-einheit-ordensverleihungen.html) (last accessed July 28, 2015).
Burkhart, Diana (2010): 'The Disposable Immigrant: The Aesthetics of Waste in "Las cartas de Alou"', in: *Journal of Spanish Cultural Studies* 6/11, pp. 153–165.
Campra, Rosalba (1991): 'Descubrimiento de América e invención del "otro"', in: *Revista de la Universidad de Puerto Rico* 5/17, pp. 77–88.
Casier, Marlies (2009): 'Contesting the "Truth" of Turkey's Human Rights Situation: State-Association Interactions in and outside the Southeast', in: *European Journal of Turkish Studies* 10 2009 (https://ejts.revues.org/4190#ftn16) (last accessed July 28, 2015).
Cha, Kyung-Ho (2010): 'Erzählte Globalisierung. Gabentausch und Identitätskonstruktion in Fatih Akın's "Auf der Anderen Seite"', in: Ezl, Özkan (ed.): *Kultur als Ereignis: Fatih Akıns Film Auf der anderen Seite als transkulturelle Narration*. Bielefeld: transcript, pp. 135–150.
Chan, Winnie (2005): 'Curry on the Divide in Rudyard Kipling's "Kim" and Gurinder Chadha's "Bend It Like Beckham"', in: *Ariel*, July 1, 2005, pp. 1–23.
Chaudhury, Parama (2003): 'Bend It Like Beckham', in: *Film Monthly* (http://www.filmmonthly.com/ video_and_dvd/bend_it_like_beckham.html) (last accessed February 12, 2015).
Dear, Michael J. (2000): *The Postmodern Urban Condition*. Oxford: Blackwell.
Delanoy, Werner (2006): 'Transculturalism and (Inter-) Cultural Learning in the EFL classroom', in: Delanoy, Werner; Laurenz Volkmann (eds.): *Cultural Studies in the EFL Classroom*. Heidelberg: Winter, pp. 233–48.
Der Spiegel (1973): 'Die Türken kommen – rette sich wer kann', in: *Der Spiegel*, July 30, 1973 (http://www.spiegel.de/spiegel/print/d-41955159.html) (last accessed October 8, 2014).
Deveny, Thomas G. (2012): *Migration in Contemporary Hispanic Cinema*. Plymouth: Scarecrow.
ECHR (2009): 'The European Court of Human Rights, Country Fact Sheets, 1959–2009' (http://www.echr.coe.int/NR/rdonlyres/59F27500-FD1B-4FC5-8F3F-F289B4A03008/ 0/Annual_Report_2007.pdf) (last accessed July 28, 2015).

Elley, Derek (2002): 'Bend It Like Beckham', in: *Variety* 386/7, p. 32.
Elsaesser, Thomas (2012): 'European Cinema and the Postheroic Narrative: Jean-Luc Nancy, Claire Denis, and *Beau Travail*', in: *New Literary History* 43, pp. 703–725.
Empresa Municipal Promoción de Madrid (2008): *esMadrid.com* (http://www.esmadrid.com/en/portal.do;jsessionid=DF9278784DAD9C5B571A08D827819E21. APP2) (last accessed August 10, 2008).
Epstein, Mikhail (2009): 'Transculture. A Broad Way between Globalisation and Multiculturalism', in: *American Journal of Economics and Sociology* 68/1, pp. 327–351.
Ezl, Özkan (ed.): *Kultur als Ereignis: Fatih Akıns Film Auf der anderen Seite als transkulturelle Narration*. Bielefeld: transcript.
Fevry, Sébastien (2014): 'Immigration and Memory in Popular Contemporary French Cinema: The Film as "Lieu d'entre-mémoire"', in: *Revista de Estudios Globales y Arte Contemporáneo* 2/1, pp. 239–263.
FILMDIENST (1989):'Abschied vom falschen Paradies', in: *FILMDIENST* 19, p. 271.
Fischer, Paul (2003): 'Gurinder Chadha - Success at Last as "Beckham" Finally Hits US', in: *Film Monthly* from *03/13/2003* (http://www.filmmonthly.com/Profiles/Articles/GChadha/ GChadha.html) (last accessed February 4, 2015).
Flesler, Daniela (2004): 'New Racism, Intercultural Romance, and the Immigration Question in Contemporary Spanish Cinema', in: *Studies in Hispanic Cinemas* 1/2, pp. 103–118.
Fouz-Hernández, Santiago (2005): 'Javier Bardem: Body and Space', in: Everett, Wendy; Axel Goodbody (eds.): *Revisiting Space. Space and Place in European Cinema*. Oxford: Peter Lang, pp. 187–207.
Fraser, Benjamin (2006): 'The Space in Film and the Film in Space: Madrid's Retiro Park and Carlos Saura's "Taxi"', in: *Studies in Hispanic Cinemas* 3/1, pp. 15–32.
García Ballesteros, Aurora; Beatriz Cristina Jiménez Blasco (2012): 'Immigrant Business Strategies in the City of Madrid', in: *International Journal of Humanities and Social Science* 2/20, pp. 86–97.
Gilroy, Paul (1999): 'Hatred of the Partially Familiar', in: *Times Higher*, June 25, 1999 (https://www.timeshighereducation.co.uk/features/hatred-of-the-partially-familiar/ 146962. article) (last accessed July 28, 2015).
Gilroy, Paul (2004): *After Empire: Melancholia or Convivial Culture?* London: Routledge.
Gilroy, Paul (2006): 'Colonial Crimes and Convivial Cultures', in: *Rethinking Nordic Colonialism Exhibition. Keynote Speech* (http://www.rethinking-nordic-colonialism.org/files/pdf/ ACT2/ESSAYS/Gilroy.pdf) (last accessed July 28, 2015).
Göktürk, Deniz (2000): 'Migration und Kino – Subnationale Mitleidskultur oder transnationale Rollenspiele?', in: Chiellino; Carmine (ed.): *Interkulturelle Literatur in Deutschland: Ein Handbuch*. Stuttgart: Metzler, pp. 329–347.
Göktürk, Deniz (2002): 'Beyond Paternalism: Turkish German Traffic in Cinema', in: Bergfelder, Tim; Erica Carter; Deniz Göktürk (eds.): *The German Cinema Book*. London: BFI, pp. 248–256.
Göktürk, Deniz (2010): 'Mobilität und Stillstand im Weltkino digital', in: Ezl, Özkan (ed.): *Kultur als Ereignis: Fatih Akıns Film Auf der anderen Seite als transkulturelle Narration*. Bielefeld: transcript, pp. 15–46.

Görling, Reinhold (2004): 'Emplacements', in: Borsò, Vittoria; Reinhold Görling (eds.): *Kulturelle Topographien*. Stuttgart, Weimar: Metzler, pp. 43–63.

Görling, Reinhold (2007): 'Topology of Borders in Turkish-German Cinema', in: Schimanski, Johan; Stephen Wolfe (eds.): *Border Poetics De-limited*. Saarbrücken: Wehrhahn, pp. 149–162.

Gómez Jiménez, María Luisa (2014): 'Diversity and the Law, Everybody Is Equal before the Law?', in: Sara Ashencaen Crabtree (ed.): *Diversity and the Processes of Marginalisation: A European perspective*. London: Whiting & Birch, pp. 1–13.

Gramling, David (2010): 'On the Other Side of Monolingualism: Fatih Akın's Linguistic Turn(s)', in: *German Quarterly* 83/3, pp. 353–372.

Greuling, Matthias (2014): 'Fatih Akın über "The Cut"', in: *Wiener Zeitung*, September 3, 2014 (https://www.youtube.com/watch?v=5XuABgQIVNs) (last accessed July 28, 2015).

Grice, Andrew (2015): 'Landlords Renting Properties to Illegal Immigrants to Face up to Five Years in Prison', in: *The Independent*, August 3, 2015 (http://www.independent.co.uk/ news/uk/politics/landlords-renting-properties-to-illegal-immigrants-to-face-up-to-five-years-in-prison-10433897.html) (last accessed August 4, 2015).

Gueneli, Berna (2014): 'The Sound of Fatih Akın's Cinema: Polyphony and the Aesthetics of Heterogeneity in "The Edge of Heaven"', in: *German Studies Review* 37/2, pp. 337–356.

Hagemann, Marie (1993): *Schwarzer, Wolf, Skin*. Stuttgart: Thienemann Verlag.

Hall, Stuart (1992): 'The West and the Rest: Discourse and Power', in: Hall, Stuart; Bram Gieben (eds.): *Formations of Modernity: Understanding the Modern*. Cambridge: Polity Press, pp. 275–320.

Hasselbach, Ingo (1993): *Die Abrechnung. Ein Neonazi steigt aus*. Berlin: Aufbau Verlag.

Hoberman, J. (2011): 'Dream Act: Town Rallies to Help an Immigrant in Utopian *Le Havre*', in: *VillageVoice*, October 19, 2011 (http://www.villagevoice.com/2011-10-19/film/dream-act-town-rallies-to-help-an-immigrant-in-utopian-le-havre) (last accessed July 27, 2015).

Hofstede, Geert (2001): *Culture's Consequences*. 2nd edition. London: Sage.

HRW (2014): 'Turkey's Human Rights Rollback', in: *Human Rights Watch*, September 29, 2014 (https://www.hrw.org/report/2014/09/29/turkeys-human-rights-rollback/ recommendations-reform) (last accessed July 28, 2015).

Huber, Christoph (2007): 'Cannes 2007 – Import Export', in: *cinema scope* 31 (http://cinema-scope.com/cinema-scope-magazine/cannes-2007-import-export-ulrich-seidl-austria) (last accessed July 28, 2015).

Huggan, Graham (2006): 'Derailing the "Trans"? Postcolonial Studies and the Negative Effects of Speed', in: Antor, Heinz (ed.): *Inter- und Transkulturelle Studien: Theoretische Grundlagen und interdisziplinäre Praxis*. Heidelberg: Winter, pp. 55–61.

Huxley, Aldous (1932): *Brave New World*. London: Chatto & Windus.

Ide, Wendy (2008): 'The Edge of Heaven; New Film Reviews', in: *The Times*, February 23, 2008, p. 9.

INE (Instituto Nacional de Estadísticas) (2013): *Madrid. Estadística del Padrón Continuo a 1 de enero de 2013. Datos a nivel nacional, comunidad autónoma y provincia* (http://www.ine.es/jaxi/tabla.do?path=/t20/e245/p04/a2013/l0/&file=00028004.px&type=pcaxis&L=0) (last accessed September 5, 2015).

INE (Instituto Nacional de Estadísticas) (2014): *Madrid. Estadística del Padrón Continuo. Datos provisionales a 1 de enero de 2014* (http://www.ine.es/jaxi/menu.do?type=pcaxis&path=/t20/e245/p04/provi&file=pcaxis) (last accessed September 5, 2015).
Invest in Madrid (2014): *Business Location* (http://www.investinmadrid.com/index.php/business-location-madrid/unique-selling-proposition) (last accessed December 19, 2014).
Isenberg, Noah (2011): 'Fatih Akın's Cinema of Intersections', in: *Film Quarterly* 64/4, pp. 53–61.
Jones, Stan (2003): 'Turkish–German Cinema Today: A Case Study of Fatih Akın's "kurz und schmerzlos" and "Im Juli"', in: Rings, Guido; Rikki Morgan-Tamosunas (eds.): *European Cinema Inside Out. Images of the Self and the Other in Postcolonial European Film*. Heidelberg: Winter, pp. 75–91.
Kaya, Ayhan (2007): 'German-Turkish Transnational Space: A Separate Space of Their Own', in: *German Studies Review* XXX/3, pp. 483–502.
Kessel, Joseph (1943): *Army of the Shadows*. New York: Alfred A. Knopf.
Lederle, Josef (2004): 'Gegen die Wand', in: FILMDIENST 57/5, pp. 28–29.
Legifrance (2015): 'Article L622-1', in: *Legifrance.gouv.fr* (http://www.legifrance.gouv.fr/affichCode.do;jsessionid=0A2E238E6C958A2C3A9FE3F10B36714E.tpdila21v_3?idSectionTA=LEGISCTA000006147789&cidTexte=LEGITEXT000006070158&dateTexte=20150601) (last accessed July 27, 2015).
Lemercier, Fabien (2009): 'Kids Living like Domestic Animals', in: *Cineuropa*, September 10, 2009 (http://www.cineuropa.org/ff.aspx?t=ffocusinterview&l=en&tid=2013&did=112474) (last accessed July 27, 2015).
Lim, Dennis (2011): 'Home Theatre; a Second Look', in: *Los Angeles Times*, October 16, 2011, p. D.6.
Löser, Claus (2008): 'Berlin am Bosporus. Spielarten und Hintergründe des deutsch-türkischen Kinos', in: *FILMDIENST* 58/5 (http://www.filmdienst.de) (last accessed October 8, 2014).
Madrid Destino (2014): *¡Madrid!* (http://www.esmadrid.com/en/) (last accessed December 19, 2014).
Malik, Sarita (1996): 'Beyond the "Cinema of Duty"? The Pleasures of Hybridity: Black British Film of the 1980s and 1990s', in: Andrew Higson (ed.): *Dissolving Views. Key Writings on British Cinema*. London: Cassell, pp. 202–215.
Malik, Sarita (2002): 'Money, Mcpherson and Mindset: the Competing Cultural and Commercial Demands on Black and Asian British Films in the 1990s', in: *Journal of Popular British Cinema* 5, pp. 90–103.
Marie, Anne (2009): 'Little Bob – Interview – October 11, 2009', in: *rockinterviews.com* (http://www.rock-interviews.com/pageart.php?page=artistes/2009/Little-Bob2&lang=eng&id=32) (last accessed July 27, 2015).
Massumi, Brian (2002): *Parables for the Virtual*. Durham: Duke UP.
Mennel, Barbara (2009): 'Criss-Crossing in Global Space and Time: Fatih Akın's "The Edge of Heaven"', in: *Transit* 5/1, pp. 1–27.
Mennel, Barbara (2010): 'The Politics of Space in the Cinema of Migration', in: *GFL* 3 (http://gfl-journal.com), pp. 39–55.
Meza, Ed (2008): 'Lolas Look to "Heaven" at German Film Kudos', in: *Daily Variety Gotham*, April 28, 2008, p. 9.
Mishra, Pankaj (2014): 'The Western Model is Broken', in: *The Guardian*, October 14, 2014 (http://www.theguardian.com/world/2014/oct/14/-sp-western-model-broken-pankaj-mishra) (last accessed July 27, 2015).

Moses, Dirk; Michael Rothberg (2014): 'A Dialogue on the Ethics and Politics of Transcultural Memory', in: Bond, Lucy et al. (eds.): *The Transcultural Turn: Interrogating Memory Between and Beyond Borders*. Berlin: De Gruyter, pp. 29–38.

Nacify, Hamid (2001): *An Accented Cinema. Exilic and Diasporic Filmmaking*. Princeton: Princeton University Press.

Naiboğlu, Gözde (2010): '"Sameness" in Disguise of "Difference"? Gender and National Identity in Fatih Akın's "Gegen die Wand" and "Auf der anderen Seite"', in: *GFL* 3, pp. 74–98.

Observatorio de la Inmigración Marroquí en España' (2007): *Extranjeros en la comunidad de Madrid, Principales nacionalidades. Evolución 1996–2006* (http://www.uam.es/ otroscentros/TEIM/Observainmigra/obsInmigra_inicio.htm) (last accessed August 10, 2012).

Observatorio de las Migraciones y de la Convivencia Intercultural de la Ciudad de Madrid (2005): *Madrid, Inmigración y diversidad: primera explotación estadística. Julio 2005*. Madrid: Observatorio (Madrid Convive 2).

Orwell, George (1949): *1984*. London: Secker & Warburg.

Özdoğan, Selim (2005): *The Blacksmith's Daughter/Die Tochter des Schmieds*. Berlin: Aufbau Taschenbuch Verlag.

Palomo, Miguel Ángel (2015): 'Mala – entretenida – interesante – buena. Las películas', in: *El País*, February 2, 2015, p. 54.

Phillips, Richard (2010): 'Welcome from France: A Compassionate Exposure of Anti-Immigrant Measures', in: *World Socialist Web Site* 17/04/2010 (https://www.wsws.org/ en/articles/2010/04/welc-a17.html (last accessed July 27, 2015).

Quandt, James (2011): 'Any Port in a Storm', in: *ArtForum* 11, pp. 75–76.

Rascaroli, Laura (2013): 'Becoming-Minor in a Sustainable Europe: The Contemporary European Art Film and Aki Kaurismäki's Le Havre', in: *Screen* 54/3, pp. 323–340.

Raschke, Jessica (2004): 'Juggling Cultures in *Bend It Like Beckham*', in: *Australian Screen Education* from 01/01/2004, pp. 123–126.

Rendi, Giovanella (2006): 'Kanaka sprak? German-Turkish Women Filmmakers', in: *GFL* 3 (http://gfl-journal.com), pp. 78–93.

Rings, Guido (2000): 'Selbst- und Fremdbetrachtungen bei Fassbinder', in: Brady, Martin; Helen Hughes (eds.): *Deutschland im Spiegel seiner Filme*. London: CILT 2000, pp. 52–80.

Rings, Guido (2005): *Eroberte Eroberer. Darstellungen der Konquista im neueren spanischen und lateinamerikanischen Raum*. Madrid, Frankfurt: Iberoamericana/ Vervuert.

Rings, Guido (2008): 'Blurring or Shifting Boundaries? Concepts of Culture in Turkish–German Migrant Cinema', in: *GFL* 1/8 (www.gfl-journal.com), pp. 6–38.

Ritzer, George (2011): *The McDonaldization of Society*. 6th edition. London: Sage Publications.

Romney, Jonathan (1997): 'The Kaurismäki Effect', in: *Sight and Sound* 7/6, p. 13.

Sáez-González, Jesús Miguel (2012): 'Críticas de Cine/Film Reviews. Enero –Marzo, 2012', in: *Revista de Comunicación Vivat Academia* XIV/118, pp. 122–144.

Said, Edward (1995[1978]): *Orientalism. Western Conceptions of the Orient*. London: Penguin.

Sandhu, Sharon (2005): *Are We Bending It Like Beckham? Diasporic Second-Generation South Asian Canadian Women in Sport*. Ann Arbor: Proquest (MA thesis from York University, Toronto).

Santaolalla, Isabel (2005): *Los "Otros". Etnicidad y "raza" en el cine español contemporáneo*. Zaragoza: Prensas universitarias de Zaragoza.
Santaolalla, Isabel (2007): 'Inmigración, "Raza", y género en el cine español actual', in: Herrera, Javier; Cristina Martínez-Carazo (eds.): *Hispanismo y Cine*. Madrid, Frankfurt/Main: Iberoamericana/Vervuert, pp. 436–476.
Schachtner, Christina (2015): 'Transculturality in the Internet: Culture Flows and Virtual Publics', in: *Current Sociology Monograph* 63/2, pp. 228–243.
Silicone team (ed./2003): 'Bend It Like Beckham', in: *siliconindia* from May 2003, p. 15.
Silvey, Vivien; Roger Hillman (2010): 'Akın's "Auf der anderen Seite" ("The Edge of Heaven") and the Widening Periphery', in: *GFL* 3/10 (http://gfl-journal.com), pp. 99–116.
Sparks, Ian (2009): 'Drive to Abolish French Law that Makes it Illegal to Help Immigrants Sneak into Britain', in: *MailOnline*, May 1, 2009 (http://www.dailymail.co.uk /news/article-1176247/Drive-abolish-French-law-makes-illegal-help-immigrants-sneak-Britain.html) (last accessed July 27, 2015).
Spivak, Gayatri Chakravorty (1999): 'Can the Subaltern Speak?', in: Spivak, Gayatri Chakravorty (ed.): *A Critique of Postcolonial Reason*. Cambridge, Massachusetts: Harvard University Press, pp. 206–236.
Stewart, Michael (2014): 'Anticipating Home: "The Edge of Heaven" as Melodrama', in: ibid. (ed.): *Melodrama in Contemporary Film and TV*. London: Palgrave, pp. 205–222.
Tageszeitung (2014): 'Das sollten sie sehen', in: *Die Tageszeitung*, November 17, 2014, p. 17.
Taubin, Amy (2011): 'All Movies Great and Small', in: *Film Comment* 47/4, pp. 56–59.
Tezcan, Levent (2010): 'Der Tod diesseits von Kultur – Wie Fatih Akın den großen Kulturdialog umgeht', in: Ezl, Özkan (ed.): *Kultur als Ereignis: Fatih Akıns Film Auf der anderen Seite als transkulturelle Narration*. Bielefeld: transcript, pp. 47–70.
Thomas, Stefan (2007): 'Exklusion und embodiment: Formen sozialen Ausschlusses im modernen Kapitalismus', in: Würmann, Carsten; Martina Schuegraf; Sandra Smykalia; Angela Poppitz (eds.): *Welt. Raum. Körper. Transformationen und Entgrenzungen von Körper und Raum*. Bielefeld: transcript, pp. 37–56.
Urban, Urs (2007): *Der Raum des Anderen und Andere Räume. Zur Topologie des Werkes von Jean Genet*. Würzburg: Königshausen & Neumann.
Vincent, Elise (2012): 'Le "délit de solidarité", outil d'intimidation des bénévoles, va être supprimé', in: *Le Monde* 28/09/2012 (http://www.lemonde.fr/societe/article/2012/09 /28/le-delit-de-solidarite-outil-d-intimidation-des-benevoles-est-supprime_1767173_ 3224.html#) (last accessed July 27, 2015).
Weaver-Hightower, Rebecca (2006): '"Cast Away" and "Survivor": The Surviving Castaway and the Rebirth of Empire', in: *The Journal of Popular Culture* 39/2, pp. 294–317.
Welsch, Wolfgang (1997): 'Transkulturalität. Zur veränderten Verfassung heutiger Kulturen', in: Schneider, Irmel; Christian W. Thomson (eds.): *Hybride Kulturen. Medien – Netze –Künste*. Köln: Wienand, pp. 67–90.
Welsch, Wolfgang (1999): 'Transculturalism – The Puzzling Form of Cultures Today', in: Featherstone, Mike; Scott Lash (eds): *Spaces of Culture: City, Nation, World*. London: Sage, pp. 194–213.

Wilkin, Peter (1996): 'New Myths for the South: Globalization and the Conflict between Private Power and Freedom', in: *Third World Quarterly* 17/2, pp. 227–238.

Wilson, Lana (2009): 'Aki Kaurismäki', in: *Senses of Cinema* (http://sensesofcinema.com/2009/great-directors/aki-kaurismaki/#b14) (last accessed July 27, 2015).

Young, Robert J. C. (1995): *Colonial Desire. Hybridity in Theory, Culture and Race.* London, New York: Routledge.

Zaimoğlu, Feridun (1998): *Koppstoff.* Hamburg, Berlin: Rotbuch Verlag.

Zaimoğlu, Feridun (1999[1995]): *Kanak Sprak. 24 Mißtöne vom Rande der Gesellschaft.* Hamburg, Berlin: Rotbuch.

Zournazi, Mary (2003): 'An Interview with Brian Massumi', in: *International Festival* (http://www.international-festival.org/node/111) (last accessed July 28, 2015).

4 Inspiration from Abroad? Cultural Boundaries in Chicano Cinema

4.1 Preliminary Remarks

So far, this study has identified numerous transcultural identity constructs in contemporary European film that are in line with conceptualizations proposed by Huggan (2006), Antor (2006, 2010) and Benessaieh (2010, 2012), but also a continuity of monocultural patterns of thought. One example is the conservation of ghetto concepts that frame people with migrant backgrounds as criminals with separatist tendencies (see Akın's *Short Sharp Shock* or Aladag's *Rage*). The presentation of assimilation as the best practice that tends to marginalize the cultural heritage of migrants and suppresses cultural difference in favor of western constructs of progress (in Chadha's *Bend It Like Beckham*) and the continuity of ethnocentric patriarchal leitmotifs in most films from Armendariz's *Letters from Alou*, and Kaurismäki's *Le Havre* are more examples. All cases reveal neocolonial continuities even in movies that concentrate on the deconstruction of 'artificial' boundaries, essentialist identity constructs, and racism in a political context shaped by xenophobia, caps on migration, and the protection of traditional borders. This chapter aims to differentiate these findings by placing them into a wider context of global migration and cinematic observations beyond European boundaries.

Migration is a particularly hot topic in the US. Despite all measures to reduce immigration, including the construction of a 2000-mile-long border fence that has been compared to the Berlin Wall, the number of residents with migrant background is on the increase. With nearly forty-five million people (Díaz de León 2011), the Hispanic population forms by far the most significant minority, making the US numerically the third biggest Spanish-speaking country on the American continent, preceded only by Mexico and Colombia. Considering the Mexican roots of the vast majority of the Hispanic diaspora, far higher than average Mexican-American birth rates and ongoing migration to the US, it is no surprise that the migration and diaspora developments remain major themes for American cinema and TV.

Chicano cinema is probably the most visible expression of this media discussion, as the growing number of directors and scriptwriters who focus on Mexican migration to and diaspora life in the US have managed to bring migrant perspectives into numerous Hollywood productions as well as TV, therefore reaching North-American mainstream population on a regular basis. Such a popularity was unthinkable for the producers of the predominantly documentary–style first phase of Chicano cinema, but there is also a potential downside to this success, which includes the danger of assimilating filmic messages to the taste of mainstream audiences.

Gregory Nava's *My Family* and *Bordertown* have been selected as key examples of Chicano cinema, because Nava is one of the most popular Chicano directors, and these films about cultural conflicts of protagonists with Mexican migrant background seem to mark the beginning and the end of his impressive Hollywood career. *My Family* has been highlighted as an excellent example of the cinematic exploration of 'artificial' boundaries that Mexican migrants to the US and their descendants have faced in the past. *Bordertown* outlines the possibilities and limits of one Mexican-American woman in her search for social justice and cultural identity. Also, *Bordertown* is probably the best-known film about the Juárez femicides and, at the same time, the worst in financial terms, despite the leading roles of Jennifer López, Martin Sheen, and Antonio Banderas. In this context, this chapter will address two key questions: 1. To what degree and how exactly does Nava's critical interrogation of Anglo-American and Mexican perspectives contribute to the blurring of traditional boundaries? 2. Where are the limits of this transcultural approach?

4.2 *My Family*, *Bordertown*, and the 'American Dream'

Although Gregory Nava is one of the most established Chicano cinema directors, especially due to *El Norte* (1983), *My Family* (1995), *Selena* (1997), *American Family* (2002–2004), and *Bordertown* (2006), his work remains difficult to categorize. Berg includes him in the 'rebellious, not separatist [...] Second Wave' of Chicano film development, which maintains a critical distance from Hollywood conventions while refusing to adapt to the radical social criticism of films of the first documentary period (2002: 186f.). Raab, however, regards him as a representative of the so-called Third Wave (2009: 177) 'made either within the Hollywood system or, if not, adhering closely to the Hollywood paradigm', which implies that the films 'do not accentuate Chicano oppression or resistance' (Berg 2002: 187).

This study will argue that none of these attempts to categorize Nava's work is ultimately convincing because films like *El Norte* and *Bordertown* are simply too different to be summarized as examples of one style. There is evidence of Nava's development from a socio-critical Chicano director to an acclaimed Hollywood director whose films are aimed more at entertainment of a mass audience. In this context, I argue that the socio-critical *El Norte* could be categorized as an example of Berg's second wave, whereas *My Family* and *Bordertown* follow in many aspects established norms of US melodrama, which allows their classification as part of the so-called third phase.

Together with his wife Ann Thomas, Nava writes the scripts for *El Norte* and *My Family*, but his international breakthrough starts with *My Family*, which generated $11 million on a budget of $5.5 million (see Llano 1995: 22, IMDB 2015). The movie makes additional money through substantial video/DVD sales and rentals, copyright allowance for dissemination on national and international TV, and sales of the film music. All this links *My Family* to a rather small group of late 20th century Chicano success stories, which include the Ritchie Valens biography *La Bamba* (Luis Valdez 1987), Cheech Marin's comedy *Born in East LA* (1987), and Edward James Olmos's *American Me* (1992).

The reasons for such a financial success are still being discussed: The convincing cast of Chicano/Latino actors (Jimmy Smits, Jennifer López) and Mexican actors (Eduardo López Rojas), the melodramatic elaboration of popular themes that were successfully explored in previous blockbusters,[1] as well as Nava's auto-biographical input and his personal fieldwork (West 1995: 26) might have facilitated this success. Probably even more important and at the same time less acknowledged is, however, the transcultural potential of the Sánchez family story, which mirrors key aspects of the 'American Dream' summarized by Ebert as the 'great American story [...] of how our families came to this land and tried to make it better for their children' (1995).

The story is about first-generation Mexican migrants José and María Sánchez who work hard to improve the lives of their six children: Paco, Chucho, Irene, Toni, Memo and Jimmy. They have great success, because at the end of the film most of them have managed to leave the Chicano ghetto: Bill alias 'Memo' works as a successful lawyer in the center of LA; 'Toni' (Antonia), her Anglo-American husband David, Jimmy, and his son Carlitos have all left the house to dream their dreams of a better life. Not only Memo's professional career but Toni's development from nun to emancipated social worker, Jimmy's transformation from embittered rogue to a man who takes his father role seriously, and Irene's decision to become a housewife and mother could all be regarded as examples of a successful pursuit of happiness encouraged by the American Dream. The same applies to their parents' decision to have such a large family and to support all of their children, because ultimately they realize that they 'had a good life'.

All of this is very much in line with the wide spectrum of individual possibilities to pursue happiness in the American Dream. Adams coins this in his classic study *The Epic of America* as 'a dream of a social order in which each man and each woman shall be able to attain to the fullest stature of which they are innately capable, and be recognized by others for what they are, regardless of the fortuitous circumstances of their birth'.[2] Very similarly, Kimmage stresses a material and a spiritual component to the dream that links consumption, property ownership and class mobility to 'a blend of optimism and happiness, alluded to in the Declaration of Independence' (2011: 27). Kimmage also examines in detail in how far the dream has been key for the political rhetoric of most American presidents in the 20th and 21st century, because it has the ability to unite Americans across class and ethnic boundaries behind a particular ideology, which promises infinite possibilities for hard working people. 'The myth of the American Dream is a myth of hard work rewarded' (2011: 36)[3]. Particularly in this respect, *My Family* transgresses ethnic boundaries and facilitates non-Hispanic spectators' identification with the protagonists, above all hard working José and María Sánchez and their favorite son Memo. Retrospectively, the casting of Jennifer López as young María also appears to be a good fit, because López could be regarded as an example of the American Dream come true, although she certainly does not start as a dishwasher on her way to becoming a millionaire. In any case, she joins a strong group of Latino actors that made it to Hollywood, including Esai Morales, Edward James Olmos, and Jimmy Smits, with Morales stressing the importance of the cast as an indicator of Latino agency ('we can tell our own stories', in: Ventocilla 1995).

Bordertown continues the American Dream saga insofar as Jennifer López is now a famous actress, who comes in as the main protagonist, and her role as the passionate *Chicago Sentinel* news reporter Lauren Adrian highlights socio-political opportunities for women in the US. This includes Latino women because Lauren is presented to be of Mexican migrant background, albeit adopted at a young age by an Anglo-American couple. This role has been categorized as a re-edition of 'the tired cliché of the American savior' (Day 2008: 9), a statement that has to be further discussed in the second part of the film analysis. However, it is worth stressing that Lauren blurs traditional boundaries insofar as she critically intervenes against 'international indifference' (García Mainou 2008) and promotes 'alternative forms of social and political membership within Mexico' (Valdes 2010: 60). Also, as one of the most iconic figures of a Latino woman, Jennifer López contributes to the cultural analysis from several points of view: On the one hand, she represents a strong and determined heroine who fights male attempts at marginalization and victimization of women and can therefore represent female agency beyond ethnic boundaries. On the other hand, as eroticized Latino woman, she returns to traditional binaries and patterns of Othering.

Nava indicated the agenda of his work shortly after the premiere of *My Family*, when he highlighted it as a 'movie about an American family', with which people of very different migrant backgrounds are able to identify.[4] He never used the term 'transcultural', and he tended to focus on the importance of his films for the visibility of Latino communities.[5] However, his definition of 'assimilation' as 'a two-way street' that allowed migrants and their descendants to make a 'contribution to this country' indicated a transcultural perspective: 'In the same way that Italian-Americans or Irish-Americans or [...] Swedish-Americans or any other group have disappeared into the melting pot [...] we all preserve to a certain extent our cultures' (Nava, in: Moyer 2002). In this context, Nava tends to regard himself both as Latino community representative and as US American,[6] and he has enhanced this transcultural line of argumentation by stressing the 'universal human' character of his drama *Why Do Fools Fall in Love*, which explored the life and music of Frankie Lymon (Nava, in: Ford 2013).

There is, however, evidence that Nava's interests mirror a cultural hierarchy that might have developed from *My Family* to *Bordertown*. In particular, the film analysis has to explore how problematic it is that *My Family* does not discuss the neoliberal and social-conservative directions of the American Dream, whereas *Bordertown* locates effective agency against neoliberal excess north of the border.

4.3 Transcultural Potential

4.3.1 'Artificial' Boundaries

My Family stresses the importance of overcoming 'artificial' boundaries and portrays the Sánchez family as an example of transcultural practice. When José Sánchez crosses the border between Mexico and the US, because the Mexican Revolution has left his family without resources, 'la frontera norte' is—in the words of the narrator—only an arbitrarily set 'line in the dust'. In East LA, a relative called 'El Californio' opts for a regional identity construct, which is enhanced by his criticism of US policy. All of this discredits the famous and in the last decades vehemently defended frontier between the two states as a political construct set and revised according to the right and might of the strongest, which should not be misinterpreted as a cultural boundary and does fight notions of 'natural' borders.

In this context, a melodramatic climax is reached when US border police force María to board a train back to Mexico. Considering her pregnancy and her US citizenship, her forced deportation is both inhuman and unlawful, and the scene criticizes the injustice of the historic mass deportation of more than 140,000 Hispanic workers and their families after the Great Depression of 1929. In that period little consideration was given to family ties or citizenship, and latino appearance was often enough to trigger deportation.[7] Also, María's return takes several years, and the border crossing is so difficult that it marks Chucho for life. Another artificial boundary appears to be the Los Angeles River that separates the house of El Californio in East LA from the Anglo-American center of LA, to which José and his new family commute to work. Over the years, the city council builds more bridges to improve the transport between these very different parts of the city, but until José's and his wife's death it is largely a one-way traffic for the poorer population with migrant background. Not by coincidence, the film stresses toward the end that—although born in LA—Memo's future parents-in-law had never been on the other side of the river. Their visit to the Sánchez family home is the rare exception to the rule, and the critical incidents that shape the encounter do not allow the spectators to regard it as the beginning of a regular cultural exchange.

The critical interrogation of boundaries increases in *Bordertown*, although in an era of enhanced glocalization with (back then) newly built factories ('maquiladoras') in Northern Mexico recruiting cheap labor and therefore reducing production costs for North American companies, the focus shifts to class divides across national borders. As 'maquiladora' owner Marco Antonio Salamanca puts it:

> There are two sets of laws in any country: the laws for people with money and the laws for everybody else. And don't think it's any different in the US because I buy politicians on both sides of the border all the time.

This is in many respects a convincing summary of the film's early focus on the objectification and brutal exploitation by socio-economic elites of vulnerable people, above all poor young women with indigenous backgrounds like Eva Jiménez. New opportunities linked to international business are a good reason for Marco to be proud of his dual citizenship, which gives him the necessary economic outreach. Not by coincidence he answers Lauren's attempt at national categorization ('Who are you? Mexican? Are you American?') with a reference to his glocal character: 'Mexican ... American ... These are very limited terms. They don't mean much in a modern world'. Although the direct link of that elite to the Juárez murders and the associated conspiracy theory appear far too simplistic and will have to be critically interrogated in the next section, Nava's wish to highlight the dangers of international business turning into international crime in a context of inefficient national monitoring and policing deserves attention. It might be worth adding that the US-Mexican border, which is so important for *My Family*, remains a topic in *Bordertown*. In the context of glocal business, however, it is highlighted as an obstacle only for the colonized poor. In her desperation toward the end of the film, Eva tries to cross the border and nearly dies in this unsuccessful attempt, whereas members of glocal elites like Marco and North American citizens like Lauren move effortlessly from one place to the next.

4.3.2 Chicano Agency

The substantially different plots of the two films lead to a different focus in the search for transcultural potential. *My Family* concentrates on the potential of first-generation Mexican migrants and their descendants in the US. As 'mestizos', José and María are shaped not only by the Catholic heritage of Spanish conquest and colonization mirrored in their names, but also by a pre-Columbian belief in nature deities. The film addresses the synthesis of both religions. As María returns to the US, the spirit of the Rio Grande, defender of the 'artificial' boundary, confronts her and threatens to kill her son, Chucho. She prays to the Virgin Mary to keep him alive. María attempts to cross the border during the daytime, but she nevertheless encounters an owl (a nocturnal animal) that Nava associates with the Aztec God of the night winds Tezcatlipoca (in: West 1995: 27) who had to be honored by human sacrifices. This connects María's fight against the river spirit with the epic fight of the God of light Quetzalcoatl against the often Satan-like 'trickster' Tezcatlipoca, (see Stocker 2002), although—in line with her name—she asks not for Quetzalcoatl's intervention, but for Virgin Mary's ('hay que tener fe en la virgen'). Although it appears miraculous that Chucho is rescued from the river's forces, there is no doubt for María that the river spirit's power remains unbroken. Consequently, she believes that Chucho's death at the hand of Anglo-American police in her East LA 'barrio' 25 years later is because of that spirit's curse. Both the narrator and the presence of an owl that—this time sheltered by the night—can quietly observe the hunt for and killing of Chucho confirm her belief. In his interview with West (1995: 27), Nava adds the possibility of a Christian connotation to the analysis when he outlines Chucho as an innocent victim of powerful social injustice that opens parallels to the story of Jesus Christ.

In this respect, the Sanchez family alludes to the founding family of Christianity, Mary, Joseph, and Jesus, but also to pre-Columbian beliefs, in which the fight between day and night symbolizing good and evil is part of the cyclical and temporal concept of nature. At the end of the day of the family reunion there has to come the night, in which the son sacrifices himself for the cardinal sins of human society, including greed, pride and wrath. In contrast to Jesus, Chucho lives these cardinal sins. His greed culminates in drug trafficking, and his pride is explicit in his fight against other street gangs, but the excessive wrath displayed against his own father seals his fate. The film does not follow Chucho's argumentation in which his responsibility appears radically diminished due to US capitalism setting materialist norms. Instead, in line with the American Dream leitmotif, individual responsibility appears key for both individual achievement and failure. Symbolic circles represent cyclical concepts of time, such as the mambo around Chucho's car, the knife fight in the dance hall, and the cultivation of maize in the back garden of the Sánchez family home, which links pre-Columbian indigenous societies, contemporary Catholic Mexico, and the Mexican diaspora in the US as it represents traditional food. It is no coincidence that Jimmy reunites with his son Carlitos in the back garden at harvest time.

José and María achieve a new dimension when they are examined as a 'creator couple' (West 1995: 27), an interpretation that I suggest taking further by exploring the individual characteristics of the four sons as children of Ometeotl. Paco reminds us in this context of Quetzalcoatl's association with light, mercy, wind, and Eastern orientation, linking to the narrator's attempt to shed light on the family history, in which he refrains from malicious comments and does not even claim a main role for himself. He is omnipresent and invisible in most of the film, while he accompanies the different protagonists of his story, and he is the only child staying in the family home in East LA. On the other hand, Chucho shows a tendency toward aggression, which culminates in a bloody conflict with another Chicano gang and indicates parallels to the Aztec God of war Huitzilopochtli. Memo can easily be linked to the God of gold, Xipe Tote, due to his materialist orientation in the West of the family home (in the center of LA), which leaves the role of Tezcatlipoca for the embittered misanthropic Jimmy.[8] This interpretation is supported by the anti-social portrayal of his son Carlitos, who loves to dress up as Aztec, shoots at neighbors and startles Memo's future parents-in-law by jumping naked on the living room table where they are sitting. All of this summarizes in a humorous way the cultural distance between hybrid imagined Chicanos and Protestant-materialist presented Anglo-Americans, an image that could be inspired by Weber's notions of the 'capitalist spirit' (1973: 359).

Bordertown draws on this opposition in its search for transcultural potential and, similarly to *My Family*, identifies individual agency first and above all in successful Chicano examples. In some respects comparable to Toni, *Bordertown*'s Lauren Adrian starts a humanitarian mission to rescue abused and threatened people South of the Mexican border. If, in opposition to Toni, Lauren shows at first a strong rejection of her Mexican heritage, then this is mainly a result of external pressures of discrimination, racism and social injustice that she seems to have experienced as Mexican in the US. Her main point of reference is the murder of her parents, illegal migrants from Mexico, who were killed when working on a field. Although these murders are only faded-in via flash-backs and Lauren never elaborates on the events, it is clear that she regards them as a consequence of wide-spread racism when she explains to George Morgan, the editor of the *Chicago Sentinel* newspaper she works for: 'I didn't want to be Mexican—not in this country'.

Latest in this scene it is clear that the young Chicana did not assimilate to Anglo-American culture out of her own free will, but because she wanted to avoid a similar tragic end for herself. Starting from the assumption that Mexicans are victimized by socio-political elites in the US, just like indigenous Eva appears victimized by socio-political elites in Mexico, Lauren identifies with Eva ('I saw myself'), which explains her motivation to publish an article on the Juárez murders: 'I could be one of those women in the factories. It could be me in one of these graves. I can't let this go'. Taking into account that only a few scenes earlier a suddenly dark-haired Lauren threw the blond hair color away, which had helped her to conceal her Mexican heritage, it is now clear that the rather reluctant search for a news story in Juárez has transformed into an ambitious quest for the protagonist's Mexican-American identity. In this context, Eva's role changes—from yet another object of a news story for the *Chicago*

Sentinel to a role model for subalterns who are not any longer willing to accept their marginalization and victimization. I argue that the traditional North-South binary with the US as maker of history and South America as sufferer from that history is at this stage replaced by a transcultural solidarity construct.[9]

Figure 4.3.2.1 Eva and Lauren in *Bordertown*.

4.3.3 Language Use, Spacing and Music

Transcultural aspects in *My Family* and *Bordertown* are also visible in bilingual language use, mixed spaces and hybrid film music. Although in the first part of *My Family* the protagonists speak Spanish and the music remains in Spanish, cultural access for an Anglo-American audience is facilitated by subtitles and comments from the English-speaking narrator, who stresses important concepts in both languages (i.e. US portrayed as 'el otro lado del mundo' and 'the other side of the world'). The more the protagonists improve their English and become embedded in Anglo-American culture, the more this rather redundant intersentential code switching from the narrator is being replaced by intrasentential code switching from the protagonists, which tends to add important information to the dialogues. The turning point is reached in the 1950s, because the viewer is now predominantly confronted with second generation protagonists like Chucho who speak English with the occasional Spanish word in particular sentences. Carty has analyzed this language use in detail and comes to the conclusion that intrasentential switching relates predominantly to expressive functions ('hijo'), friendly exhortations ('ándale') and insults ('puto'), but it also includes words for law enforcement institutions ('la Migra') and Anglo culture (pinche) (2012: 75). One particularly interesting example of the expressive function is the conflict between José and Chucho, in which José argues: 'I didn't raise my children to be sinvergüenzas', and to which Chucho responds: 'Fuck la dignidad. Fuck your struggle'. Intrasentential code switching indicates here 'extreme anger' (ibid.), but also excellent intercultural competence in so far as key concepts from José's cultural background are for the bilingual speaker best understood untranslated ('vergüenza', 'dignidad').

Very similarly, bilingual code switching in *Bordertown* starts intersentential and is mainly aimed at improving communication. Lauren does the first step when she draws on her suppressed Spanish language knowledge in her conversation with Eva and Eva's mother. This switch is motivated by commercial interests that reflect her key interests at this stage of the plot ('¿Has hablado con otro periódico?'). Far less convincing is, unfortunately, the switch back to English, because this leaves the viewer puzzled as to how both the young Mayan Eva and her mother, who are being presented as poor, marginalized and isolated in the slums of Juárez, might have managed to develop good English language competence. In particular Eva speaks very fluent English after only a few conversations with Lauren, and there is no explanation with regard to the origins of this foreign language knowledge and/or the strong learning curve. Similarly unbelievable is towards the end of the film Lauren's impressive knowledge of Spanish, which allows her to work as editor of the Mexican newspaper previously run by Alfonso Díaz (Antonio Banderas). However, despite the significant shortfalls in *Bordertown*, the use of code-switching in both films draws attention to the importance of the Spanish language as a key aspect of Chicano life, which mirrors multilingual reality in the US.

In *My Family*, the blurring of spatial boundaries is particularly explicit in the Sánchez family home. The wooden house and its small terrace fit easily into films about the 'Wild West' and therefore establish a link to the American frontier with its expansion of migrant settlements but, behind the house, José starts to cultivate maize in the tradition of his rural Mexican ancestors. The interior of the house is shaped by American furniture of the time, as well as indigenous and Catholic symbols, including masks, the cross and pictures of Virgen Mary. There is a reduction in the portrayal of Catholic attributes when the camera moves from the parents' bedroom (with two pictures of Virgen Mary next to the bed) to the living room, in which Chucho, Jimmy and Toni rebel against family traditions. However, even the final shot in this sequence reveals a cross on the inner part of the exterior door, which stresses the Catholic mentality inside the family house, outside of which the viewer can see the skyscrapers of the center of LA with their reference to spaces dominated by Weber's capitalist spirit (1973: 359). Here and elsewhere, the house exemplifies Bhabha's 'Third Space' (1994), in which the hybrid use of language, a polycultural mix of music, diverse patterns of behavior, and ultimately different identity constructs in dynamic interaction are mutually enriched and can develop further. Taking into account that the house is an example of life in the 'barrio' and East LA as a whole, it can be regarded as a laboratory of transcultural encounters.

Bordertown takes the idea of marginal places as potential spaces for cultural encounters further, but at the same time class boundaries are stressed, and marginality becomes the key theme. Most of the film is shot south of the US-Mexican border and outside of Juárez's city center (in its slums, the surrounding desert, a waste disposal site, or one of the maquiladoras located in the desert). The scenes in the city are predominantly shot in places that have no major appeal to the privileged parts of Mexican society or tourists. These include areas of low-level prostitution and the simple offices of Díaz's newspaper, which stand in sharp contrast to the luxury restaurant in which Marco seduces Lauren and the offices of the *Chicago Sentinel* in the US. If in *My Family* most poorer Chicanos are in East LA, in *Bordertown* the place for poorer Mexicans is south of the US-Mexican border and outside of the Juárez city center. However, the two films portray questions of mobility very differently: Whereas My Family presents the poorer Sánchez family more mobile than Karen's well-off Anglo-American parents, social movement in *Bordertown* tends to be associated with higher economic capital, although the film mentions a history of working class migration.[10] The differences in mobility include unlimited border crossings for Lauren and Marco, but not for Eva, which mirrors an imbalance in social and economic opportunities: Lauren has a chance for promotion in the *Chicago Sentinel,* and Marco thrives on global business, but Eva and her mother are likely to remain in poverty in the slums of Juárez. Significantly, there are no more bridges for poorer people to use to find decent work in better areas, as José Sánchez did, and transcultural encounters have to take place in marginal places if/when the privileged (often reluctantly) go there. This is what happens when Lauren, who does not volunteer to go to Juárez, never mind its slums, gets to know Eva in the marginal spaces that shape her life. In contrast, Memo and Karen's relationship develops in LA's city center.

Finally, the use of music mirrors the potential and limits of transculturality in *My Family* and *Bordertown*. In *My Family*, the shift of boundaries from predominantly indigenous-Mexican environments to a Mexican-American household is accompanied by a change of music from *Rosa de Castillo* in P'urhépecha language to *Angel Baby* in English. The director's choice of *Angel Baby*, a popular Rock and Roll song interpreted here by Chicano singer Jeanette Jurado but later also by John Lennon, is significant because it supports the portrayal of Chucho as a rebellious character. Consequently, the song is played at the beginning of the 1950s episode and then again immediately before the climax of that episode, which ends with Chucho's death.[11] In line with the rock 'n' roll movement, Chucho rejects the 'establishment', which includes the generation of his parents. In particular, he dislikes the view of life built on manual work and

Christian-bourgeois morals, which his father defends as an expression of dignity. Interestingly enough, dignity is a key concept for Chucho too, but he defines it as masculine freedom and pride that should not be limited by manual work or social laws. The necessity to confirm his gang leadership role on a daily basis leads to irreconcilable conflicts with likeminded machos like Butch, while his absurd position in relation to capitalist norms remains similarly destructive. On the one hand, he rejects and despises these norms ('this is the only thing that counts here'), but on the other hand he has internalized them. He cannot imagine a leadership role with limited economic means, hence his decision to opt for a career as a drug dealer. Chucho mirrors here the fate of numerous rock 'n' roll singers who present themselves as rebels but then take on the capitalist spirit of the establishment and ultimately die from drugs, like Frankie Lymon and Elvis Presley. The love story from *Angel Baby* ('You're like an angel, too good to be true') can be interpreted as a reference to the relationship between Chucho and Jimmy, because the cool gang leader does virtually everything for his little brother—he even irons his trousers. At the end, Jimmy is Chucho's only link to the family, and Chucho's death transforms Jimmy into an embittered lone wolf.

Rock 'n' roll is, however, not the only musical metaphor for the rebellion of Chicano youth against traditional boundaries. Particularly significant is the scene in which Chucho plays Pérez Prado's *Que Rico El Mambo* on his car radio and encourages children from the neighborhood to dance to it.[12] There are parallels to rock 'n' roll insofar as conservative groups in the US rejected mambo dance—due to its 'erotic' hip movements—at least as much as the supposedly immoral acrobatic in rock 'n' roll. In contrast, the children's performance in *My Family* supports the interpretation of mambo as an expression of love of life, which destabilizes the bourgeois hypocrisy frequently associated with conservative perspectives. At the same time, it allows viewers to reconsider Chucho's example as a rebellion against traditional boundaries set by older generations, because it happens roughly 10 years before the impact of the '68 generation. The 'clash' of generational cultures is enhanced by ethnic considerations insofar as the young Chicano fights against his marginalization, suppression, and finally, elimination by the white Anglo-American power structures. The scene in which an Anglo-American mother storms out of her house when she sees that her son has joined the group of Latino children dancing mambo and pulls him back in a desperate effort to re-establish cultural boundaries confirms this interpretation. I argue that both rock 'n' roll and mambo mirror hybrid identities that critically interrogate the monocultural construct of white Anglo-American power centers.

Considering *Bordertown*'s strong appeal for transcultural solidarity in its exploration of the murders of Juárez, it is no surprise that the only musician to appear on stage is a well-known political activist from Latin America. In the years leading up to the production of the film, Juanes was one of the most widely celebrated Latin American musicians[13] whose career peaked with the album *Mi Sangre* (2004) and its most famous song *La Camisa Negra*. Juanes established a well-funded foundation in support of victims of land mines in Colombia. He was honored for his activism at the *Adopt-A-Minefield* gala in November 2005 and was invited to Brussels to join the EU's campaign against landmines with a concert in the European Parliament in April 2006 (European Parliament 2006). In *Bordertown*, he performs *La Camisa Negra* on the birthday party of Don Felipe Salamanca's daughter but, Lauren's intervention makes it possible for Eva to attend as well. The song seems to give Eva, a major fan of Juanes, a moment of happiness greater than anything has experienced so far, which reminds us of the importance of affects in films like *The Edge of Heaven* and *Le Havre*. At the same time, the song blurs culture- and class-related boundaries insofar as it appeals to the more privileged guests as much as it appeals to Eva. Finally, due to its influence by *raspa*, a style of tropical music that is also known as chucu-chucu in Colombia and a particular *cumbia* style in other parts of Latin America,[14] *La Camisa Negra* could be regarded as an excellent example of hybrid music, which opens up parallels to *Angel Baby* and *Que Rico El Mambo* in *My Family*. However, Juanes's recruitment for a private party of the rich Salamanca family, the lack of direct political references in Juanes's appearance on stage and in his song, the extremely short and superficial contact between Eva and Juanes in the autograph scene, and Eva's distress at recognizing her rapist immediately after the song indicate the limits of transculturality in *Bordertown*. Similarly, the framing of José Sánchez and his children highlights the continuity of boundaries in *My Family*.

4.4 Transcultural Limits

4.4.1 Uncle Tom, Ghetto Kids, and the Failure of Intercultural Examples

For his exploration of a 'barrio' in East LA as microcosm of Chicano diaspora in the US, Nava can draw on numerous cinematic examples, including Cheech Marin's highly successful comedy *Born in East LA*. However, in contrast to Marin's parody of the American Dream, which starts with the title (*Born in East LA* as response to Springsteen's *Born in the U.S.A.*), *My Family* continues to disseminate the idea of never-ending opportunities for hard working and ambitious Chicanos, and this message limits the transcultural potential of the film. I argue that José Sánchez could be regarded as a Chicano version of the protagonist of Harriet Beecher Stowe's *Uncle Tom's Cabin* (2015 [1852]), as he remains extremely passive if not apathetic and 'obedient', despite the forced and illegal deportation of his pregnant wife and then later Chucho's execution by police. Admittedly, the film indicates social injustice when close-ups of the modest wooden family house in East LA are placed immediately before a long shot of the palace of the white US family in the center of LA, for whom María works as a servant. However, the usually vocal narrator neither comments on these differences in housing nor criticizes the power structures that separate the city into the poorer Eastern part and the much richer city center, from where the police are sent to discipline the cheap labor reserves the Chicano minorities provide. Overall, the passivity advocated by José Sánchez in these scenes reminds us of the double standards disseminated by Uncle Tom, which early reviews of Stowe's novel detected, for example back in 1852 in the *Liberator*:

> Is there one law of submission and non-resistance for the black man, and another of rebellion and conflict for the white man? When it is the whites who are trodden in the dust, does Christ justify them in taking up arms to vindicate their rights? And when it is the blacks who are thus treated, does Christ require them to be patient, harmless, long-suffering, and forgiving? Are there two Christs? (in: Rosenthal 2005: 35)

It seems that the replacement of 'black' by 'colored' allows us to see an astonishing parallel between the two protagonists, which *My Family* enhances through the socio-politically similarly passive behavior of María. Another example is Irene, who follows in her mother's footsteps by marrying within the local Chicano community and remaining for the rest of her life in East LA. She is such a marginal character that she is hardly mentioned in the second part of the film.

Clear exceptions to this family portrayal are Chucho und Jimmy, but their anti-capitalism is limited by their ghetto mentality. Chucho is a particularly sad example of self-isolation because he remains unable to develop the transcultural potential of his music into a convincing alternative lifestyle. He fails to see the similarities between his personal rebellion and the indignation voiced by other young people within and beyond the Chicano community, and he cannot bridge the gaps that separate the marginalized characters in his surroundings. Consequently, there is no attempt to search for solidarity among white, black, and Chicano youngsters fighting the establishment. Instead of trying to enhance the links between Chicanos, Chucho seems to find personal satisfaction as the leader of an insignificant Chicano gang. The machismo underpinning the gang's fights is not only destructive (e.g., when Chucho kills the leader of the rival gang) but also self-destructive insofar as it leads to Chucho's persecution and execution by police.

Due to the violent death of his older brother, Jimmy develops an even stronger self-isolation and fundamental rejection of white Anglo-American society. He becomes an embittered small-time criminal, who repeatedly spends time in jail and seems to receive more inspiration from the indigenous masks that decorate his room than from any other source.[15] This all leads to the reconstruction of a cultural dichotomy between Chicanos and Anglo-Americans that is frequently so strong that viewers could regard Jimmy as an excellent example of Huntington's *Clash of Civilizations* (2007), were it not for the occasional distractions the director puts in place. In the jail scene, the culture conflict is reduced by the presentation of a Hispanic prison guard; in other scenes it is up to his wife Isabel (an illegal immigrant from San Salvador) to make Jimmy's human nature more accessible, which again helps to dissolve cultural tension. However, it is worth stressing that Jimmy is only able to open up within a Latino environment, and Isabel's death again increases his self-isolation and facilitates parallels to ghetto protagonists in Akın's *Short Sharp Shock*, Aladag's *Rage,* and Tasma's *Fracture*. Despite all differences, the young people with migrant background presented in these films tend to define themselves via petty crime and/or violence vis-à-vis the host culture, never mind if that host culture is being presented as indifferent and part of the problem (e.g.. in *My Family*) or relatively empathetic and interested in problem-solving but ultimately helpless (in *Short Sharp Shock*, *Rage,* and *Fracture*).

On the other hand, *My Family* provides potential examples of transcultural relations in its portrayal of Memo and Karen as well as Toni and David. Memo, who becomes a successful lawyer by the end of the film and attempts to marry into a wealthy Anglo-American family from the city center, has the potential to blur LA's East-West boundaries for the Sánchez family. José is proud of his son's success, and the narrator indicates the importance of the visit from the center when he stresses that this is the first time Karen and her parents cross the bridges into East LA. However, Bhabha's 'Third Space' remains an illusion because Memo opts for assimilation with the Anglo-American center when he attempts to suppress his Mexican background. Instead of negotiating his cultural heritage, Memo denies the funeral of 'El Californio' in the back garden as well as Jimmy's jail sentences. Both the declaration of the funeral as family fantasy and the cover-up of the jail sentence as further education could be regarded as desperate attempts to support Memo's (Guillermo's) new identity construct as Anglo-American 'Bill'. Memo shares this radical rejection of cultural heritage in favor of imagined US Americanness with other protagonists in contemporary migrant cinema, including Lauren in the first part of *Bordertown*, but also with British-Asian Jess in *Bend It Like Beckham*, who rejects her Sikh heritage. Rather than helping to blur cultural boundaries, Memo and Jess ultimately reconstruct and stabilize traditional binaries, be it the North-South divide in American relations or the West-East divide in British-Asian encounters. Consequently, Jimmy's son Carlitos shows a hostile attitude toward Memo's future parents-in-law when he jumps with indigenous feather headdress but otherwise naked onto the living room table facing the 'invaders', yet another example of Huntington's view of new culture conflicts ahead (2007).

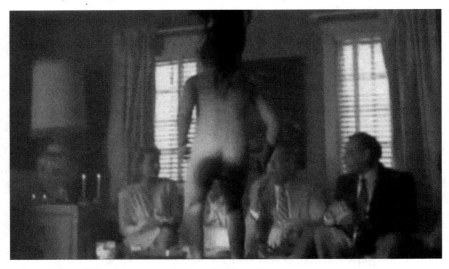

Figure 4.4.1.1 The Aztec encounter in *My Family*.

This leaves only Toni's relationship with David, who shares concerns for socio-political reforms and human rights protection in Latin America, as a potential example of transculturality in *My Family*. As former catholic nun and priest, both had to give up their posts in order to marry and start a new life together. This means a rupture with catholic family traditions and viewpoints: Abandoning the order is as unacceptable to Toni's mother María as the marriage Toni arranges for her brother Jimmy and illegal migrant Isabel to protect her from deportation back to San Salvador. 'There are certain things in life that are sacred … sagrados', argues María, and José agrees. Also, in contrast to the older generation's acceptance of political authority, but in line with Chucho's and Jimmy's critical distance from the Anglo-American 'establishment', Toni and David object to laws that defend existing power hierarchies and the status quo, here in particular US migration laws that allow for Isabel's deportation. Although Toni and David even share a healthy distance from religious fundamentalism and superstition with Chucho and Jimmy, they are very different in the cognitive defense of their resistance. In opposition to the personal and often egocentric emotional rebellion of the two small-time criminals, Toni and David's fight for solidarity with victims of human right abuse indicates a transcultural intervention 'in-between' traditional boundaries and identity constructs (Bhabha 1994: 2, 180–181).

Unfortunately, the two characters receive only marginal roles in the film, and it remains unclear why their socio-political and cultural intervention remains limited to victims of socio-political injustice in Latin America. Based on their objection to US immigration laws requiring the deportation of Isabel, reconsidering laws that facilitated María's deportation in the

1930s and Chucho's execution in the 1950s could have been a logical step. However, as it stands, the focus on social injustice south of the border helps to distract viewers from socio-economic injustice, political discrimination, and cultural racism in the US. In addition, Toni and David's characters are not well developed. Toni appears to be a contemporary edition of Sor Juana Inés de la Cruz when she decides on convent life in order to escape the traditional roles of an apolitical homemaker and mother that her parents had chosen for her and Irene, but the potential and limits of her rebellion are not elaborated.[16] Similarly, the motifs for David's rebellion against religious and political authorities remain unclear. Furthermore, the couple's viewpoint is weakened by the fact that they do not seem to engage in a meaningful dialogue with the victims of abuse. Instead, they continue to objectify these victims by attempting to speak on their behalf, rather than with them.[17] Although this reminds us of Spivak's negation of the question 'can the subaltern speak' (1999: 230), Toni and David's distraction from social injustice in the US should above all be interpreted as an expression of Nava's interest in containing the socio-political criticism of his film and disseminating assimilation as the best route for Chicano minorities. Nava showed that he has chosen assimilation for himself when he fought for Hollywood recognition and an international career through *My Family*. The melodramatic excess, which includes the simultaneous abandonment of two religious vocations by Toni and David, might form part of this strategy of assimilation into 'the Hollywood paradigm' (Raab 2009: 177), but it does not increase the credibility or the transcultural potential of the film.

Particularly interesting is Paco's role as narrator. He reminds us of 19th century documentary-realist narrative styles and is in this respect not a convincing choice. However, his role is not limited to comments from outside the plot, and as one of the members of the Sánchez family he offers more than the 'trite, overblown narration', James rejects (1995: 18). Also, his comments add important metafictional perspectives, for example when he stresses the subjectivity of his father's stories on which the filmic plot rests. He even highlights repeatedly his own subjectivity as a member of the family by indications of kinship such as 'my father', 'our mother', and 'my brother Chucho', which could be regarded as a rejection of traditional omniscient narrators. From this subjective viewpoint, Paco mediates migrant history between viewers and the Sánchez family, while trying to balance the different angles from which other members of the family tell the story. While visiting Jimmy in jail, Paco reminds him of his responsibility as the father of little Carlitos and complies with his role as older brother acting on behalf of wider family concerns regarding Jimmy's criminal career. However, overall, he marginalizes this role to give his parents, brothers, and sisters more space for their perspectives. He tends to accept his role with tolerance and invites viewers to do the same. Rather than assessing other people's behavior, his aim is to understand their often very different life scripts. This includes his mother's religious viewpoint, within which the family history appears as a product of divine intervention, be it by Virgin Mary or the river spirit, but there is similar openness for Chucho's and Jimmy's rebellions and for the life-styles chosen by Memo and Toni. Ultimately, Paco attempts to give everybody a voice, regardless of their ideological perspective (conservative in the case of José, María and Irene, but liberal-individualist for Chucho, Jimmy and Toni), and their status in the family (Isabel is an in-law). It could be argued that next to Toni, Paco most addresses Antor's requests for enhanced cultural understanding by 'willingly embracing the unfamiliar' (1996: 73). This implies an expansion of cultural knowledge both in cognitive and emotional respects correlating with travel experiences, be it from José's and María's migrant history, Toni's convent life, or Memo's education and working life in the center of LA. After his experiences with jail life, even Jimmy decides to broaden his horizons by leaving the family home and starting a journey with his son Carlitos. At the end, only Paco stays in the family home, but his literary work on the family history means that he has travelled as well (and with him the viewers), which links up to Antor's statement on the importance of journeys in postcolonial pedagogy: 'We have travelled and therefore our horizon has widened' (1996: 72).

Less convincing is the strong marginalization of Anglo-Americans in Paco's story and the enhancement of religious discourse. The former means that Karen and David have hardly anything to say; the latter is visible in a shift of perspective. In the first part of the film we see Maria's interpretation of Chucho's death as predestined ('She knew he was meant to die at the river'). In the second part a similar scheme is used to explain Jimmy's criminality from the narrator's viewpoint and, therefore, as a consequence of his research on family history:

> Jimmy carried a lot of shit for the rest of us. All the hate, all the rage and injustice. And somehow, if it wasn't for him, we couldn't have gone on to do all the things we did. Me with my writing and Tony with her politics, and most of all Memo, the pride and joy of the family.

The idea that Jimmy's distress allows the rest of the Sánchez family to lead a better life can be seen as a parallel construct to the sufferings of Christ, in which case the Christian view of ultimate sacrifice passes from Chucho to Jimmy. While this interpretation of Chicano machismo and criminality remains extremely questionable, there can be little doubt that its fatalistic take confirms the Uncle Tom strategy of political passivity and cultural assimilation proposed by José and María Sánchez.

4.4.2 *The Savior from the North*

The most widely disseminated *Bordertown* movie poster, which is also the international DVD cover, shows Jennifer López as Lauren Adrian in the foreground and the bus used for the kidnapping of female workers in the middle of the Mexican desert in the background. While López dominates the right part of the picture, her gaze to the left, the camera in her hand, and her walking posture (right arm and leg forward) indicate her strong will to fully shape the rest of that picture. Despite the transcultural solidarity message outlined before, neither this, nor any other movie poster shows indigenous Eva in the foreground. All of this correlates with Eva's role in the film as a victim of low class and high class Mexican machos, in need of protection by US journalist Lauren and her North American newspaper. It also summarizes the question of agency, which can be linked to bilingual competence, lighter skin color, a certain economic and cultural capital, and above all, US citizenship. Nava's film neglects to mention the huge spectrum of national and regional associations in which Mexican women from different social classes organize themselves to fight social injustice and offer protection to other women. These associations range from *AMAM* (2015) to *Nuestras Hijas de Regreso a Casa* (2015), which continues to draw international attention on the missing women from Juarez and other areas of the Mexican province Chihuahua.[18] Furthermore, not a single Mexican police officer, government representative, or other politician in *Bordertown* seems to be interested in exploring the murders in Juárez. Apart from Teresa Casillas, who plays only a minor role and seems unable to protect Eva from her enemies, the only other Mexican willing to investigate the crimes is Alfonso Díaz. However, in both cases Lauren has to fight to get their support, and she has to lead the small team.

Mata summarizes such images in *Bordertown* as a reconstruction of the stereotypical 'Savior from the North' theme that 'reinforces the racist portrayal of the Mexican people as inept' (2010: 16). I argue that such a binary correlates with powerful portrayals of US individualism in Hollywood Westerns and Science Fiction,[19] which have survived the economic, political, and moral crisis of the US that gained momentum well before *Bordertown* with the highly criticized US led invasion of Iraq in 2003 and continued with the 'global crisis' from 2008.[20] However, Nava's choice of Jennifer López as 'savior' is as unconvincing as the outline of her role in the script. The star's public image as sex symbol and demanding diva is a difficult fit for the human rights role she is asked to play. Also, the key aspects of that role lack credibility: Lauren introduces herself as a North American business woman who rejects her Mexican heritage, which is in line with her poor knowledge of the Spanish language and Mexican culture. On the other hand, she appears shortly afterwards as female undercover agent in a maquiladora and, at the end of the film, leads Díaz's Mexican newspaper. It is worth stressing that Nava's choice of actors for the leading Mexican roles does not help to destabilize US-centric perspectives, because the two non-Mexican Hollywood stars (Brazilian actress Sonia Braga and Spanish actor Antonio Banderas) are not best suited to exemplify Mexican agency.

146 *Inspiration from Abroad?*

Finally, although Nava is right in questioning the efficiency of Mexican intervention in the historical investigation and prosecution of the Juárez murders, it can be argued that patterns of traditional patriarchy and racialization (see Avila 2012: 129) might explain the challenges on the ground much better than *Bordertown's* global capitalist conspiracy theory. Furthermore, there are questions of governability (especially but not exclusively) in Juárez during its most recent key period of drug wars, which are not mentioned in the film: Between 2006 and 2010 alone, i.e., in the main production and dissemination period of Nava's film, the rivalry between the Juárez cartel and the Sinaloa Federation led to around 6,500 deaths in the city, and the cartels remain powerful.[21]

Admittedly, *Bordertown* proposes a much more critical interrogation of the American Dream than *My Family*, which has an impact on the development of the US savior leitmotif. If *My Family* proposed hard work as the key to success for everybody, especially poor Mexican migrants from the South, *Bordertown* concentrates on the numerous obstacles that lead to their failure in the pursuit of happiness. One example is the murder of Lauren's parents, who were—just like José and María Sánchez—poor Mexicans and migrated to the US in search of a better life. Lauren explicitly criticizes widespread racism ('I didn't want to be Mexican, not in this country'), which is likely to be the reason behind her parents' murders and leads to Lauren suppressing her Mexican heritage. Other examples include the numerous maquiladora workers, who earn so little in the US companies south of the border that they are left without dreams. While waiting at the bus stop in one of the poorest areas of Juárez, Eva tells Lauren her perspective:

> They tell us go to work in the maquiladoras, make money to keep your land, but there is no money. The government and the factories take everything. All the money is for them. For us, nothing. [...] We have no land, we cannot go home.

The poor background, the red illumination, and the close-up of Eva's face stress the despair that will increase later on in the film, when Eva recognizes her rapist and when she attempts to cross the border to save her life. However, even that border crossing fails, which confirms unsurmountable obstacles for poor non-white people to pursue happiness, be it south or north of the border, whereas richer protagonists like Marco Salamanca seem to be able to live the American Dream in Mexico as well as in the US.

Thanks to her adoption by a wealthier, white, Anglo-American couple, which helped her get the right education and a job she likes, Lauren is able to dream her dream, but it is very materialistic and comes at a price. Her decision in favor of a career means not having a family or embracing her Mexican heritage. When she discovers that the price is too high, she suddenly shifts from US-centric materialism to a similarly homogenous and separatist but spiritual Mexican ethnocentrism. This implies a sharp South-North divide of the two basic components of the American Dream with superior spiritualism in the former and inferior materialism in the latter[22] and leaves little space for transcultural identity construction. At a symbolic level, the radical shift is highlighted by Lauren's change in hair color, from a blonde toner—which she quickly washes out in one scene—to the black original, as well as by her decision to use the Spanish language again and to stay in Juárez as head of Díaz's newspaper. Although this has to be interpreted in the context of Lauren's fight for a more inclusive, collective, and spiritual American Dream, it correlates with monocultural notions of US individualism and agency that seem hard to overcome.

4.5 Concluding Remarks

The foregoing highlights continuities in the portrayal of neo-colonial binaries this study has found in all previously explored European films. In *My Family*, minority ghetto culture and concepts of assimilation to mainstream society appear to be complementary insofar as the latter appears to be the way to pursue happiness beyond the boundaries of East LA. Memo's ambitions are a particularly good example of this tendency, but his parents' work ethic and the presentation of traditional family structures as universal life style is also very much in line with key aspects of an American Dream that aims to further enhance monocultural notions of the 'melting pot', rather than negotiations of identities in a culturally diverse society. *Bordertown* shows similar tendencies when its hero Lauren at first suppresses her Mexican heritage in order to fully assimilate into US society but then inverts her position by going back to her Mexican 'roots' without allowing much space for Mexican agency, never mind hybrid Chicano identity. Transculturality remains in these contexts often a rather superficial exterior phenomenon, or it appears as a temporarily limited process that remains unable to replace the traditional North-South dichotomy with US cultural values and work ethics leading the way to a better society. The failure, marginalization, or simply lack of elaboration of transcultural ways of life suggested through Toni and David's social work and through Lauren and Eva's joint fight against neo-colonial exploitation correlates with the director's preference for melodramatic excess, mass audience success, and his own ambition to assimilate into Hollywood society. This culminates in identity constructs that might be more oriented toward mainstream audience tastes than empirically proven hybridity.

Nava's films also stress aspects for the negotiation of identities in contemporary migrant cinema that have been marginalized in European film. One example is the examination of 'collective aspirations' reflected in 'mediascapes' and 'ideoscapes' of modern mass media,[23] which Nava includes in his reflections on different concepts of the American Dream. In *My Family* and *Bordertown* the American Dream is explored not only as a main factor of migration to and permanent settlement in the US, but as a key to the collective imagination that shapes highly individual ways of life in the so-called host country. Europeans might not have a comparable European Dream, although the European Commission enhances a secularized vision of European identity in diversity that links up to the common heritage of European Enlightenment shared by many. However, African, Asian, and Latin-American migrants aiming for Europe certainly have their dreams, which could be summarized as a 'European Dream' that has either replaced the American Dream or given it a new home.[24] All this is mirrored and shaped by European mass media, including migrant cinema and TV, and it is particularly obvious in *Bend It Like Beckham*, in which the film music encourages British-Asian Jess 'to dream the dream'.

The exact nature of this dream and its correlation with social, economic and symbolic capital, which depends on gender, age and race, as well as the difficulties in establishing a space and a place for it (e.g. in England/Europe/the US/'the West'/inside/outside the family) remains to be further explored, and Nava's filmic reflection of the American Dream offers an excellent starting point for such a debate. There is at first the nearly naïve belief in the feasibility of the American Dream reconstructed in *My Family* and confirmed by most family members' successful pursuit of individual happiness. The dream is then destabilized in the 'mise-en-scène' of brutal suppression of the poor by neoliberal global elites in *Bordertown*, in which the arbitrary abuse of power on both sides of the US-Mexican border not only stops the poor from achieving their dream but enhances their misery and even allows murderers to go unpunished.[25] Finally, there is the partial reconstruction of the dream in the same film, when Eva's murderers receive their well-deserved punishment, Lauren finds her Mexican Self and then continues the fight against the ongoing abuse of power as Head of Díaz's Mexican newspaper. Similarly, we can analyze the individual pursuit of happiness in *Letters from Alou*, *Taxi*, *The Edge of Heaven*, and *Le Havre* as part of a desirable but under neo-colonial capitalism utopic dream linked to concepts of human rights and secular Christianity as part of a shared legacy of European Enlightenment.

In this context, *Bordertown* is an excellent example for a serious attempt to address contemporary concerns over the lack of postcolonial responsibility (Wallerstein 2003, Lazarus 2012, Menozzi 2014). In a framework of increasing globalization the growing power of transnational corporations, and political volatility, for which the expansion of maquiladora industries in the late 1990s and the poor and dangerous working conditions of their predominantly younger female staff could be symbolic,[26] Nava accepts major personal and economic risks to intervene critically on behalf of that workforce. These risks start with arrests, a burglary, and death threats[27] and end in a major financial set-back, which might partially be the result of political pressures to silence a film that has most likely upset many (usually

North American) maquiladora owners as well local politicians.[28] Not by coincidence, Jennifer López received the "Artists for Amnesty" award for her role as producer and star of *Bordertown* at the Berlin International Film Festival.

Although the film's conspiracy theory is far too simplistic, and there are numerous other weaknesses (discussed above), there can be no doubt that Nava makes here a serious attempt to tackle social inequality, intercommunal violence, and economic exploitation on a global scale. He also suggests a rethinking of intellectual commitment, which lies at the heart of a debate on the meaning of democracy and associated concepts of political participation, responsibility, and freedom of expression in a world interconnected but still very much marked by forms of exclusion and inequality. All of this is in line with Armendáriz's, Saura's and Kaurismäki's socio-critical auteur cinema (see *Letters from Alou, Taxi, The Match Factory Girl* and *Le Havre*), but it goes well beyond the critical engagement of many other and often more popular European films (e.g., Chadha's *Bend It Like Beckham* and *It's a Wonderful Afterlife* or Akın's *In July* and *Solino*).

Finally, a key strength of leading Chicano directors' productions is their immediate impact. Whereas most European films—including *Taxi, The Edge of Heaven* and *Le Havre*—reach a relatively modest amount of viewers in cinemas, reflected in a box office gross of less than one million dollars, Nava's *My Family* and *Bordertown* have generated the better part of 20 million dollars together.[29] There is certainly no monocausal explanation for cinematic success, and there are exceptions to the rule on both sides of the Atlantic. However, the Hollywood studio production system and its financing offer advantages in dissemination and impact that should not be ignored. Requests for more generous and more centralized economic support of European cinema have been made regularly, and some important steps toward enhanced European funding have been taken, but there are socio-economic, political and—above all— national cultural concerns with regard to more centralized film production, that remain difficult to overcome.

Notes

1. See for example in *Born in East LA* the conflict between Chicanos and 'la migra' and the unlawful expulsion of a US citizen, which are key themes in *My Family* as well.
2. Adams (1941: 404); for an introduction to the American Dream's origins see Lallas (2014).
3. See also Weber's examination of the development of the 'capitalist spirit' from Protestant working ethics (1973: 359).
4. Latinos, Greeks, and Hungarians are mentioned explicitly; see Nava (1995).
5. See Nava (1995). Adopting a Latino perspective, he stressed on the National Hispanic Media Coalition Impact Awards 2014: 'We don't get the same opportunities […] we got to fight for the film and TV industry to create more opportunities, more jobs for Latinos on both sides of the camera' (Nava 2014).

150   *Inspiration from Abroad?*

6. In his interview with Moyer (2002), Nava outlines 'the thing about the Latino culture is that we assimilate very, very quickly', shortly before he comments on the US 'our culture is very, very pervasive all over the world'.
7. Although the exact number of forced deportees remains unclear (estimates range from 140,000 to 400,000), there is no doubt about illegal aspects of the process. Even the National Commission on Law Observance and Enforcement, established by US President Hoover, reports 'illegal searches and seizures' (1931: 133), 'inquisitorial examinations' (ibid. 137) and a 'lack of customary safeguards' under exclusion of the public (ibid. 143).
8. See Smith (2003: 193ff.) for an introduction to the mythological background.
9. See also Sadowski-Smith, who discusses the relationship between Lauren and Eva as 'transnational solidarity' (2009: 81), and the *Artists for Amnesty* award given to Jennifer López for her role as protagonist and producer of *Bordertown* in 2007.
10. Like many maquiladora workers, Eva migrated to Juárez, and Lauren's family migrated to the US.
11. *Angel Baby* is the only song in the film performed on screen, and its montage immediately before the decisive knife fight between Butch and Chucho stresses its importance even more.
12. Pérez Prado's own migration and success story mirrors the dissemination of mambo from Cuba to Mexico and the US. In addition, as 'King of Mambo', Prado exemplifies the movement associated with provocative Latin music and dance style.
13. Juanes appears in *TIME* magazine from 2005 as one of the 100 'most influential people' and 'the leading music artist in the Spanish-speaking world' (TIME 2005).
14. See the song's categorization as 'el chucu-chucu mayor de Juanes' (SHOCK 2015), and the discussion of raspa in Waxer (2002: 61).
15. The connection of Jimmy with Tezcatlipoca is further enhanced by the indigenous decoration of his room, which is particularly visible in the scene, in which he leans over Isabel and covers her with a blanket.
16. Toni decides to join a convent shortly after catching Irene's wedding bouquet, which suggests that she might be the next woman to prolong conservative mother and housewife ideals. Her rejection of Irene as a role model is highlighted when she starts crying and refuses to accept the bouquet.
17. Toni's father indicates the challenges associated with Isabel's lack of consent regarding the marriage for papers: 'Hija, you just messed up this girl's life without even asking for her permission'.
18. For an overview of more than 100 associations, see *Directorio de mujeres por y para las mujeres* (Amigos contra el SIDA 2015).
19. Particularly good examples are classic Westerns, such as Aldrich's *Vera Cruz* (1954), Sturges's *The Magnificent Seven* (1960), and Kennedy's *Return of the Seven* (1966), but the concept is also supported in more recent Science Fiction like Bay's *Armageddon* (1998), Spielberg's *War of the Worlds* (2005), and Nolan's *Interstellar* (2014).
20. See also Mishra's 'The Western model is broken' (2014).
21. The Juárez cartel has been weakened due to the arrest of its leader Alberto Carrillo Fuentes in 2013, but it has not been dissolved. See CBC News (2014).
22. See Kimmage (2011: 27) and our discussion in 4.2 for characteristics of the American Dream.

23. Appadurai (1996: 31); see also Appadurai (2012: 98) and Bachmann-Medick (2006).
24. See Villa Martínez's comments on shifts from an American Dream to a European Dream (2011: 340).
25. The film constructs a linear history from the killing of Lauren's parents in the US, which Lauren does not remember as having led to any arrests, to the Juárez murders in Mexico that appear as similarly marginalized and/or ignored.
26. For an introduction into the working conditions in the maquiladora industries that *Bordertown* addresses, see Bacon (2004), Lugo (2009), and Hendricks (2010).
27. Johnson informs about the arrest of a movie production assistant, a burglary—in which $100,000 worth of equipment was stolen, and there were death threats against Nava and the cast (2007).
28. MGM and New Line decided against US theatrical release, which meant that *Bordertown* was never shown in US cinemas and went straight to DVD. In Mexico, the film was only accepted by a few theaters with more than one year delay after international distribution had started in Europe, and co-star Maya Zapata argued that the Mexican government banned *Bordertown* for political reasons (see FNS 2008, Day 2008). It remains, however, difficult to prove how much of such decisions were a consequence of political pressure.
29. See IMDB (2015), which indicates a box office gross of $502,000 for *Taxi*, $741,000 for *The Edge of Heaven*, and $612,000 for *Le Havre*, in opposition to $11 million for *My Family* and $8.3 million for *Bordertown*. If *Bordertown* has to be considered a financial failure, then this correlates with the substantial and not very well spent budget ($21 million vis-à-vis $5.5 million for *My Family*, particularly due to high expenses for Hollywood stars Jennifer López and Antonio Banderas). One of the few exceptions to the norm of modest income in European migrant cinema is Chadha's *Bend It Like Beckham*.

Filmography

Akın, Fatih (1998): *Short Sharp Shock/kurz und schmerzlos*. BRD: Wüste Filmproduktion.
Akın, Fatih (1999): *In July/Im Juli*. Germany: Wüste Filmproduktion.
Akın, Fatih (2002): *Solino*. Germany: Wüste Filmproduktion.
Akın, Fatih (2007): *The Edge of Heaven/Auf der anderen Seite*. Germany/Turkey: Anka Film.
Aladag, Züli (2006): *Rage/Wut*. BRD: Köln Media Filmproduktionen GmbH.
Aldrich, Robert (1954): *Vera Cruz*. US: Hecht-Lancaster Productions.
Armendáriz, Montxo (1990): *Letters from Alou/Las cartas de Alou*. Spain: Elías Querejeta Producciones Cinematográficas S.L., Televisión Española (TVE).
Arslan, Thomas (2001): *A Fine Day/Der schöne Tag*. Germany: Pickpocket Filmproduktion/zero-film/ZDF.
Bay, Michael (1998): *Armageddon*. US: Touchstone Pictures.
Bochert, Marc-Andreas (2015): *Krüger aus Almanya*. Germany: Provobis.
Bouchareb, Rachid (2006): *Days of Glory/Indigènes*. Algeria, France: Tessalit Productions, Kiss Films, France 2 Cinéma.
Bresson, Robert (1959): *Pickpocket*. France: Agnès Delahaie Productions.

Bresson, Robert (1969): *Mouchette*. France: Argos-Films, Parc Film.
Bresson, Robert (1983): *Money/L'argent*. France/Switzerland: Marion's Films, France 3, EOS Films.
Chadha, Gurindher (2002): *Bend It Like Beckham*. UK, Germany, US: Kintop Pictures.
Chadha, Gurindher (2010): *It's a Wonderful Afterlife*: US: Goldcrest Pictures.
Denis, Claire (1988): *Chocolat*. France, West Germany, Cameroon: Caroline Productions, Cerito Films, Cinémanuel.
Denis, Claire (2008): *35 Shots of Rum/35 rhums*. France, Germany: Soudaine Compagnie, Pandora Filmproduktion.
Haneke, Michael (2000): *Code Unknown/Code inconnu*. France, Germany: Canal+, Bavaria Film.
Kahane, Peter (2015): *The Blind Flyers/Blindgänger*. Germany: Polyphon.
Kaurismäki, Aki (1990): *The Match Factory Girl/Tulitikkutehtaan tyttö*. Finland, Sweden: Esselte Video, Finnkino, Svenska Filminstitutet.
Kaurismäki, Aki (2011): *Le Havre*. Finland, France, Germany: Sputnik, Pyramide Productions, Pandora Filmproduktion.
Kennedy Burt (1966): *Return of the Seven*. US, Spain: Mirisch Production Company.
Marin, Cheech (1987): *Born in East LA*.US: Clear Type Productions.
Nakache, Olivier; Eric Toledano (2014): *Samba*. France: Quad Productions, Ten Films, Gaumont.
Nava, Gregory (1983): *El Norte*. US: American Playhouse, Channel Four Films, Independent Productions.
Nava, Gregory (1995): *My Family*. US: American Playhouse, American Zoetrope, Majestic Films International.
Nava, Gregory (1997): *Selena*. US: Q Productions, Esparza, Katz Productions.
Nava, Gregory (1998): *Why Do Fools Fall in Love*. US: Rhino Films, Warner Bros.
Nava, Gregory (2002–2004): *American Family* (TV series). US: 20th Century Fox Television, El Norte Productions, KCET.
Nava, Gregory (2006): *Bordertown*. US: Möbius Entertainment, El Norte Productions, Nuyorican Productions.
Nolan, Christopher (2014): *Interstellar*. US: Paramount Pictures.
Olmos, Edward James (1992): *American Me*. US: Olmos Productions, Universal Pictures, YOY.
Saura, Carlos (1996): *Taxi*. Spain: Canal+.
Spielberg, Steven (2005): *War of the Worlds*. US: Paramount Pictures,.
Sturges, John (1960): *The Magnificent Seven*. US: Mirisch Company.
Tasma, Alain (2010): *Fracture*. France: ACSE, CNC.
Valdez, Luis (1987): *La Bamba*: US: Columbia Pictures Corporation, New Visions Pictures.
Zeïtoun, Ariel (2001): *Yamakasi – Les samouraïs des temps modernes*. France: Leeloo Productions, TF1 Films Productions, Canal+, Digital City.
Zübert, Christian (2011): *Three Quarter Moon/Dreiviertelmond*. Germany: BR, ARTE.

Bibliography

Adams, James Truslow (1941): *The Epic of America*. Garden City: Blue Ribbon Books.
AMAM (2015): *Asociación Internacional Mujeres Abrazando México A.C.* (http://mujeresamamasociacion.jimdo.com) (last accessed July 27, 2015).

Amigos contra el SIDA (2015): *Directorio de mujeres por y para las mujeres* (http://www.aids-sida.org/dir-mujeres-f.html) (last accessed July 27, 2015).
Antor, Heinz (1996): 'The Ethics of Criticism in the Age after Value', in: Ahrens, Rüdiger; Laurenz Volkmann (eds.): *Why Literature Matters: Theories and Functions of Literature.* Heidelberg: Winter, pp. 65–85.
Antor, Heinz (2006): 'Multikulturalismus, Interkulturalität und Transkulturalität. Perspektiven für interdisziplinäre Forschung und Lehre', in: Antor, Heinz (ed.): *Inter- und Transkulturelle Studien: Theoretische Grundlagen und interdisziplinäre Praxis.* Heidelberg: Winter, pp. 25–39.
Antor, Heinz (2010): 'From Postcolonialism and Interculturalism to the Ethics of Transculturalism in the Age of Globalization', in: Antor, Heinz; Matthias Merkl; Klaus Stierstorfer; Laurenz Volkmann (eds.): *From Interculturalism to Transculturalism: Mediating Encounters in Cosmopolitan Contexts.* Heidelberg: Universitätsverlag Winter, pp. 1–14.
Appadurai, Arjun (1996): *Modernity at Large. Cultural Dimensions of Globalization.* Minneapolis: University of Minnesota Press.
Appadurai, Arjun (2012): 'Disjuncture and Difference in the Global Cultural Economy', in: Lechner, Frank; John Boli (eds.): *The Globalization Reader.* Chichester: Wiley & Sons, pp. 94–104.
Avila, Edward A. (2012): *Conditions of (Im)possibility: Necropolitics, Neoliberalism, and the Cultural Politics of Death in Contemporary Chicana/o Film and Literature.* San Diego: University of California (ProQuest Dissertations).
Bachmann-Medick, Doris (2006): *Cultural Turns. Neuorientierungen in den Kulturwissenschaften.* Reinbek: Rowohlt.
Bacon, David (2004): *Children of NAFTA: Labor Wars on the U. S.-Mexico Border.* Berkeley: University of California Press.
Benessaieh, Afef (2010): 'Multiculturalism, Interculturality, Transculturality', in: Benessaieh, Afef (ed.): *Transcultural Americas/Amériques transculturelles.* Ottawa: Ottawa University Press, pp. 11–38.
Benessaieh, Afef (2012): 'Après Bouchard-Taylor: multiculturalisme, interculturalisme et transculturalisme au Québec', in: Imbert, Patrick; Fontille, Brigitte (eds.): *Trans, multi, interculturalité, trans, multi, interdisciplinarité.* Québec: Presses de l'université Laval, 2012, pp. 81–98.
Berg, Charles Ramírez (2002): *Latino Images in Film: Stereotypes, Subversion, Resistance.* Austin: University of Texas Press.
Bhabha, Homi (1994): *The Location of Culture.* New York: Routledge.
Carty, Gabrielle (2012): 'Language, Space and the Evolving Chicano Family in Nava's "My Family"', in: *iMex* 1/2, pp. 73–85.
CBC News (2014): 'Mexico's Cartels: Behind the Drug War' (http://www.cbc.ca/news/world/mexico-s-cartels-behind-the-drug-war-1.2549149) (last accessed July 27, 2015).
Day, Mark R. (2008): 'Why Did Bordertown Do a Belly Flop?', in: *La Prensa* (San Diego) 32/12, p. 9.
Díaz de León, Javier (2011): 'Migration, Cooperation and Development: the Role of the Mexican Government', presentation at *Dealing with the Causes: Mexico's Economic Policy and Migration*, organized by Center for Strategic and International Studies on January 11, 2011 (http://csis.org/files/attachments/110111_DiazdeLeon_Presentation.pdf) (last accessed August 2, 2015).
Ebert, Roger (1995): 'My Family', in: *Chicago Sun-Times*, May 3, 1995 (http://www.rogerebert.com/reviews/my-family-1995) (last accessed October 8, 2014).

European Parliament (2006): 'EP and Juanes Say "No" to Landmines', in: *European Parliament*, April 19, 2006 (http://www.europarl.europa.eu/sides/getDoc.do?type=IM-PRESS& reference=20060418STO07401&format=XML&language=EN) (last accessed July 27, 2015).

FNS (2008): 'Death Threats and E-Mail Warnings in Juarez', in: *Newspaper Tree. El Paso's Online Newspaper* 23/05/2008 (http://archive.newspapertree.com/news/2481-death-threats-and-e-mail-warnings-in-juarez) (last accessed July 27, 2015).

Ford, Franco (2013): 'Interview with Gregory Nava', in: *Medium Rare* 16/04/2013 (http://www.mediumraretv.org/2013/04/interview-with-gregory-nava-2) (last accessed July 27, 2015).

García Mainou, Ricardo (2008): 'Temas fronterizos', in: *Economista*, November 19, 2008 (http://search.proquest.com/docview/336466197?accountid=131239) (last accessed March 14, 2014).

García Pullés, Josefina (2008): 'Bordertown, ciudad al límite', in: *El Amante Cine* 189, p. 35.

Hendricks, Tyche (2010): *Wind Doesn't Need a Passport: Stories from the U.S.-Mexico Borderlands*. Berkeley: University of California Press.

Huggan, Graham (2006): 'Derailing the "Trans"? Postcolonial Studies and the Negative Effects of Speed', in: Antor, Heinz (ed.): *Inter- und Transkulturelle Studien: Theoretische Grundlagen und interdisziplinäre Praxis*. Heidelberg: Winter, pp. 55–61.

Huntington, Samuel (2007[1996]): *The Clash of Civilizations and the Remaking of World Order*. London: Simon & Schuster.

IMDB (2015): *International Movie Database* (http://www.imdb.com/?ref_=nv_home) (last accessed August 12, 2015).

James, Caryn (1995): 'A Mexican-American Journey of Generations', in: *The New York Times*, May 3, 1995, C. 18.

Johnson, Reed (2007): 'Mexico's Murdered Women Find a Voice in "Bordertown"', in: *Los Angeles Times*, February 14, 2007, E1 (http://articles.latimes.com/2007/feb/14/ entertainment/et-bordertown14) (last accessed May 21, 2015).

Kimmage, Michael C. (2011): 'The Politics of the American Dream', in: Hanson, Sandra; White, John (eds.): *American Dream in the 21st Century*. Philadelphia: Temple University Press, pp. 27–39.

Lallas, Demetri (2014): '"From the People, by the People, to the People": The American Dream(s) Debut', in: *The Journal of American Culture* 37/2, pp. 162–171.

Lazarus, Neil (2012): *The Postcolonial Unconscious*. Cambridge: Cambridge University Press.

Llano, Todd (1995): 'How Hispanic Films Make It to the Big Screen', in: *Hispanic* 7/95, p. 22.

Lugo, Alejandro (2009): *Fragmented Lives, Assembled Parts*. Austin: University of Texas Press.

Mata, Irene (2010): 'Writing on the Walls: Deciphering Violence and Industrialization in Alicia Gaspar de Alba's "Desert Blood"', in: *MELUS* 35.3 (Fall 2010), pp. 15–40.

Menozzi, Filippo (2014): *Postcolonial Custodianship: Cultural and Literary Inheritance*. New York: Routledge.

Mishra, Pankaj (2014): 'The Western Model Is Broken', in: *The Guardian*, October 14, 2014 (http://www.theguardian.com/world/2014/oct/14/-sp-western-model-broken-pankaj-mishra) (last accessed July 27, 2015).

Moyer, Bill (2002): 'Bill Moyers Interviews Gregory Nava', in: *Public Broadcasting Service* (PBS) (http://www.pbs.org/now/transcript/transcript_nava.html) (last accessed July 27, 2015).

National Commission on Law Observance and Enforcement (1931): *Report on the Enforcement of the Deportation Laws of the United States*. Washington: Government Printing Office (http://pds.lib.harvard.edu/pds/view/4673882?n=1&s=4&print Thumbnails=no) (last accessed February 17, 2015).

Nava, Gregory (1995): '"Mi Familia": Casting for Authenticity', in: *Los Angeles Times*, June 4, 1995, p. 14.

Nava, Gregory (1997): 'Gregory Nava: Selena es la historia del sueño americano', in: *El Latino* (San Diego), April 17, 1997, p. 13.

Nava, Gregory (2014): 'Gregory Nava: Red Carpet Interview at NHMC Impact Awards' (https://www.youtube.com/watch?v=Lgqyc5nsl6c) (last accessed June 7, 2015).

Nuestras Hijas de Regreso a Casa (2015): *Asociación civil fundada por familiares y amistades de jovencitas desaparecidas o asesinadas en el Estado de Chihuahua* (http://nuestrashijasderegresoacasa.blogspot.co.uk/p/quienes-somos.html) (last accessed July 27, 2015).

Raab, Josef (2009): 'Latinos and Otherness: The Films of Gregory Nava', in: Thies, Sebastian; Josef Raab (eds.): *E Pluribus Unum?: National and Transnational Identities in the Americas/Identidades nacionales y transnacionales en las Américas*. Tempe: Bilingual Press/Editorial Bilingüe/Münster: LIT Verlag, pp. 175–192.

Rosenthal, Debra J. (ed./2005): *Harriet Beecher Stowe's Uncle Tom's Cabin*. New York: Routledge.

Sadowski-Smith, Claudia (2009): 'Imagining Transnational Chicano/a Activism against Gender-Based Violence at the U.S.-Mexican Border', in: Concannon, Kevin; Francisco A. Lomelí; Marc Priewe (eds.): *Imagined Transnationalism: U.S. Latino/a Literature, Culture, and Identity*. New York: Palgrave MacMillan, pp. 75–94.

Smith, Michael Ernest (2003): *The Aztecs*. 2. Auflage. Oxford: Blackwell.

SHOCK (2015): 'Lo de Juanes es el chucu-chucu', in: *SHOCK*, January 29, 2015 (http://www.shock.co/cultura/articulos/lo-de-juanes-es-el-chucu-chucu-69138) (last accessed July 27, 2015).

Spivak, Gayatri Chakravorty (1999): 'Can the Subaltern Speak?', in: Spivak, Gayatri Chakravorty (ed.): *A Critique of Postcolonial Reason*. Cambridge, Massachusetts: Harvard University Press, pp. 206–236.

Stocker, Terry (2002): 'The Aztec Trickster on Display: The Darkest Side', in: *Trickster's Way* 1/1 (http://digitalcommons.trinity.edu/trickstersway/ vol1/iss1/2/) (last accessed October 8, 2014).

Stowe, Harriet Beecher (2015[1852]): *Uncle Tom's Cabin*. (https://www.gutenberg. org/files/203/ 203-h/203-h.htm) (last accessed August 12, 2015).

TIME (2005): 'Time Magazine Celebrates New Time 100 List of Most Influential People with Star-Studded Event April 19th', in: *TIME*, April 15, 2005 (http://content.time.com/time/ press_releases/article/0,8599,1049613,00.html) (last accessed July 27, 2015).

Valdes, Julio (2010): *El Jardín del Edén, Bordertown, and the United States – Mexico Border Region: Representations of Integration and the Changing Nation-State*. Ann Arbor: ProQuest Dissertations.

Villa Martínez, Marta Inés (2011): 'Desplazados y refugiados: Entre ser, merecer y ocultar su situación. A propósito de la migración forzada de colombianos en Colombia, Ecuador y Canadá', in: Feldman-Bianco, Bela et al. (eds.): *La construcción social del sujeto migrante en América Latina: Prácticas, representaciones y categorías*. Buenos Aires, Quito: CLACSO, FLACSO, pp. 339–366.

Wallerstein, Immanuel (2003): 'Knowledge, Power, and Politics. The Role of an Intellectual in an Age of Transition', in: Opening Presentation at UNESCO Forum on Higher Education, Research and Knowledge Global Research Seminar "Knowledge Society vs. Knowledge Economy: Knowledge, Power, and Politics", Paris, 8–9 December 2003 (http://unesdoc.unesco.org/images/0018/001833/183329e.pdf) (last accessed July 27, 2015).

Waxer, Lise A. (2002): *The City of Musical Memory. Salsa, Record Grooves, and Popular Culture in Cali, Colombia*. Middletown: Wesleyan University Press.

Weber, Max (1973): *Soziologie. Weltgeschichtliche Analysen. Politik*. Stuttgart: Alfred Kröner.

West, Dennis (1995): 'Filming the Chicano Family Saga: Interview with Director Gregory Nava', in: *Cineaste* 21, 4, pp. 26–28 (http://billbarry.net/laborinmovies/GregoryNava-1.doc) (last accessed July 27, 2015).

Conclusion

This study argues that contemporary European cinema shows a new interest in the Other, possibilities for multi-ethnic conviviality, and the need for a re-definition of the Self in the context of enhanced globalization, international mass migration, and expansion of the European Union. The fluid and transgressive character of migrant Others appears to be a fruitful starting point for the critical interrogation of monocultural identity constructs, neo-liberal politics, and neocolonial structures in contemporary Europe, which tend to be particularly popular in times of crisis and are thus likely to come back periodically. Many films dramatize forms of resistance against monocultural continuities, which are reflected in recent political turns toward xenophobia, cultural racism, and 19th century nationalism. The aim is to redefine a new role for Europe in our transcultural modernity and to support alternative perspectives better suited to address the opportunities and challenges in our highly dynamic societies.

I argue that most films contribute to this agenda by individualizing and humanizing migration as well as life in mainstream societies, which subverts the binaries set by nationalist, neoliberal, and neocolonial discourses. Rather than following popular portrayals of mass migration as a mass problem for the host societies and subdividing sharply into legal and illegal migrants, which allows for the latter to be persecuted as criminals, the wide spectrum of films from *Letters from Alou* (1990) to *Le Havre* (2011) and beyond highlights the individuality and humanity of its protagonists. This approach draws the viewers' attention to shared features underpinning our transcultural modernity. More recent films like *The Edge of Heaven* (2007) and *Le Havre* tend to include the isolation, incommunication, and personal impotence of individuals without migrant background. This draws on criticism of the 68 generation, *New German Cinema* perspectives, and/or earlier cultural criticism and allows for the (re-)conceptualizations of both migrants and non-migrants as outsider-protagonists in search of a better life. All of this correlates with Deleuze's and Guattari's postcolonial project of becoming 'nomads' of Europe (1986: 380), which suggests that we radically rethink established boundaries and the sedentary model of land distribution they are based on.[1]

Conclusion

All films from our case study analysis and most recent examples from the wider cinematic context, including *Leave to Remain* (2013), *Samba* (2014), *Blindgänger* (2015) and *Krüger from Almanya* (2015), send clear messages against ethnocentrism, discrimination, and racism, but there appears to be a paradigmatic change in identity construction. I argue that most European migrant films until the end of the 1990s—from Baser's *40 Square Meters of Germany* (1985) to Armendáriz's *Letters from Alou* and Saura's *Taxi* (1996)—operate largely within a traditional multicultural or traditional intercultural framework that follows an agenda of enhanced peaceful coexistence, mutual respect, and limited interaction. Within it, island concepts of cultures, which frame collective identities as relatively homogenous, essentialist, and therefore separatist entities, continue to mark conviviality constructs. Although many of these older films present attempts at bridging differences, from the anonymous German kid's innocent greeting of Turna in *40 Square Meters of Germany* to Carmen's relationship with Alou, the individual, temporary, and contingent nature of their success highlights the limits of cultural exchange in ethnocentric environments. This includes the continuity of cultural dichotomies that divide people into Self and Other, with migrants and subcultures usually summarized as the latter and exemplified or protected by outsider-protagonists.

In contrast, most post-2000 films from our text corpus aim to further explore transcultural features of our increasingly global environment. This is particularly obvious in British, French, and German contexts explored in films like *Ae Fond Kiss* (2004), *Le Havre*, and *The Edge of Heaven*, i.e., in cinematic landscapes shaped by the critical mass of productions from popular directors and scriptwriters with and without migrant backgrounds. It is, however, visible in other European countries, with *Princesses* (2005) and *Un franco, 14 pesetas* (2006) as particularly good examples of more recent films with transcultural agendas in Spain, and *Import/Export* (2007) as an outstanding work from Austria. Migrant cinema in these countries is still largely left to directors and scriptwriters without migrant background, and there are on average fewer films with migration topics, but demographic tendencies suggest that especially in Western European nations, in which immigration is likely to remain a hot topic, film production will catch up in the next decades.

In view of monocultural continuities, most transcultural relations in European film remain coincidental as well as individually and temporally limited, for example in the cultural adoption processes developed in *The Edge of Heaven*, *Le Havre*, *Welcome* (2009), *Hands Up* (2010), *Leave to Remain*, and *Blindgänger*, but also in the interethnic relationships explored in *Last Resort* (2000) and *Samba*. However, they include convincing suggestions for the development of a new Europe, such as the need to replace nationalist history constructs with ethics of transcultural memory. Whereas the former displays a preference for governmentally prescribed 'top-down' commemorations of highly selected events of a distant past, the latter aims at 'bottom-up' analyses of themes that help to address the multiethnic character of contemporary Europe within the context of increasing globalization and international mass migration. *The Edge of Heaven* and *Le Havre* are good examples of this tendency insofar as—in Akın's film—Ayten and Yeter flag up memories of Kurdish and Alevi rights violations (including 'disappearance' and the Maraş massacre of 1978) that do not form part of state commemorations. In Kaurismäki's work—Marcel comments on the contrast between homeless refugees fighting for basic rights such as family unification and a mechanical system of exclusion that reminds us of Vichy France. Whereas the former tends to be marginalized in governmental discourse, Vichy injustice is well remembered in commemorations and school books, and this contrast has also been criticized in *Welcome* and *Hands Up*. Other examples are the exploration of traumatic memories in *Leave to Remain* and personal memories of an interethnic relationship in *35 Shots of Rum*. All these films suggest the rejection of traditional dichotomies of Self and Other, because the Other is always part of the Self and vice versa, which discredits nationalist history construction. More precisely, they recommend to explore our own shared memories of human loss and happiness, based on which we might be able to find ways out of our outsider experiences and develop a more sustainable future together.

New ethics of affect, which are particularly explicit in *The Edge of Heaven*, support such a reorientation by suggesting that we explore existential situations based on the (negative and positive) impacts of affects. On the one hand, the film examines individual loss of control as a key challenge because this can lead to chain reactions, which are here responsible for two deaths: In the case of Yeter, an old man reacted violently, whereas in Lotte's death, a child lost control. These and numerous other cases stress that nobody is free from such tendencies, and that significantly more self-control is needed to reduce such tragedies. On the other hand, affects open the way for new feelings and new emotions that culminate in the cross-cultural bond between Ayten and Lotte as well as the construction of Susanne's and Ayten's cross-cultural patchwork family. Both relationships suggest a multiple break with traditional boundaries, which this study has traced back to deconstruction in Fassbinder's work, and which also links up to cross-cultural solidarity constructs in *Le Havre*, *Welcome*, *Hands Up*, *The Blind Flyers*, and *Last Resort*.

These constructs indicate alternatives to contemporary monocultural tendencies in European politics and media discourse. The latter are exemplified by conservative anti-immigration politics in the UK, which include proposals to jail landlords for renting accommodation to illegal migrants and to cut benefits for EU migrants, and different referendums in Switzerland, from the minaret ban in 2009 (sharply criticized by Akın in an open letter) to the re-introduction of immigration quotas in 2014. In these and many other cases, nationalist politics are in tension with European Union interests in reducing national boundaries and free movement agreements. In the last decade, however, the Commission has arguably shown more interest in EU enlargements (2004 and 2007) and strategic Eastern outreach (Ukraine crisis since 2014), than in the removal of remaining boundaries between its core member states. Amendments to anti-discrimination laws might be a common feature, but key amendments can often be traced back to public pressure, which includes the intervention of migrant cinema directors. In particular, the attention drawn to discriminatory legislation by films like *Days of Glory* (2006), *Welcome, Hands Up,* and *Le Havre* has facilitated changes in French law allowing former WWII soldiers with African background to receive pensions that are comparable to pensions of French veterans, and humanitarian aid for migrants is now explicitly excluded from government persecution. Also, in the context of growing media interest, there is an increased public awareness of the need to overcome the human tragedies associated with existing boundaries, including migrant victims in the Mediterranean, but also deaths in attempts to cross the channel from Northern France to the UK and challenges for refugees on Greek and Italian islands.

On the other hand, transcultural orientations can be found in earlier films. It is no coincidence that Kaurismäki returns to films from Renoir and Bresson, whereas Akın receives inspiration from Fassbinder. Particularly productive periods for the exploration of transcultural features of outsider-protagonists are the Nouvelle Vague, which has been inspired by Bresson, and the New German cinema, which has been shaped by Fassbinder with classics like *Katzelmacher* (1969) and *Fear Eats the Soul* (1974). Outstanding films in the 1980s and 1990s include Stephen Frears and Hanif Kureishi's *Sammy and Rosie Get Laid* (1987), Claire Denis's *Chocolat* (1988), and Gianni Amelio's *Lamerica* (1994). This indicates that it would be blatantly wrong to understand the above-mentioned tendencies as indications of new exclusive boundaries for the categorization of developments in European cinema.

The interest in cultural exchange leads to a more comprehensive interrogation of patterns of exclusion, which include colonial continuities highlighted by Echevarría's *Cabeza de Vaca* (1991). The film reconstructs cultural and biological racism, cultural hierarchies, and other aspects of European colonial discourse for the purpose of deconstruction, but it also offers a transcultural alternative exemplified by the protagonist's opening up to shared affects and shared memories. This way, *Cabeza de Vaca* highlights the fragility of powerful self-portrayals and self-glorification but also the vicious cycles of human violence, which link up to more contemporary patterns of suppression and exclusion presented in *Letters from Alou, Taxi, Last Resort, Welcome, Le Havre, Samba, My Family* (1995) and *Bordertown* (2006). These films reconstruct marginality via poor, temporally limited, and usually collective migrant housing. Migrants live on plantations, in refugee camps, and low-class suburbs outside city centers that correlate either directly with different forms of neo-colonial exploitation, for example in *Letters from Alou, Samba,* and *Bordertown,* or they concentrate on monocultural exclusion mechanisms that allow for colonial continuities—in *Taxi, Last Resort, Welcome,* and *Le Havre.*

On the other hand, *Bend It Like Beckham* supports neocolonial agendas by recommending ways for successful assimilation to Western capitalist concepts of modernity, which prolong Orientalist binaries and reveal an astonishing ignorance of 20th and early 21st century developments that have discredited Western leadership. *My Family* reconstructs a similar binary, but it indicates at least some aspects of neocolonial suppression in the past (e.g., María's deportation and Chucho's killing) more forcefully than *Bend It Like Beckham*. The latter concentrates on first- and second-generation migrant protagonists in contemporary Britain who have reached slightly more than average living standards—semi-detached house with Mr. Bhamra working in a white-collar profession. In this context, it seems easier to present monocultural attitudes within the diaspora as the only remaining hurdle to take.

However, the dissemination of separatist identity concepts goes well beyond films like *Bend It Like Beckham* and *My Family*. Although most contemporary directors stress the need to blur cultural boundaries, their work does not always manage to stick to the transcultural agenda they originally aimed for, and sometimes they quite directly support a monocultural Western agenda. Unfortunately, such portrayals not only start but frequently end in reaffirmations of traditional dichotomies. One example is the presentation of first-generation migrants as the stagnant, suppressive, and ethnocentric Rest vis-à-vis a progressive, liberal and understanding West in *40 Square Meters Germany*, *Farewell to a False Paradise* (1988) and *Yasemin* (1988), which continues in *Samia* and *Bend It Like Beckham*. In such microcosms, Western-oriented younger representatives like Elif, Yasemin, Samia, and Jess lead the way, whereas older members of the diaspora are encouraged to either follow the younger generation's drive toward assimilation or remain excluded and left behind. Other neo-colonial aspects include the framing of migrant Others as children in need of white adult protection, even in films with a strong transcultural agenda like *Welcome* and *Le Havre*. Also, women are frequently left in supporting roles (e.g., in *Le Havre* and *Samba*), whereas *The Edge of Heaven* subscribes to a particular nationalist discourse that continues to discriminate ethnic minorities and other opposition.

Similarly problematic is the portrayal of second-generation migrants as representatives of a criminal parallel world to mainstream society. Examples include *Short Sharp Shock* (1998), *Kanak Attack* (2000), *Ghettokids* (2002), and *Rage* (2006), but also more recent films like *Tough Enough* (2006) and *Fracture* (2010), which correlates with the 'mise-en-scène' of criminal migrant milieus in *The Albanian* and *El Niño*. Although it is important for European cinema to include less privileged people with migrant backgrounds as active subjects attempting to negotiate their identities, the portrayal of migrant communities as criminal cultures remains misleading and offensive in its marginalization of integrated, educated, and hardworking representatives. In addition, the marginalization of the mainstream population with migrant backgrounds in migrant cinema is in its dichotomy and exclusionary practice comparable to the marginalization of diasporas in majority culture discourse, against which the same cinema objects. In this context, ghetto films should be analyzed not only as expressions of interest in subalterns and the deconstruction of mainstream cinema, but also as a growing tendency toward melodramatic excess. The latter often sells very well and correlates with attempts to simplify binary oppositions of the complex set of human relationships in societies marked by mass immigration, which destabilizes visions of multi-ethnic conviviality pursued by most directors in this study.

In this context, Nava's films may be inspirational for European directors insofar as they explore the importance of migrants' dreams as a key factor for mass migration and the negotiation of identities in postcolonial diaspora. Nava highlights the need to interrogate these dreams, exemplified by the development from a belief in the American Dream in *My Family* to its destabilization and partial reconstruction in *Bordertown*. The more recent film shows also a serious attempt to address contemporary concerns over the lack of postcolonial responsibility in media discourse, and there is always a chance to learn from its basic mistakes in plot, montage, and character construction to make the next attempt more credible.

Finally, popular Chicano cinema in the US, for which most of Nava's films are good examples, tends to achieve substantially more impact than its European counterpart, which correlates with its tendency to draw on the Hollywood studio system. If the European Union has a genuine interest in European film competing on equal footing with Hollywood, it will have to radically rethink and restructure its current approach to funding and production. Some inspiration for this could come from the constant reinvention of the Hollywood studio system, which has managed to incorporate the impressive and highly diverse work of Steven Spielberg, Robert Rodríguez, Quentin Tarantino, Steven Soderbergh, and Spike Jonze. I argue that films from Montxo Armendáriz, Fernando León de Aranoa, Fatih Akın, Thomas Arslan, Stephen Frears, Ken Loach, Aki Kaurismäki, and Rachid Bouchareb, to name just a few outstanding European directors highlighted in this book, deserve at least a similarly wide audience.

Note

1. For a recent discussion see Aldea (2014).

Filmography

Akın, Fatih (1998): *Short Sharp Shock/kurz und schmerzlos*. BRD: Wüste Filmproduktion.
Akın, Fatih (1999): *In July/Im Juli*. Germany: Wüste Filmproduktion.
Akın, Fatih (2002): *Solino*. Germany: Wüste Filmproduktion.

Conclusion   163

Akın, Fatih (2007): *The Edge of Heaven/Auf der anderen Seite*. Germany/Turkey: Anka Film.
Aladag, Züli (2006): *Rage/Wut*. BRD: Köln Media Filmproduktionen GmbH.
Amelio, Gianni (1994): *Lamerica*. Italy, France, Switzerland: Alia Film, Cecchi Gori Group Tiger Cinematografica, Arena Films.
Armendáriz, Montxo (1990): *Letters from Alou/Las cartas de Alou*. Spain: Elías Querejeta Producciones Cinematográficas S.L., Televisión Española (TVE).
Arslan, Thomas (2001): *A Fine Day/Der schöne Tag*. Germany: Pickpocket Filmproduktion/zero-film/ZDF.
Baser, Tefvik (1985): *40 Square Meters of Germany/40 Quadratmeter Deutschland*. Germany: Letterbox Filmproduktion.
Baser, Tefvik (1988): *Farewell to False Paradise/Abschied vom falschen Paradies*. Germany: Letterbox Filmproduktion/ZDF.
Becker, Lars (2000): *Kanak Attack*. Germany: Becker & Häberle Filmproduktion GmbH.
Bochert, Marc-Andreas (2015): *Krüger aus Almanya*. Germany: Provobis.
Bohm, Hark (1988): *Yasemin*. Germany: Hamburger Kino Kompanie/ZDF.
Bouchareb, Rachid (2006): *Days of Glory/Indigènes*. Algeria, France: Tessalit Productions, Kiss Films, France 2 Cinéma.
Buck, Detlev (2006): *Tough Enough/Knallhart*. Germany: Boje Buck Produktion.
Chadha, Gurindher (2002): *Bend It Like Beckham*. UK, Germany, US: Kintop Pictures.
Denis, Claire (1988): *Chocolat*. France, West Germany, Cameroon: Caroline Productions, Cerito Films, Cinémanuel.
Denis, Claire (2008): *35 Shots of Rum/35 rhums*. France, Germany: Soudaine Compagnie, Pandora Filmproduktion.
Echevarría, Nicolás (1990): *Cabeza de Vaca*. Mexico, Spain, US, UK: Producciones Iguana.
Fassbinder, Rainer Werner (1969): *Katzelmacher*. Germany: Antitheater-X-Film.
Fassbinder, Rainer Werner (1974): *Fear Eats the Soul/Angst essen Seele auf*. Germany: Filmverlag der Autoren.
Faucon, Philippe (2000): *Samia*. France: Canal+.
Frears, Stephen (1987): *Sammy and Rosie Get Laid*. UK: Channel Four.
Glenaan, Kenneth (2004): *Yasmin*. UK, Germany: Parallax Independent, EuroArts Medien.
Goodison, Bruce (2013): *Leave to Remain*. UK: Indefinite Films.
Goupil, Romain (2010): *Hands Up/Les mains en l'air*. France: Les Films du Losange, France 3 Cinéma, France Télévision.
Haneke, Michael (2000): *Code Unknown/Code inconnu*. France, Germany: Canal+, Bavaria Film.
Iglesias, Carlos (2006): *Un franco, 14 pesetas*. Spain: Adivina Producciones.
Kahane, Peter (2015): *The Blind Flyers/Blindgänger*. Germany: Polyphon.
Kaurismäki, Aki (2011): *Le Havre*. Finland, France, Germany: Sputnik, Pyramide Productions, Pandora Filmproduktion.
León de Aranoa, Fernando (2005): *Princesses/Princesas*. Spain: Reposado Producciones.
Lioret, Philippe (2009): *Welcome*. France: Nord-Ouest Productions, Studio 37, France 3 Cinéma.
Loach, Ken (2004): *Ae Fond Kiss*. Great Britain, Belgium, Germany, Italy, Spain: Bianca Film.
Monzón, Daniel (2014): *El Niño*. Spain: Telecinco Cinema, Ikiru Films, Vaca Films.

Naber, Johannes (2010): *The Albanian/Der Albaner*. Germany, Albania: ARTE.
Nakache, Olivier; Eric Toledano (2014): *Samba*. France: Quad Productions, Ten Films, Gaumont.
Nava, Gregory (1995): *My Family*. US: American Playhouse, American Zoetrope, Majestic Films International.
Nava, Gregory (2006): *Bordertown*. US: Möbius Entertainment, El Norte Productions, Nuyorican Productions.
Pawlikowski, Pawel (2000): *Last Resort*. UK: BBC.
Samdereli, Yasmin (2011): *Almanya – Willkommen in Deutschland*. Germany: Roxy Film, Infa Film.
Saura, Carlos (1996): *Taxi*. Spain: Canal+.
Seidl, Ulrich (2007): *Import/Export*. Austria, France, Germany: Ulrich Seidl Filmproduktion GmbH, Pronto Film, Société Parisienne de Production.
Tasma, Alain (2010): *Fracture*. France: ACSE, CNC.
Valdez, Luis (1987): *La Bamba*: US: Columbia Pictures Corporation, New Visions Pictures.
Wagner, Christian (2002): *Ghettokids*. France, Germany: ARTE, BR.
Zeïtoun, Ariel (2001): *Yamakasi – Les samouraïs des temps modernes*. France: Leeloo Productions, TF1 Films Productions, Canal+, Digital City.
Zübert, Christian (2011): *Three Quarter Moon/Dreiviertelmond*. Germany: BR, ARTE.

Bibliography

Aldea, Eva (2014): 'Nomads and Migrants: Deleuze, Braidotti and the European Union in 2014', in: *Open Democracy*, July 10, 2014 (https://www.opendemocracy.net/can-europe-make-it/eva-aldea/nomads-and-migrants-deleuze-braidotti-and-european-union-in-2014#_ftn1) (last accessed July 27, 2015).
Deleuze, Gilles; Felix Guattari (1986): *A Thousand Plateaus*. Translated by Brian Massumi. London: Athlone Press.

Index

Acting Our Age (documentary film) 62
Adams, James Truslow: *The Epic of America* 129
Adorno, Theodor 9
Ae Fond Kiss (film): Pakistani community and 10; rejects monoculturality 76; transculturality 158
Afghanistan: cultural transitions 16
Africa: postcolonial immigration 14; Spanish immigration 50
agency: Chicano cinema 132–35; having a voice 83, 143; northern saviour in *Bordertown* 145–47
Akın, Fatih: audience for 162; career of 77; *Crossing the Bridge* 11; Fassbinder and 88, 89; *Head-On* 85–86; *In July* 5, 84; second-generation background 20; *Solino* 5, 84, 85 see also *The Edge of Heaven*; *Short Sharp Shock*
Aladag, Züli: *Rage* 81, 141
The Albanian (film) 84, 161
Alevi: rights violations against 159
Alfonso XII of Spain 59
Algeo, Katie 64
Algerian immigrants 14
alienation, Brechtian techniques of 78
Allen, Stuart: *Love Thy Neighbour* 10
Almanya (film) 5, 67
Alvaray, Luisela 34
AMAM 145
Amelio, Gianni: *Lamerica* 3, 160
American Me (film) 129
Amnesty International 149; Turkey and 92
Anderson, Benedict: the imagined community 84; nationalism 9–10
Angel Baby (song) 137–38, 139
Angus, Thongs and Perfect Snogging (film) 62

Antor, Heinz 8, 10, 127; embracing the unfamiliar 144; global interconnectedness 11
appearance: Native American dress 41
Appiah, Kwame Anthony 13
Aranoa, Fernando León de: audience for 162; *Princesses* 3
Arletty 101–102
Armas Marcelo, Juan José: *Burnt Ships* 32
Armendáriz, Montxo: audience for 162; internal displacement of 20 see also *Letters from Alou*
Armenia: Turkey and genocide 93
Army of the Shadows (film) 98, 101; adapted from Kessel's book 106
Arslan, Thomas: audience for 162; *Dealer* 82; *A Fine Day* 86; *Geschwister - Kardesler* 81
Ashcroft, Bill 14, 15
assimilation 141; *Bend It Like Beckham* 93, 127, 161; as best practice 127; or exclusion 161 see also monoculturality
Asturian, Miguel Angel 35
auteur cinema: European tradition of 18–19

Bagh, Peter 100
Ballesteros, Isolina 57; *Letters from Alou* 51
La Bamba (film) 129
Banderas, Antonio 145; *Bordertown* 19, 135
Bangladeshi immigrants 14
Baser, Tevfik 10, 76, 78; compared to Fassbinder 78; migrant's perceptions of Other 80 see also *40 Square Meters of Germany*; *Farewell to a False Paradise*
The Beach (film) 70
The Beatles 103

166 Index

Beau Travail (film) 98
Becker, Lars: *Kanak Attack* 82–83
Beckham, David 69, 70; *Bend It Like Beckham* and 63; Englishness of 65; as a guru 72
Belgium 14
Ben Seni Sevdugumi (song) 87
Bend It Like Beckham (film): assimilation and 93, 127, 161; bending football norms 65–66; budget for 19; cultural hierarchies 68, 79; the 'European Dream' 148; exclusion and 52, 68–70; football as cultural mediator 16; generational conflict 67; guarding monoculturality 72–76; identity construction 79; ignores capitalist criticism 70, 71; lack of hybridity 75–76; neo-capitalism models of culture 16; postcolonial diaspora and 12; protagonist between cultures 64–67; S. Asian women in the diaspora 64; sexual orientations and 63; story of 62–63; transculturality 4; treatment of Sikh heritage 141; treatment of Sikhism 64–65
Bend it Like Beckham (film): context of Chadha's career 62
Benessaieh, Afef 11, 127; intercultural bonds 89
Berg, Charles Ramírez 131
Berges, Paul Mayeda 62
Bergfelder, Tim 18–19
Berghahn, Daniela: cultural dichotomies 64, 66
Berlin in Berlin (film) 81
Berlin International Film Festival: Artists for Amnesty award 149
Bhabha, Homi: hybrid societies 11; ongoing colonialism 14; Third Space 94, 136, 141
Bhaji on the Beach (film) 62; hybrid identity 66
Bianchini, Franco 51
Bindra, Guljit 62
The Blacksmith's Daughter (Özdogan) 94
The Blind Flyers (film) 5; cross-cultural solidarity 159
Blindgänger (film): cultural adoption 158; identity construction 158; new wave and 2; solidarity 96
Bochert, Marc-Andreas: *Krüger aus Almanya* 91
Bohm, Hark 4, 10, 79–80; *North Sea Is Dead Sea* 79 see also *Yasemin*

Bollywood films 19
Bordertown (film) 19; the American Dream and 130–31, 146–47, 162; bilingualism 135–36; boundaries and globalizations 132; capitalist conspiracy theory 146, 148–49; example of Chicano cinema 128; individual agency 134–35; movie poster for 144–45; spatial boundaries 137; suppression and exclusion 160; transculturality 137, 138–39
Born in East L.A. (film) 129, 139
Bouchareb, Rachid: audience for 162; *Days of Glory* 102
Bourdieu, Pierre: cultural capital 51
Braga, Sonia 145
Brave New World (Huxley) 106
Brazilian immigrants 14
Brecht, Berthold: alienation techniques 78
Breger, Claudia 94; definition of narrative 13–14; on *The Edge of Heaven* 90; implicit dialogicity 93; trans-ethnic relations 13
Bresson, Robert: *The Devil, Probably* 97, 100; influence of 160
Bride and Prejudice (Chadha) 62
Bridging Differences (Gudykunst) 10
Britain: anti-immigration politics 159; cricket and Empire 68–70; ethnicity and class 69; ex-colonial migration 9; ideas of Englishness 69–70; migrant mediascape 2–3; nationalism 9; non-EU migrants 17; Pakistani community 10; postcolonial migration 14; and US culture 70
British East Africa Company 69
British National Party (UK) 103
Bruce-Novoa, Juan 30
Bry, Théodore de 40
Buck, Detlev: *Tough Enough* 84
Burnt Ships (Armas Marcelo) 32
Bwana (film) 55, 107; city narratives and 60; racist violence in 56

Cabeza de Vaca (film) 3; colonialism and 12; compared to *Le Havre* 109; conqueror as migrant Other 29–32; deconstructing stereotypes 42–43; Estebanico's origins 39; inequality and exclusion 4; narrative of 31–32; neocolonialism 160; New World emigration 51; Othering in conquest 32–35; post-colonial discourse 29; subsidies for 30–31

Cabeza de Vaca, Álvar Núñez: *Shipwrecks* 30–31, 36
Calderson, Felipe 146
Campra, Rosalba 57
Cannes Film Festival: *Le Havre* and 98
cannibalism 38
Captain from Castile (film) 37, 39
Carbonell, Pedro 59–60
Carlos I, King of Spain 30
Carné, Marcel: *Children of Paradise* 101
Carpentier, Alejo: *The Harp and the Shadow* 32
Carrasco, Salvador: *The Other Conquest* 29
Carty, Gabrielle 135
Cast Away (film) 70
Cetin, Sinan: *Berlin in Berlin* 81
Cha, Kyung-Ho 94
Chadha, Gurinder 4; food and culture 65; life and career of 62; second-generation background 20; 'twice' immigrant parents 69 *see also Bend It Like Beckham*
Chaudhury, Parama: on *Bend It Like Beckham* 64
Chicano cinema: agency and 132–35; the American dream and 129–30; assimilation of Hollywood paradigms 131; *Cabeza de Vaca* 30; debates about 19–20; Hispanic diaspora and 127–28; Hollywood system and 149, 162; success of 128–29; Uncle Tom 139–40 *see also Bordertown; My Family*
Children of Paradise (film) 101
Chinese cinema 19
Chocolat (film) 107, 160
Christianity: *Ae Fond Kiss* 76; Christianizing the 'pagans' 33–35; as European heritage 18; hybrids with native cultures 36; and pagan Others 53
Christopher Columbus (film) 30–31
Christopher Columbus: The Discovery (film) 29, 37
Cimeno, Michael: auteurism and 19
cinema: cultural and commercial pressures 1; embracing diversity 1; 'European' 17–18; interest in Otherness 1; language and 16
Clash of Civilizations (Huntington) 141
class: the American Dream 129–30; ethnicity in Britain and 69; Mexican migrants 137; solidarity and 100–04

colonialism and imperialism 3; contemporary Europe 1; hybrid culture and 15; language and 15–16; media discourse 29–32; migration from 12; ongoing 14–16; white patriarchal protection 57–58 *see also* neocolonialism; postcolonial identity theory; postcolonialism
Columbus, Christopher 29
community, imagined 84
Cortés, Hernan 29
cosmopolitanism: transculturality 13
Council of Europe: Eurimages fund 2; multicultural/rights mandate 18
cricket in English culture 68–70
The Crime of Monsieur Lange (film) 97, 100
Crossing the Bridge: The Sound of Istanbul (documentary film) 11
culture: adoption of 158–59; clashes of 96; difference 1; embracing the unfamiliar 144; McDonaldization of 70; notions of 8–10; rejection of heritage 141; rejection of hosts' 141; Third Space 79; Third Space of 94, 96, 136, 141 *see also* identity; interculturality; monoculturality; multiculturality; Other and Othering; transculturality
The Cut (film): 'love, death, devil' trilogy 77

Danquart, Pepe: *Fare Dodger* 56
Days of Glory (film) 102; discrimination legislation 160
De Palma, Brian 19
De Sica, Vittorio 98
Dealer (film) 83
Decolonising the Mind (Thiong'o) 15
decolonization: public acceptance of diversity and 9
Delanoy, Werner 8, 10; on intercultural learning 10; process of transculturality 12–13
Deleuze, Gilles 157
Denis, Claire 160; *Beau Travail* 98
Deveny, Thomas G.: Franco's ideology 53
The Devil, Probably (film) 97
difference: globalization and 11; identity of 83; interculturalists' focus 10; reconciliation and 91; scales of 13 *see also* culture; identity; Other and Othering
directors: cultural and commercial pressures 1; displacement of 20

Index

discrimination 3; anti-immigration politics 160; past and present forms of 98; portrayals of 95
Dogs of Paradise (Posse) 33
Dörrie, Doris: *Happy Birthday, Turk/ Happy Birthday, Türke* 81
Doulos: The Finger Man (film) 97–98

East Is East (film) 62; assimilation 4; cultural hierarchies 79; guarding monoculturality 73, 75, 76; hybridity 67; neo-capitalism models of culture 16; Pakistani community and 10
Ebert, Roger 129
Echevarría, Nicolás 3; deconstructing stereotypes 42–43; European colonialism 20; Self and Other 41–42 *see also Cabeza de Vaca*
economics: alternatives to capitalism 86; *Bordertown* conspiracy theory 132–33, 146, 148–49; boundaries and globalizations 132; Eurozone crisis 17; interrogation of neo-liberalism 157; marketing hybrid consumption 15; neo-liberalism 103–04; Spain and crisis 48; US capitalist norms 133
The Edge of Heaven (film) 5; awards for 77; concepts of culture 10; cultural adoption 158; ethics of affect 159; the 'European Dream' 148; global context 159; identity and stereotypes 91–95; narrative of 86–91; nationalist discourse 161; original title of 91, 96; part of 'love, death, devil' trilogy 77; perceptions of immigration 52; portrayal of Turkey 96; transculturality 4, 85, 86–91, 95, 158
Elley, Derek 64
Elsaesser, Thomas: European cinema 17–18; European nostalgia 98; New German cinema 78
Epstein, Mikhail 11
Erdogan, Recep Tayyip 92
Erkan & Stefan (television) 16
ethics of affect 159
Eurimages: aim of funding 2; foundation of 18
Europe: Christianity and 18; discourse of superiority 57; the European Dream 148; immigration to Spain 50; integration of migrants 1; as makers of history 29–32; migration as hot topic 158; migration from colonial lands 12; as multicultural 17; multidirectional memories 11–12 *see also* European Union
European cinema: art-house design 62; box office and 19
European Convention on Human Rights 103
European Court of Human Rights 103; Turkey and 92
European Film Distribution Office (EFDO) 18
European Script Fund (SCRIPT) 18
European Union: anti-immigration politics 159–60; Euroscepticism and migration 1; Eurozone crisis 17; film funding and awards 18; Maastricht Treaty 2; Schengen Agreement 2; Single European Act 2
Everett, Wendy: auteur cinema 18–19; European cinema 17–18
exclusion: in *Bend It Like Beckham* 52; in *Cabeza de Vaca* 4; Madrid as melting pot 61; Nava tackles 149; portrayals of 95

Fare Dodger (film) 56
Farewell to a False Paradise (film) 78, 95; assimilation 161; interculturality 79; shifting from monoculturality 80
fascism 3; *Lamerica* and 12; neo-nazis in unified Germany 81; neofascism and *Taxi* 55–60; social Darwinism and 57
Fassbinder, Rainer Werner: Akın and 88, 89; compared to Baser 78; deconstruction of 159; *Fear Eats the Soul* 3, 78; German xenophobia and 80; influence of 160; influence on New German cinema 77–78; *Katzelmacher* 78, 80; *The Marriage of Maria Braun* 78; transcultural deficiency 88
Faucon, Philippe: *Samia* 4, 67
Fear Eats the Soul (film) 3, 95; 21st century Turkey and 93; German guest-workers 78; influence of 160; transcultural deficiency 88; xenophobia 80
Federal Cross of Germany: award for Akın 77
FELIX 18
Fernández, Enrique: on *Cabeza de Vaca* 31

Fevry, Sébastien 99
films: low-budget and small scale 18
financial matters: international inequality 14; low-budget films 18–19
A Fine Day (film) 95
Fischer, Paul 63
Flesler, Daniela 61
Floeck, Wilfried 42
food: as cultural code 65, 74, 75–76
football: bending the norms 65–66; cultural and gender openness 67–68; as cultural mediator 16; place in English culture 68
40 Square Meters of Germany (film) 10, 78, 95; assimilation 161; intercultural clashes 96; multicultural framework 158; shifting from monoculturality 80
1492 (film): post-colonial discourse and 29; Spanish subsidies for 30
Fracture (film) 84; criminality and 161; the ghetto and 141
France: discrimination laws 160; ex-colonial migration 9; *Le Havre* and penal code 97, 100, 108; migrant mediascape 2–3; non-EU migrants 17; postcolonial immigration 14
Frears, Stephen: audience for 162; *Sammy and Rosie Get Laid* 160

García Canclini, Néstor: *Hybrid Cultures* 11
García Mainou, Ricardo 130
gender issues: openness 67–68; othering female sexuality 39; stereotyping 3; transculturality and 67
Germany: German-Turkish TV comedy 16; guest workers 9, 78; interest in the Nazi past 98; loneliness of migrants 88; migrant mediascape 2–3; nationalism of immigrants 10; New German Cinema 77–80, 157; non-EU migrants 17; shifting portrayals 95; solidarity messages 5; Turkish-German films 77; from Weimar to Nazism 16; xenophobia 80
Ghettokids (film) 84; criminality and 161
Gilroy, Paul: conviviality 13, 96; half-difference 91
Glen, John: *Christopher Columbus* 29, 30–31, 37

global society: communications 12–13; interconnectedness 11; transculturality 71
Goethe, Johann Wolfgang von: anti-revolutionary perspective 94
Gordon, Richard Allen 38
Göktürk, Deniz 78, 96; saving women 80
Goupil, Romain 98 *see also Hands Up*
Gramática castellana (Nebrija) 15
Gramling, David: on Akın's trilogy 77; multilingualism 88, 89, 95
Greece 17
Grenier, Richard 37
Griffith, Gareth 15
Guattari, Felix 157
Gudykunst, William B.: *Bridging Differences* 10
Gueneli, Berna: on Akın's films 77; on *The Edge of Heaven* 95; fake Goethe 94; polyphony of Europe 89
Gutiérrez Aragón, Manuel: *Poniete* 34; *Things I Left in Havana* 53
Gutiérrez, Chus 52
Guzmán, Martín Luis: *La querella de México* 39

Ha, Kien Nghi: on hybridity 15; hybridity and 16
La Haine (film) 81, 82
Hall, Stuart: the West and the rest 71
Hands Up (film) 98; cross-cultural solidarity 159; cultural adoption 158; discrimination legislation 160; *Le Havre* and 106; Vichy injustices 159
Hans Staden's True History: An Account of Cannibal Captivity in Brazil (Staden) 38
Happy Birthday, Turk/Happy Birthday, Türke (film) 81
The Harp and the Shadow (Carpentier) 32
Le Havre (film) 5; characters and monoculturality 104–08; class solidarity and 100–04; concepts of culture 10; cross-cultural solidarity 159; cultural adoption 158; discrimination legislation 160; the 'European Dream' 148; fascism and imperialism and 12; French penal code and 101; global context 159; humanity of 157; neocolonialism 109, 161; new wave example 2; perceptions of immigration 52;

reception and awards 98; settings and influences 97–98; socio-politicial institutions 108–09; solidarity and 91, 96; suppression and exclusion 160; transculturality and 4, 158; white protection for Others 106–07, 109, 161
Head-On (film) 5; part of 'love, death, devil' trilogy 77; transculturality and 85–86
Herder, Johann Gottfried 10; defining monoculturalism 9
Hijos del Viento (film) 39
Hillman, Roger 94
Hoberman, J. 98, 100
Hollywood system: auteurism and 19; box office and 19; Chicano cinema and 149, 162
Holocaust: European interest in 98
Holtz, Stefan: *Kiss Me Kismet* 85
How Tasty Was My Little Frenchman (film) 38
Huber, Christoph 88
Huggan, Graham 8, 10, 127; football and culture 68
Huitzilopochtli 134
Human Development Indexes 17
Human Rights Watch 92
Huntington, Samuel: *Clash of Civilizations* 141
Huxley, Aldous: *Brave New World* 106
Hybrid Cultures (García Canclini) 11
hybridity: the American Dream 5; Chicano identity 147; Chicano music 139; cultural choices 68; football and 67–68; 'going native' 35–36; music 87; neo-imperialism 15–16; the second generation 66; transcultural exchanges 11

identity: colonialism and 29–32; of difference 83; *The Edge of Heaven* and 91–95; essentialist constructs 127; Mexican-American 135–36; negotiation of 148; separatist 161; shift in film approaches 158 *see also* culture; Other and Othering
I'm British But... (documentary film) 62
immigration: public acceptance of diversity and 9; Spanish discourse 48 *see also* migrants
Import Export (film) 88; transculturality 158
In July (film) 5, 61, 84; erotic Other 91

In Search of Intercultural Understanding (Schmidt) 10
Indian immigrants *see Bend It Like Beckham;* South Asian migrants
indigenous societies: *Cabeza de Vaca* and 32–38; Native American magic 40; Spanish conquest 32–35
inequalities: in *Cabeza de Vaca* 4; Nava tackles 149; Nkrumah criticizes 14
interculturality 8; *Farewell to a False Paradise* 79; notions of 50; tensions of globalism 14
International Cricket Conference (ICC) 68
International Federation of Film Critics prize: *Le Havre* and 98
Iraq 16
Isenberg, Noah 77, 88
Islam: *Ae Fond Kiss* 76
Islamist movements: cultural transitions 16; global communication 12
Israel 16
Italy: non-EU migrants 17
It's a Wonderful Afterlife (film) 62

Jäckel, Anne 18
Jamal, Ahmed A.: *Majdhar* 10
James, Caryn 143
Jamon Jamon (film) 54
Jericho (film) 29
Juanes (Juan Vásquez): *La Camisa Negra* 138–39
Juárez, José Miguel: *Hijos del Viento* (film) 39
Jurado, Jeanette 137

Kachru, Braj B. 16
Kahane, Peter: *The Blind Flyers* 5
Kanak Attack (film) 82–83, 95; criminality and 161; voice of immigrants 83
Kanak Sprak (film): the ghetto 84; influence of 82–84
Kassovitz, Mathieu: *La Haine* 81, 82
Katzelmacher (film) 95; German guest-workers 78; influence of 160; xenophobia 80
Kaurismäki, Aki 4, 5; audience for 162; French penal code and 101, 102; influences 97–98; internal displacement of 20 *see also Le Havre*
Kaya, Ayhan 96
Kenya: Sikhs and the railway 69
Kessel, Joseph: *Army of the Shadows* 106

Kimmage, Michael C. 129–30
King, Henry: *Captain from Castile* 37, 39
Kiss Me Kismet (film) 85
Knightly, Keira 63
Krüger from Almanya (film) 91, 158; new wave and 2; solidarity 96
Kurds: in *The Edge of Heaven* 96; rights violations against 159
Kureishi, Hanif: *Sammy and Rosie Get Laid* 160
Kuyuncu, Kazim: *Ben Seni Sevdugumi* 87

La Camisa Negra (song) 139
Lamata, Luis Alberto: *Jericho* 29
Lamerica (film) 3, 160; fascism and imperialism and 12
language: Chicano bilingualism 135–36; of colonizers 15–16; indigenous societies 41; multilingualism 88, 89, 95; P'urhépecha 137; transcultural 89; widespread Spanish 51
Las Casas, Bartolomé de 33, 57, 58
Last Resort (film): cross-cultural solidarity 159; cultural adoption 158; suppression and exclusion 160
Latin America: 'discovery' of 51; immigration to Spain 50; post-colonial migration 14
Leave to Remain (film): cultural adoption 158; identity construction 158; traumatic memories 159
Lennon, John 138
Letters from Alou (film): anti-racism 51; compared to *Le Havre* 109; concepts of culture 10; the 'European Dream' 148; example of European diversity 2; humanity of 157; image of harmony undermined 60; key film in Spanish cinema 48; multicultural framework 158; multiculturality 4; neocolonialism and migrants 51–55; postcolonialism 12; story of 52–55; suppression and exclusion 160
Life Belongs to Us (film) 97, 100
Lioret, Philippe: *Welcome* 98, 101, 102
Loach, Ken: *Ae Fond Kiss* 10, 76; audience for 162
Locarno Film Festival: award for Akın 77
López, Jennifer 129; Artists for Amnesty award 149; *Bordertown* 19, 144–45; in *My Family* 130
Love Thy Neighbour (television) 10

LUX prize 18
Lymon, Frankie 138; *Why Do Fools Fall in Love?* 131

Majdhar (film) 10
Malik, Sarita 66
marginalization: ghetto films 161–62; government policies and 104; past and present forms of 98; US-Mexican border 137
Marin, Cheech: *Born in East L.A.* 129, 139
The Marriage of Maria Braun (film) 78
Marxism 20
Massumi, Brian: connecting to Others 99; transculturality 13
MEDIA: foundation of 18
Melville, Jean-Pierre: *Army of the Shadows* 101, 106; film noir crime dramas 97–98
Mennel, Barbara 96
Mexico: the American Dream and 146–47; native cultures and Echevarría 30; powerful drug cartels 146; privilege and marginalization 137 *see also* Bordertown; My Family; Nava, Gregory
migrant cinema: categorizing 20
migrants: challenges for refugees 160; the children 98–99; European financial crisis and 17; European integration of 1; exploitation of 61; as hot topic 158; humanizing 157; perceptions of Self and Other 80; portrayals of 3; rejection of host culture 141; returning home 61–62; in victim role 57–58, 61
monoculturality: the American Dream 146–47; assimilation as best 127; changing perspectives on 1; characters in *Le Havre* 104–08; compared to transculturality 8; cultural adoption 158–59; culture of 'wogs' 83–84; current interrogation of 157; guarding in *Bend It Like Beckham* 72–76; Herder on 9; hierarchies within 79; historical perspective of change 16; resistance to deconstruction 3; tensions of globalism 14 *see also* assimilation
Monzón, Daniel: *El Niño* 84
Morales, Esai 130
Moroccan immigrants: postcolonialism 14; *Taxi* and 56

Moses, Dirk 105; transcultural memory 89
multiculturality: European film funding/awards 18; Madrid melting pot 49–51; notions of 50; shift in film approaches 158; Spanish cinema 48; tensions of globalism 14
music: Chicano cinema 137–38; hybrid 11, 87; transculturality 140
My Big Fat Greek Wedding (film) 76
My Family (film): the American Dream 130, 162; assimilation 161; bilingualism 135–36; Chicano agency and 132; example of Chicano cinema 128; glocal businesses 132–33; narration of 143; solidarity in 142; spatial boundaries 136–37; story of 129–30; success of 128–29; suppression and exclusion 160; transculturality 137–38, 141–43; Uncle Tom-ism 139–40
My Son the Fanatic (film): Pakistani community and 10

Naber, Johannes: *The Albanian* 84
Nacify, Hamid 20
Nagra, Parminder 62
narrative: Breger's definition of 13–14; New Historical 31, 32
Narváez, Pánfilo de 32
National Front Party (UK) 103
National Institute of Statistics (Spain) 49–50
nationalism: Anderson on 9–10; colonialism and 59; contemporary politics and 157; European migration and 1; historical perspective of 8–9; transculturality and 13
Nava, Gregory 5; agenda of 130; assimilation and 143; *Bordertown* 128; career of 128; cinematic success 149; migrant dreams 162; negotiation of identities 148; tackling exclusion and inequality 149 *see also Bordertown*; *My Family*
Nebrija, Antonio: *Gramática castellana* 15
neocolonialism: Echevarría deconstructs stereotypes 42–43; framing Self and Other 14; global experience and 14; *Le Havre* and 106–07; ongoing colonialism 14–16; Spanish cinema and 48; suppression and exclusion 160
neoliberal economics 1

Netherlands 14
Neubert, Stefan 8
Nice Arrangement (documentary film) 62
1984 (Orwell) 106
El Niño (film) 84, 161
Nkrumah, Kwame: inequality of wealth 14
El Norte (film) 128
North Sea Is Dead Sea (film) 79
Nuestras Hijas de Regreso a Casa 145

Observatorio de la Immigración Marroquí en España 56
O'Donnell, Damian: *East is East* 4, 10, 62
Offside (film) 79
Olmos, Edward James 130; *American Me* 129
Organization for Economic Cooperation and Development (OECD) 17
Orwell, George: *1984*, 106
Other and Othering: adoption of 99; binary with Self 11; cinema's interest in 1; conquerors as migrants 29–32; cultural dichotomies 158; dehumanization of Self and 41–42; European interest in 157; female sexuality 39; 'going native' 35–36; *Le Havre* 108; humanization of Self and Other 34–35, 41–42; Indians not negation of West 71; migrant's perceptions of 80; ongoing colonialism 14–16; perfect/imperfect dichotomy 33–34; purity and superiority 9; religion and 40; Self and 159; solidarity and 100–04; Spanish conquest and 32–35; superiority in colonial discourse 57; wide spectrum of 3–4
The Other Conquest (film) 29
Ottoman Empire: transition to Turkish Republic 16
Özdogan, Selim: *The Blacksmith's Daughter* 94

Pacino, Al: *Scarface* 82
Pakistani immigrants 14
Palestine 98; cultural transition to Israel 16
Palomo, Miguel Ángel 98
Panahi, Jafar: *Offside* 79
Pereira dos Santos, Nelson: *How Tasty Was My Little Frenchman* (film) 38

Pérez Prado, Dámaso: *Que Rico El Mambo* 138
Pérez Rosado, Pedro: *Salt Water* 53
Peter-Weiss Award 77
Pitman, Thea 19–20
Pizarro, Francisco 29
Poniente (film) 52; Christianity and 34; city narratives and 60; racist violence in 56
Portugal 14
Posse, Abel: *Dogs of Paradise* 33
postcolonial identity theory 3
postcolonialism: global experience and 14; importance of journey to 144; lack of responsibility 148–49; responsibility and 3
Prasad, Udayan: *My Son the Fanatic* 10
Presley, Elvis 138
Princesses (film) 3, 54–55; transculturality 158
P'urhépecha language 137

Que Rico El Mambo (song) 138, 139
La querella de México (Guzmán) 39
Quetzalcoatl 133–34

Raab, Josef 128, 143
race and ethnicity: agency and 107–09; the American Dream and 129–30; essentialist debates 19–20; ghettos and 141; ideas of Englishness 69–70; interethnic relationships 159; Uncle Tom-ism 140; white patriarchal protection 57–58
racism 3; biological 10; contemporary politics and 157; cultural 10; German anti-racist attacks 81; *Letters from Alou* and 51–55; neofascism and *Taxi* 55–60; Spanish cinema and 48
Rage (film) 81; criminality and 161; the ghetto and 84, 141
Rascaroli, Laura: on *Le Havre* 99, 104; transcultural cinema 97
The Red Circle (film) 97–98
religion: Aztec and Christians 133, 134; Catholicism in *My Family* 136–37; interrelatedness of 89; Native American magic 40; pagan Others 53
Renoir, Jean: *The Crime of Monsieur Lange* 97; influence of 160; *Life Belongs to Us* 97, 100
Restrepo, Luis Fernando 41
Rings, Guido: fear in cinema 61

Ritzer, George 70
Robinson, Douglas: *Translation and Empire* 14
Rojas, Eduardo López 129
Rooney, Wayne 69
Roth, Hans-Joachim 8
Rothberg, Michael 11–12, 105; multidirectional memory 36; transcultural memory 89
Rubio, Ingrid 55
Rulfo, Juan 35

Said, Edward: ongoing colonialism 15; the West and the rest 70–71, 89
Salt Water (film) 53; city narratives and 60
Samba (film): agency of ethnic groups 107; cultural adoption 158; identity construction 158; suppression and exclusion 160
Samdereli, Yasmin: *Almanya* 5, 67
Samia (film) 67; assimilation 4; guarding monoculturality 73
Sammy and Rosie Get Laid (film) 160
The Samurai (film) 97–98
Sanchis Sinisterra, José: *Shipwrecks of Álvar Núñez* 31
Sanders-Brahm, Helma: *Shirin's Wedding* 77
Sandhu, Sharon: negotiating identity 74; S. Asian women in the diaspora 64
Santaolalla, Isabel 55
Sarkozy, Nicolas 98
Saura, Carlos 4; racism and neofascism in *Taxi* 55–60 *see also Taxi*
Scarface (film) 82
Schachtner, Christina 108
Schäffauer, Markus K. 32
Schmidt, Patrick: *In Search of Intercultural Understanding* 10
Schygulla, Hanna 88
Scorcese, Martin 19
Scott, Ridley: *1492*, 29, 30
scriptwriters 1
Seidl, Ulrich: *Import Export* 88
Selena (film) 128
Sensin... You're the One! (film) 77
separatism: deconstruction of concepts 4
Sepúlveda, Juan Ginés de 33, 57, 58
sex and sexuality: in *Bend It Like Beckham* 63; neocolonial fantasies 55
Shankar, Shalinki 14, 15
Sheridan, Guillermo 30

Shipwrecks (Cabeza de Vaca) 30–31, 36, 39
Shipwrecks of Álvar Núñez (play) 31
Shirin's Wedding (film): German guest-workers 78
Short Sharp Shock (film) 5; criminality and 161; the ghetto and 84, 141; Locarno award for 77; migrants and criminals 91; portrayal of exclusion 95; voice of migrants 81–82, 83
Sikhism: in *Bend It Like Beckham* 64–65, 71–72; construction of Ugandan railway 69; guarding culture of 72–75
Silvey, Vivien 94
Smits, Jimmy 129, 130
social Darwinism 57
Sociedad Estatal de Quinto Centenario 30
Soehring, Hans-Jürgen 101
solidarity: class and 100–04; conviviality and 96; cross-cultural 159; in *My Family* 142
Solino (film) 5, 84, 85
SOS Racismo: *Letters from Alou* and 51
South Asian migrants 14; former British colonies 9; not a negation of the West 71; working class and 69
Spain: 'discovery' of America 50; emigration in Civil War 52; Eurozone crisis 17; image and facts of Madrid 49–51; image of harmony undermined 60; Isabel and Ferdinand's fundamentalism 33; Madrid as melting pot 60–61; migrant mediascape 2–3; Muslim to Catholic culture 16; non-EU migrants 17; Othering in conquest 32–35; social status of Madrid workers 49
Spanish cinema: development of migration themes 4; multiculturality of 48; tolerance and respect 48
Spivak, Gayatri Chakravorty: allowing subalterns to speak 83; saved by white men 80; subalterns speaking 143
sport: identity construction 79 *see also Bend It Like Beckham*
Springer, Bernd: *Das kommt mir Spanisch vor* 10
Staden, Hans 38
stereotypes: *The Edge of Heaven* and 91–95
Storaro, Vittorio 59

Stowe, Harriet Beecher: *Uncle Tom's Cabin* 139
Susanna (film) 61
Switzerland: anti-immigration politics 159
Syria: cultural transitions 16

Die Tageszeitung 97
Tallmer, Jerry: on *Cabeza de Vaca* 31
Tasma, Alain 141; *Fracture* 84
Taxi (film): compared to *Le Havre* 109; the 'European Dream' 148; image of harmony undermined 60; key film in Spanish cinema 48; multicultural framework 158; neo-fascism 33; postcolonialism 12; racism and neofascism 55–60; separatism unchallenged 59; suppression and exclusion 160; transculturality 4; white protection and 106
Tezcatlipoca 133, 134
The Epic of America (Adams) 129
Things I Left in Havana (film) 53, 54; city narratives and 60
Thiong'o, Ngugi wa: *Decolonising the Mind* 15
Third Cinema: Marxism and 20
35 Shots of Rum (film) 159
Thomas, Ann 128
Three Quarter Moon (film) 5
Tiffin, Helen 14; language and colonization 15
Tough Enough (film) 84; criminality and 161
transculturality: *Bordertown* 137, 138–39; *Cabeza de Vaca* 4; conviviality and solidarity 96; defining 10–11; historical perspective of change 16; humanity and 157; language and 88, 89; multidirectional memories 11–12; music 140; *My Family* 137–38, 141–43; Nava's *My Family* and 131–32; neocolonialism and 161; notions of 50; post-2000 films 158; postcolonial identities 10–17; potential and limits of 2; process of 12–13; shifting German images and 95; tensions of globalism 14
Translation and Empire (Robinson) 14
Turkey: Armenian genocide 93; emigration to Germany 9; human rights and 92; portrayal in *Edge* 92–94

Turkish migrants 14; portrayal of Turkey and 92–94
Two for Tea (film) 61
Tyndall, John 103

Uganda: Sikhs construct railway 69
Ukraine crisis 160
Un franco 14 pesetas (film) 61; transculturality 158
Uncle Tom's Cabin (Stowe) 139
United States: the American Dream 129–30, 133, 139, 146–47, 162; bilingualism 135–36; British culture and 70; Chicano cinema 132–33; Hispanic diaspora 127–28; hybrid cultures 5; marketing hybrid consumption 15; the Mexican border 132–33; migration as hot topic 127–28; nationalism 9
Uribe, Imanol: *Bwana* 55, 107

Valdes, Julio 130
Valens, Ritchie 129
Valverde, César 42
Venice International Film Festival: award for Akın 77
Vera, Pedro de 35

Weaver-Hightower, Rebecca 70
Weed (film) 77
Welcome (film) 98, 101, 102; cross-cultural solidarity 159; cultural adoption 158; discrimination legislation 160; *Le Havre* and 106; suppression and exclusion 160; Vichy injustices 159

Welsch, Wolfgang: cultural differences 10; globalization and transculturality 12; increase in transculturality 71; monoculturality 9; notions of culture 8; transculturality 32
West, Dennis 133
Wheatley, Catherine 18
Why Do Fools Fall in Love? (film) 131
Wilkin, Peter 103–04
Wilms, André 97
women 144–45; portrayal in *Le Havre* 107–08, 109; saved by white men 80; suppression of 79

xenophobia 3; contemporary politics and 157; culture clashes 16; Europe and 1; in Germany 80–81; neocolonialism and 127

Yamakasi (film) 81, 82
Yáñez, Agustín 35
Yasemin (film) 10, 67; assimilation 4, 161; Christianity and 34; guarding monoculturality 73, 76; hero rescuer 85; interculturality 79–80; shifting from monoculturality 80; white patriarchal protection 58
Yildiz, Erol 8

Zaimoglu, Feridun: on difference 83; *Kanak Sprak* 82–84
Zavattini, Cesare 98
Zeïtoun, Ariel: *Yamakasi* 81, 82
Zemeckis, Robert: robinsonades 70
Zübert, Christian: *Three Quarter Moon* 5